# Lonsdale's Belt

The Earl of Lonsdale
President of the National Sporting Club

# Lonsdale's Belt

## The Story of Boxing's Greatest Prize

John Harding

Robson Books

First published in Great Britain in 1994 by Robson Books Ltd, Bolsover House, 5–6 Clipstone Street, London W1P 7EB

**British Library Cataloguing in Publication Data**.
A catalogue record for this title is available from the British Library

ISBN 0 86051 846 9

Phototypeset by Intype, London
Printed in Great Britain by St. Edmundsbury Press, Bury St. Edmunds, Suffolk.

# Contents

# TABLE FOR BELT AND WEIGHTS DIVISION

## BBBC Standard Weights

| | |
|---|---|
| Flyweight | 8 st and under |
| Bantamweight | 8 st 6 lb and under |
| Super-bantamweight | 8 st 10 lb and under |
| Featherweight | 9 st and under |
| Super-featherweight | 9 st 4 lb and under |
| Lightweight | 9 st 9 lb and under |
| Light-welterweight | 10 st and under |
| Welterweight | 10 st 7 lb and under |
| Light-middleweight | 11 st and under |
| Middleweight | 11 st 6 lb and under |
| Super-middleweight | 12 st and under |
| Light-heavyweight | 12 st 7 lb and under |
| Cruiserweight | 13 st 8 lb and under |
| Heavyweight | Any weight |

# Acknowledgements

I have many people to thank for help and advice during the writing of this book. Alan Roderick, Arthur Watkins, Brian Donald, Brian Nobile, Fred Deakin, Bill Matthews, Stan Shipley, Pat Woods, Dr Donmall, Sid Mander, Doug Hindmarsh, Peter Jones, Edward Robinson (at Fattorini's), Victor Barley (at Mappin and Webb), Bert Daly, Jack Doughty, Phillip Paul in the USA, Andy Ward and Joe Aitcheson all provided either information or pointed me in the right direction.

The late Frank Duffett spent many hours chatting to me in his tiny AMPRO sports shop at Waterloo – once such a distinctive feature of the British boxing scene but now, alas, demolished. Frank also lent me programmes and photos from his collection and I am grateful for all his help.

Morton Lewis talked of his famous father, Ted Kid, and of promoting in the post-war years; Sam Burns and Jarvis Astaire recalled Jack Solomons and the 1960s; while at the British Boxing Board of Control, Ray Clarke OBE and John Morris were extremely helpful, allowing me access to the Board's minutes and memorabilia.

Bernard Hart of Lonsdale Sports read the manuscript and gave helpful criticism, John Gilbert did an invaluable job making an untidy manuscript readable in the first place, while *Boxing News* editor Harry Mullan has been unfailingly kind and generous in allowing me unlimited access to the paper's files and photos.

The following belt owners all provided fascinating information and photos: Mrs Jack Hood, Chas Taylor, Sam Bowater, Cmdr Dick Pearson (Woolwich Officers' Mess), Elsie Shephard, Kitty Flynn, Mrs Maria Traynor, Alan Stratton, Ed J. Brown, Mrs Nel

Tarleton and Jack Trickett, while a special mention must be made of Mr Wolfendon, who passed on Tommy Bloggs's belt cuttings, drawings, etc. to the BBBC and thus helped preserve a unique fragment of sporting history.

Ron Olver has been of particular help, ever willing to supply a name or a telephone number, while his numerous articles in *Boxing News* (not to mention his Old Timers page) have been essential reading, a history of British boxing in themselves.

Finally, I must pay tribute to Gilbert Odd, whose idea this book originally was; a great boxing writer and journalist and still an enthusiast for the sport. I only hope this book matches up to his high standards.

# Foreword

The Lonsdale Belt has been called the finest individual trophy in the world of sport and it is difficult to disagree with that description when one realizes the awe with which our British championship trophies are regarded throughout boxing.

I will always remember a comment made at an annual meeting of one of the world organizations. A delegate was extolling the virtues of their championship belts but then he added, possibly for my benefit, '. . . but nothing to compare with the Lonsdale Belts of course'.

Old-stagers may yearn for past glories – after all everything acquires extra stature in the memory – but I am confident the Lonsdale Belts of today will stand comparison. Many fine craftsmen have worked to produce the belts first sponsored by Lord Lonsdale back in 1909 but few finer than those who worked for the present manufacturers of the belt, Thomas Fattorini Limited of Birmingham.

Every British champion wears a belt with pride and those with the skill to win three title contests in one weight division make the belt their very own property.

John Harding has told a story that has been there for the telling for a long time and I am glad that at last someone has finished the research and produced a collection of fascinating facts on those who triumphed, those who failed and those who carved a special place in the fabulous history of British boxing.

John Morris
General Secretary, British Boxing Board of Control

# Introduction

In recent years, the organization of world pro-boxing has descended into chaos. A profusion of governing bodies offer a bewildering variety of titles; World champions are ten-a-penny; skulduggery and sleaze are rife. What, the cynic might ask, is new?

From a strictly ethical point of view, it would be hard to argue that pro-boxing has fallen from some great height in recent years: Golden Ages, as we all know, are the products of middle-aged nostalgia. And yet . . . there was once a time, not so long ago, when the words 'World champion' meant just that; when a title belt was an emblem of merit, not a crudely shaped cash-card.

There was also a time, within living memory, when the distinction between a genuine title fight and a music-hall exhibition was strictly preserved; when, if one wished to see a pro-boxer knock over a series of crude no-hopers, one visited a fairground boxing booth rather than tune in to watch the latest TV 'World' title offering.

Where British titles are concerned, thankfully, there is no such confusion and little, if any, of the skewed matchmaking presently doing the sport so much harm. The British Board of Control, linked to an honourable tradition and answerable to no commercial interest, awards its titles without fear or favour, and whatever the individual quality of the holder, the timeless glamour of the Lonsdale Belt ultimately triumphs.

Which is some achievement for a trophy first awarded by a private club composed of middle-class businessmen and gamblers, paid for by a spendthrift one-time risqué sporting lord.

The National Sporting Club pretensions were once mocked

and scoffed at, its autocratic ways considered unacceptable in a democratic society. How grateful boxing fans would be if such an institution were to rise again and seize global control of a sport in danger of destroying itself! How gratifying if the principles and aspirations that underpinned the launching of that first belt were finally to be realized almost 100 years on.

# 1

# A Belting Good Idea

In mid–1909 The National Sporting Club announced that it would be offering a championship belt for each of its own chosen eight standard weight divisions.

There were conditions attached to the winning of such belts: any boxer holding one had to defend within six months after the receipt of a challenge for a minimum stake of £100 a side (£200 for heavies, £50 for flyweights). Before each defence, he had to deposit the belt with the manager of the Club; and he was also obliged to insure the trophy 'against loss or damage by larceny and fire in the sum of £200' – this amount to be deposited with the NSC as security.

The belt could be won outright, however, if the holder were declared the winner of three championship contests, consecutive or not, held under the auspices of the NSC. If there were no challenges he could still become absolute owner if he remained undisputed holder for three consecutive years. Once undisputed owner, he was entitled to a pension of £1 a week for life on reaching the age of fifty.

Most significant of all, however, the holder of the NSC belt (soon dubbed the Lonsdale Belt, after the Club's president and donor of the first belt) could claim to be the undisputed champion of England. . . .

The Lonsdale Belts were by no means the first such trophies to be presented to boxing champions. Indeed, throughout the early history of the noble art, from bare-knuckle up to the introduction of the Queensberry Rules, it had been the custom to award trophies to those boxers who had become public heroes as a result of their prowess in the ring. Such trophies were usually

1

intended for individual boxers, however, and were not meant to be passed on.

But as bare-knuckle fighting faded in popularity, and as the Queensberry Rules introduced a semblance of continuity and shape to the fledgling sport, so belts came to be awarded on a more regular, even systematic basis. In the 1880s, for instance, promoter Bob Hajjiban presented belts for specific weights: Bill Baxter won England's 8 st 6 lb championship in 1885 and Jack Davis won the 9 st championship in 1887, both receiving belts that they were expected to defend; and in the early 1900s, with rival venues such as Wonderland in London's East End, the Cosmo in Plymouth and the National Sporting Club itself seeking attractive 'lures' for particular star boxers, the number of belts on offer proliferated alarmingly.

It was because of the confusion caused by such random 'championship' belts that the National Sporting Club decided to institute its own 'official' series. The necessity for such a move can be demonstrated by looking at the progress of the lightweight title in the years prior to 1909.

In 1891 (the year of the NSC's foundation) Dick Burge beat Jim Carney to claim the crown – which he continued to claim until his retirement in 1897. However, from 1894 he clearly fought at welterweight and above – during his two 'title' fights with Tom Causer in 1897 he weighed 142 lb, 2 lb over the existing limit for lightweights. Not surprisingly, during his reign at least four other boxers claimed the title. Between 1897 and 1901 the picture gets even more confused. No fewer than nine men were declared lightweight champion at venues ranging from London (NSC, Wonderland) to Sheffield and Newcastle. In 1901 Jabez White emerged from the scrum to be hailed as 'legitimate' lightweight champ and defended it a number of times, but still, at one time or another, Young Joseph, Tommy Hogan, Jack Goldswain, Johnny Summers, Joe Fletcher and Jack Ward all laid claim to the title.

Such confusion, while good for individual promoters and boxers, was clearly damaging to the long-term credibility of the relatively new commercial sport. The NSC, in deciding on eight specific weight divisions with a trophy attached to each, was thus presenting the professional sport with a challenge: either concede to it the right to crown English champions and, in effect, grant it the authority akin to that wielded by the FA in soccer or the MCC in cricket; or continue to behave in random fashion, recognizing no central authority and thus running the risk of seeing boxing eventually outlawed – a prospect by no means impossible during the first decade of the century.

The belts thus highlighted two conflicting – perhaps ultimately irreconcilable – images of the Club. The generally accepted 'establishment' view saw it as the 'Home of Boxing', an institution that set standards, defined and refined codes, with officers and members whose conduct was above reproach, being wealthy, middle-class businessmen. This view, not surprisingly, was perpetuated by the Club's founders and officials: indeed, the most famous and influential Club man, 'Peggy' Bettinson, wrote in his history of the Club, *The Home of Boxing*: 'We would not have the Club's worth judged by great enterprises – its aim was to uphold and conserve all that is best in British Boxing.'

The alternative, essentially regional, point of view pointed to the fact that, unlike the FA, which was a truly amateur body, the NSC was a private business that promoted professional boxing primarily for the entertainment of its exclusively middle-class clientele, many of whom were drawn in by the opportunity to gamble. This alternative point of view stressed the way the Club used its powerful, albeit benevolent, dictatorship virtually to control pro-boxing at the highest level purely for its own amusement.

Between these two extremes – the romantic elitist and the pragmatic commercial – the truth undoubtedly lies.

The Club could not have been as influential as it was without possessing a wealth of boxing know-how. Men like Bettinson, C.H. Douglas, Lord Lonsdale, etc. were vastly experienced. All had fought successfully at amateur level in the days when professionals and amateurs mixed freely (indeed, regularly fought exhibitions) and their concern for the rules and regulations undoubtedly served the fledgling sport well during the 1880s and 1890s.

The NSC built upon the Queensberry Rules and possessed both determination and wealth enough to resist legal moves that might have strangled the game at birth. Whether one can completely accept Bettinson's claim in his book that 'It were well that boxing ceased to be a creation of the pub; it were well that boxers were rescued from the gutter' is irrelevant. The point is that the NSC provided an influential 'respectable' focus for the sport.

The epithet 'Headquarters' suited it perfectly. Here kings and princes could and often did come to watch boxing; here, in the eerie silence insisted upon by Club rules, referees (though seated outside the ring) could be seen to be completely in control of whatever went on inside it; here were no unsightly brawls – instead, contests of high skill between men of courage and character. And during almost two decades from its foundation in 1891, the NSC paraded a series of champions and great fighters who swiftly took on almost immortal status: Frank Slavin, Peter Jackson, Pedlar Palmer, Digger Stanley, the 'Coffee Cooler' Frank Craig, Dick Burge, Tommy Burns, Sam Langford – the romance of such names, amplified by the purple prose chronicling their various titanic battles, helped confirm the NSC as the country's premier boxing venue and boxing as an acceptable, legal sport.

The Club's glorious history persuaded many members that its purpose was not purely commercial. The writer Bohun Lynch, a Club member and chronicler, wrote: 'Boxing is a sport and a sport only . . . first and foremost it is an amusement – good fun. . . .' Bettinson himself, though not so starry-eyed, certainly remained ambivalent towards the purely commercial side of pro-boxing. He had, he declared, no objection to men making all the money they could out of the game, 'but for goodness sake, gentlemen, let us have honest sport first and foremost. . . .' In 1909, Bettinson's outlook on the boxing scene in general – and on commercial promoters in particular – was decidedly jaundiced. In October 1909 he was quoted in *Boxing* as saying: 'The boxing promoter is, I suppose, necessary in most cases but this does not prevent him often being an evil.'

Bettinson was worried that the rapid changes then occurring in professional boxing, due to its dramatic commercial 'take-off', were threatening to undermine the 'sport'. His comments on the increasing use of film to record contests illustrates this. While he welcomed the extra revenue film companies brought in, he saw dangers:

I would never allow the pictures to come first. When they are

BOXING AUGUST 13 1910. Vol. II.—No. 49.

**DID JEFFRIES QUIT?** By Hugh D. McIntosh.

# BOXING

EVERY WEDNESDAY.     ONE PENNY.

*The only Paper in the World solely devoted to Boxing.*

Vol. II.—No. 49.     13TH AUGUST, 1910.     Registered at the General Post Office as a Newspaper and for Canadian Magazine Post

## THE WORLD'S GREATEST PROMOTERS.

Mr HUGH D. McINTOSH     Mr. A. F. BETTINSON     Mr. G. L. ("TEX") RICKARD
(Australia).     (England)     (America)

placed in that position you can generally rest satisfied that the contests will go some distance. Pictures don't prove so extra profitable if a fight only goes a short journey. . . . Now if you want real genuine sport you can't carry on boxing on these lines.

Thus Bettinson was anxious that rules and regulations be standardized and universally accepted, and the introduction of a new series of English championships at eight specific weights was, for him, the key to reform not only in Britain but also abroad.

The launching of the belts was initially seen by some as the basis for an international authority that would rule boxing, and an International Board – or the suggestion of something similar – was certainly mooted in late 1909.

Bettinson, however, tended to back away from an actual organization, claiming that its establishment would entail 'too many difficulties'; and he evidently saw the institution of the Lonsdale Belt system as complicated enough for the Club, an organization that, as *Boxing* put it in October 1909, '. . . rules the boxing world without governing. That is to say, its committee never interferes with anyone else. Their motto is (or rather would be if they cared to have one): "We act in this manner simply because it is the square thing. Other people can do as they like. . . ." '

Awarding a series of trophies on a regular basis certainly laid extra responsibility on the Club. It meant organizing and overseeing various eliminating contests; it meant selecting men who would satisfy everyone's idea as to who should or should not be eligible (rather than indulging Club favourites); it meant collecting money from boxers or their backers (£200 being required as 'insurance' on the trophy); it even meant organizing a pension scheme that was attached to winning the trophy outright (an uncharacteristically 'modern' touch, this, as state pensions had only just been introduced by the Liberal Government, and were highly controversial).

One suspects that Bettinson foresaw such implications and did not relish them, whereas the man whose name would grace the belts and who would be paying for them (at least in the first instance) harboured grander, more extravagant ambitions for the trophies. But then, Lord Lonsdale was inclined to impulsive gestures without worrying too much as to the practical consequences. As he himself put it in his autobiography: 'Most things I have done have been a matter of chance. The moment comes to you, all in a rush, and you seize it. . . .'

There is a great deal of mythology attached to the reputation of Lord Lonsdale, much of it of his own creation. Although he inherited a title that brought with it vast tracts of land and buildings (including Lowther Castle), etc., he had no access to the vast wealth such estates represented. The terms of his inheritance were designed (sensibly, as it turned out) to prevent any particular earl from impoverishing his successors by running up crippling debts that could only be paid off by mortgaging or selling land.

Lonsdale was thus paid a pension (never less that £80,000 per annum) by the estate trustees and expected to get along as best he could. Nevertheless, he pursued a life of luxury in which the pursuit of sport and ostentatious living were the principal goals.

He was, to quote his biographer Lionel Dawson, 'over-exuberant all his life but he was also naive, single-minded and extravagant . . . and had always spent beyond his means. . . .' Throughout his life he was in constant financial difficulties – not surprising since he kept a personal entourage of over one hundred and when he moved between his houses a special train was allocated to the party. On an overnight journey a special sleeper was reserved for himself and another for his dogs.

As a young man – although married – he had scandalized Victorian society by having a series of affairs with prominent actresses, culminating in 1888 in a court case in which an aggrieved husband had sued him for adultery – and won. Lonsdale went abroad for a year to allow the scandal to die down. He travelled to the Arctic to collect various specimens of flora and fauna for a naturalist society, and later claimed to have discovered gold, to have begun the Klondike Gold Rush and actually to have reached the North Pole.

However, despite the exaggerations, the debts and the scandal, not to mention the increasingly anachronistic life-style, Lonsdale's love of boxing was genuine and his knowledge extensive. Boxers, he declared in his autobiography, were the salt of the earth and he enjoyed following the sport so much because 'I like the company of real men who have made their way through the world with their fists'. Moreover, 'Boxing is, I think, one of the sports that must always remain dear to an Englishman's heart – simply because it is such a purely personal matter for the man concerned.'

He was taught to box by Jem Mace, the last bare-knuckle champion of England and widely acknowledged as the 'father of boxing' in its twentieth-century form. During the period when boxing was still not a respectable sport, Lonsdale was one of the few wealthy aristocrats determined to change its image by ensuring that contests took place under properly constituted rules. His name thus became associated with 'fair play' and his presidency of the NSC lasted thirty-eight years.

In his efforts to have boxing accepted in law, he appeared in court on a number of occasions when prosecutions were brought following the deaths of boxers during contests. Today's rules, based on the original Queensberry Rules, owe their existence at least in part to Lonsdale's work, in addition to which he helped develop the padded glove, that crucial piece of equipment that marked the game's transition from bare-knuckle to Noble Art.

Whether or not the belts that were to carry his name into perpetuity were his own idea, or that of someone else on the NSC ruling committee is unknown – although had he thought the idea up he would doubtless have laid claim to the distinction in his famous memoirs written in 1936.

What is certain, however, is that he paid for the first one, ordered from the royal jewellers Mappin and Webb in the summer of 1909, and offered up as prize for the winner of the lightweight championship of England.

On 26 June 1909 the following paragraph appeared in the *Mirror of Life's* Note Book column:

On Friday last a meeting was held at the National Sporting Club between Freddie Welsh and Johnny Summers for the purpose of discussing conditions and terms for a match for the lightweight championship of England. Nothing definite, however, was arranged though articles were drawn up calling for a contest between the men to be decided on Monday 18 October but these articles were not signed, and Welsh took home with him on Saturday morning a copy of the proposed agreement to which he would not consent to affix his signature until he had first consulted his Fidus Achates, Mr Harry Marks.

Welsh and his manager Marks had much to discuss before agreeing to the terms offered by the NSC. Although keen to seize the chance to become undisputed lightweight champion of England, Welsh was already contracted to fight Young Joseph a fortnight hence in Wales, not to mention a match with European lightweight holder Piet Hobin in August. How would the results of those matches affect the proposed Belt contest?

Then there was the question of the new lightweight limit of 9 st 9 lb (down some 5 lb from the old limit of 10 st), not to mention the stipulation that he would have to defend the title within six months. What about the cinematic film rights? And would Summers be able to match the suggested £1,000 side bet?

Summers himself had plenty to think about on his own account. The new weight limit would be particularly hard on him as he had not fought below 10 st for some years. (He would argue with the NSC about this but in vain.) He was also contracted to fight Jimmy Britt, ex-USA World champ in mid-July, after which a punishing music hall tour would commence, to be followed by a trip – already signed and sealed – to Australia under the promotional banner of Hugh D. McIntosh.

In the event, the various complications involved almost resulted in the title fight – the first-ever Belt contest – being cancelled. The two men signed for 18 October but with three weeks to go, Summers was forced to ask for a postponement. Illness had led to an extension of his music hall tour contract, but the new date stipulated by the Club for the match with Welsh – November – threatened to lead to a clash of dates with promoter McIntosh, who expected him to be well on his way to Australia by then.

With hundreds of pounds in forfeits looming, Summers seemed helplessly tied up, but McIntosh magnanimously waived his claim to Summer's services: the NSC contract should take precedence, he declared. Thus it was one of the new breed of commercial showmen then transforming professional boxing who paved the way for the first Belt contest – an ironic twist not lost on 'Peggy' Bettinson.

The contractual wrangles leading up to the inaugural Lonsdale Belt contest illustrate, if nothing else, the legal and financial jungle in which pro-boxing, even in 1909, was deeply entangled. Not that the importance of this first Belt match was being underestimated. In fact, unusually for a British title fight, the Summers-Welsh clash was soon capturing world attention.

Welsh, though born in Wales, had fought almost all his contests in the USA and had been beaten only once in over sixty contests. He was a genuine world-rated contender, a British fighter who adopted the all-action American style, well managed and possessing wealthy backers. He also had an acute publicity sense: he regarded the lightweight title as the perfect stepping stone to World title bouts.

Summers, too, was in the top half-dozen world-ranked lightweights. He had already been an English champion – at featherweight in 1906 and, unofficially, at lightweight in 1908. In 100 contests between 1900 and 1909 he had been beaten just fifteen times and had recently impressed in the USA, while his two victories over ex-World champion Jimmy Britt during 1909 had made him the darling of the East End. Thousands had flocked to the West Ham Memorial Grounds to watch him hammer the gallant Britt to defeat in nine rounds amid wild scenes.

Pre-fight analyses presented the fight as the classic clash between 'science' – in the shape of Welsh – and strength – in the shape of Summers. With the added interest generated by the new weight division stipulation, the compulsory defence clause, not to mention the new belt, the eyes of the boxing world were focused on 'Headquarters' that November evening.

Publicity for the fight was unprecedented. *Boxing* – a magazine that was a product of the public's new-found obsession with the sport – devoted page after page to the contest build-up, including full-length profiles, coloured portraits of the two fighters and 'indepth' interviews carried out by roving reporters. Freddie Welsh was visited at his health farm in Chesham, the 'Fruitarian Fighter' being famous as a vegetarian and as someone who utilized all the latest 'scientific' methods of training. Summers, meanwhile, was a more traditional fighter, basing himself in Brighton where he was tracked down preparing with his East End trainers. An ex-stoker in the Merchant Marine and noted for his stamina and immense strength, Summers was concerned that a prolonged struggle to make the new weight might rob him of one of his main advantages.

On the night itself, Welsh, flamboyant as ever, made a grand entrance flanked by four corner-men all wearing jackets emblazoned with the Welsh dragon. The overall effect was spoiled, however, by the peculiar colour of Welsh's legs, which had been coated with iodine after being cut and scratched in a motor-car accident some days earlier.

Summers, meanwhile, entered in more prosaic style, accompanied by NSC corner-man Arthur Gutteridge plus ex-champs Bill Baxter and Jack Goldswain. He immediately pulled a psychological stroke, however, by raising objections to Welsh's hand-bandages. Welsh thus had to leave the arena to have them fixed and while everyone waited, the glittering Lonsdale Belt was carried around the ring for all to gaze upon approvingly.

When at last the fight commenced it was clear within minutes that Summers was going to be outthought and, for the majority of the contest, would be on the receiving end of Welsh's faster, sharper punches. Though regularly shaken, bruised and battered, Summers was able on occasions to shake the Welshman with some heavy shots. But Welsh was a supreme defensive boxer, able to block and stop the majority of Summers's punches, always moving skilfully and cleverly about the ring, 'dancing in and out, checking even Summers's most rapid dashes in such a wonderful style that when Johnny had safely calculated to meet his rushes with a vicious hook or uppercut he would be right out of distance and would nearly over-balance and fall from his effort. . . .'

Welsh was repeatedly cautioned for using his head, boring into Summers's chest, then hooking to head and face as they broke. As Summers commented afterwards: 'I don't remember ever meeting anyone who had just the same style – a crouching, creeping way of getting at you. . . .'

Thus, at the end of twenty hard-fought rounds, no one was surprised when Bettinson announced that the winner on points was Welsh – the first holder of a Lonsdale Belt.

Interviewed afterwards in his dressing-room, Welsh was diplomatic about the standard of refereeing at the Club but commented on how difficult it was to fight in the NSC's stuffy, smoke-filled atmosphere. Meanwhile his seconds carried on a brisk trade in the sale of his bloodied and sweat-stained inter-round handkerchiefs.

After a few days' delay in London, while the belt was taken off to be engraved and photographed, he took it in triumph back to Wales, his spiritual if not his actual home.

There followed a period of feverish negotiations as Welsh attempted to maximize his earnings. He returned to the NSC the following year to fight Packy MacFarland for the 'World' lightweight title, following this up with a much-heralded but dis-appointing non-title fight with featherweight Jim Driscoll. He then toyed with the idea of taking on Young Joseph at Wonderland – the Jewish East End's 'alternative' NSC – where promotor Jack Woolf was offering a sizeable purse, and a belt. The idea came to nothing, however, as did attempts to set up World title fights with Abe Attell and Ad Wolgast. Thus, some sixteen months after his first Belt fight, Welsh somewhat reluctantly re-entered the NSC ring to make his first, belated defence of his title against Matt Wells.

Although the same age as Welsh, Wells had been a professional for just two years, having already had a long and distinguished career as an amateur. In truth, no one gave Wells a chance and the expectation was that Welsh would be too quick, too clever, too ringwise. In the event, the bout proved to be the first major upset in Belt history.

Wells danced around Welsh for twenty rounds, scoring with speed and accuracy as well as demonstrating a tight defence. Welsh, on the other hand, started slowly and over-confidently, as he commented afterwards: 'Had I started after him sooner, there would have been a different result.' In time-honoured fashion, Welsh still claimed to have 'edged it', but referee Douglas gave Wells twelve rounds to Welsh's six. Other experts made the margin even greater.

Inevitably, both men set off for the USA, Wells hoping to meet various top-liners in lucrative no-decision bouts (Abe Attell, Leach Cross, Pal Moore, Packy McFarland) but his grand plans were upset when he fell ill with erysipelas. By the time the two men re-entered the Covent Garden ring in November 1912, Welsh had learned from his previous mistakes, had trained

BOXING, NOVEMBER 16, 1912
Vol. VII.—No. 167.

# THE GREAT LIGHT-WEIGHT BATTLE.

# BOXING

**PUBLISHED EVERY TUESDAY IN LONDON; EVERY WEDNESDAY IN THE PROVINCES.** | **ONE PENNY.**

THE ONLY PAPER IN THE WORLD SOLELY DEVOTED TO BOXING.

VOL. VII.—No. 167. ~ NOVEMBER 16TH, 1912. Registered at the General Post Office as a Newspaper and for Canadian Magazine Post.

## THE LIGHT-WEIGHT BELT CONTESTANTS,
### FRED WELSH AND MATT WELLS.

properly and now demonstrated his championship calibre (helped also by the defection of Wells's trainer to the Welsh camp) by imposing his own US style on the more traditional English method of Wells. Welsh also appeared to have studied Wells closely, particularly where in-fighting was concerned.

Welsh came out on top in the first clinch and ultimately Wells began to avoid coming in close, a psychological victory for Welsh upon which he gradually and relentlessly built. It was a close fight but once again there were no complaints when Welsh's hand was raised at the end of twenty rounds.

Welsh's challenges were now all directed at American and Australian opponents; and though no one knew it at the time, the Lonsdale Belt he had regained would never be fought for again. In June 1914 at Olympia, Welsh met and beat Willie Ritchie to become the undisputed World champion. His designated challenger for the British title – one Jerry Delaney from Bradford – who had waited patiently while Welsh had pursued his World title ambitions, thus looked forward to a Belt match that would carry with it a World title. But Welsh saw no financial incentive in meeting Delaney, and under existing NSC regulations the Club either felt it could not, or decided that it would not, insist on Welsh immediately accepting a challenge from Delaney.

Welsh therefore left for the USA, the First World War broke out and he never fought in the UK again. Poor Jerry Delaney was to be doubly unfortunate. In 1913, when fighting at featherweight, he had been nominated as challenger for the featherweight title then held by Ted Kid Lewis. Lewis, however, also decided to head abroad in search of money, first to Australia and then to the States, arriving just as war in Europe began.

Thus Delaney was left high and dry by two belt-holders, both of whom would spend the duration of the war earning good money in the States, capitalizing on their Lonsdale Belts. Delaney, by contrast, joined the Bradford Pals Battalion, won the DCM and was killed on the Somme in 1916.

Welsh's Lonsdale Belt (along with a second belt he had won when defeating Hughie Mehegan for the British Empire title) would remain with him in the USA. The Club rules at that point were vague concerning mandatory defences; and preoccupied as it was with raising money for ambulances during the war, it ultimately allowed him to keep the belt.

In 1920 Welsh retired, a rich man. By 1927, however, he was dead, bankrupted by the failure of his New York health farm business. His wife, left to cope as best she could, was eventually forced to sell the belt to a fight promoter who offered it to the winner of the Tony Canzoneri v Kid Chocolate World lightweight bout in 1931. It was handed over to Canzoneri and thereafter was never seen again.

# 2

## Boxing Booming

The introduction of the Lonsdale Belts was both a result of, and a contributory factor to, the British pro-boxing 'boom'; and in the two years that followed the inaugural Belt match, British boxing would experience a rapid, unregulated expansion that would bring, on the one hand, ever more pressure on the NSC to take more responsibility for 'controlling' the sport, while on the other increasing criticism of its 'domination' of championship contests.

The rise in the sport's popularity drew bigger audiences at fight venues up and down the country and presented anti-boxing forces with a variety of opportunities to highlight their case concerning the moral dangers posed by the sport (the drinking, the gambling, the associated skulduggery), while civil authorities – police and local authorities – expressed fears concerning large numbers of people gathering to watch an event that could, in certain circumstances, lead to widespread violence.

In this respect, the activities of the new breed of boxing entrepreneurs who were more businessmen than sportsmen hardly helped matters. Hugh McIntosh had shown what could be done in Australia in 1908 when he had promoted the famous Jack Johnson v Tommy Burns World heavyweight title fight. But with the US boxing scene in the doldrums following moves to outlaw the sport and to curtail large 'purse' fights, and with the Australian authorities determined to prevent another fight on the scale of the Johnson v Burns contest, McIntosh headed for England in 1910 and began preparations for a series of World championships, focusing on the search for a 'White Hope' to regain the heavyweight title from Johnson.

The resultant increase in 'hype' and excitement galvanized home promoters to step up their operations and by mid–1911 the talk was all of syndicates and gigantic new venues, enormous 'purses' and World titles. It was a relative newcomer – Jimmy White – who appeared, however, to have secured the biggest one of all: an £8,000 purse match between Jack Johnson and Bombardier Billy Wells to take place at the Earls Court Arena.

In the event, the Wells v Johnson fight was banned at the last moment by the then Home Secretary Winston Churchill (after taking advice from, among others, Lord Lonsdale). The reasons given concerned fears about the impact such a contest might have on delicate race relations throughout the Empire, particularly in view of the extraordinary coverage the contest was already receiving in the rapidly expanding popular press.

Confirmation that the authorities were unhappy about any such large-scale contests rather than simply those involving black fighters came a couple of months later with a magistrate's injunction (both men being bound over to keep the peace) that effectively halted the Owen Moran v Jim Driscoll contest scheduled to be held in Birmingham.

This decision, plus the actions of various police commissioners in Yorkshire and South Wales to allow only 'amateur' contests to proceed, confirmed certain NSC members in their belief that restricting British championship contests to the confines of the Club was prudent and indeed necessary.

As for the demands that the Club become the FA/MCC of boxing, regulating and controlling the sport from the grass-roots up – even those who might have hankered after such a role would have been daunted by the prospect in those 'boom' years just prior to the First World War. Hundreds of new venues were opening their doors to boxing, with many new halls being created specifically for the sport. In 1909 alone, Newcastle's St James, Manchester's Belle Vue, the Stadium in Liverpool and the Ring, Blackfriars began long and distinguished 'careers' as top venues, but many more smaller halls and stadia, including dozens of new skating rinks then being built, were hired and adapted by promoters.

It was the proliferation of music hall matinee shows that caused many complaints in 1910–11 concerning both the level of enter-

BOXING, DEC. 17, 1910. Vol. III.—No. 67.

# SPECIAL CHRISTMAS ISSUE.

With Coloured Supplement of Bombardier Wells.

Price 2d.

# BOXING

SPECIAL CHRISTMAS ISSUE. Price 2d.

THE ONLY PAPER IN THE WORLD SOLELY DEVOTED TO BOXING.

Vol. III.—No. 67.    17TH DECEMBER, 1910.    Registered at the General Post Office as a Newspaper and for Canadian Magazine Post.

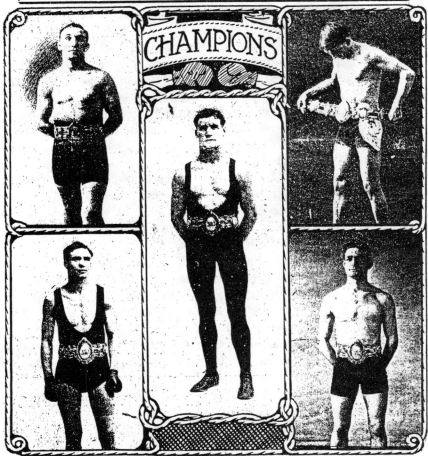

CHAMPIONS

YOUNG JOSEPH (*Welter-weight*).    JIM SULLIVAN    FRED WELSH (*Light-weight*).
DIGGER STANLEY (*Bantam*).    (*Middle-weight*).    JIM DRISCOLL (*Feather*).

tainment and the conditions under which boxers were expected to perform. Too often those putting on the shows knew little or nothing about the sport: mismatches were commonplace, as was the two-minute round – leading to farcical contests for which many men rarely bothered to prepare. There was also widespread abuse of contracts, with boxers either being grossly underpaid or not paid at all. As there was little hope of their obtaining redress in the courts, since many magistrates were not prepared to recognize boxing as a bona-fide 'trade' it can be no coincidence that 1910 saw the formation of the first Boxer's Union, in an attempt to bring some sort of basic regulation to an increasingly anarchic sport.

The anarchy, however, was by no means confined to the afternoon shows or the behaviour of fly-by-night promoters with little interest in the sport. The boom period and the arrival of Hugh McIntosh saw competition among the established boxing promoters hotting up considerably, competition that all too often spilled over into intimidation and 'spoiling' tactics that did boxing no good at all.

Notorious during these years was the rivalry between Harry Jacobs and Jack Woolf – once partners in running the famous Wonderland in the Whitechapel Road – but by 1910 arch enemies.

When Jacobs had been forced out of Wonderland that year, *Boxing* commented in an editorial: 'He has done his best to damage boxing and his enforced retirement has been followed by a boom that augurs well for everyone.' Unfortunately for his critics, Jacobs soon began operating at the Paragon Music Hall, also on the Whitechapel Road,

Jack Woolf of Wonderland.
*Boxing*, June 1910

where he advertised mammoth shows in direct competition to those at nearby Wonderland.

Before Jacobs was eventually forced out once again – this time by the LCC after complaints from local inhabitants – the rival promoters engaged in sporadic poster battles (plastering each other's bills with advertisements for tonic pills and even *Boxing* magazine itself) which led, in 1910, to *Boxing* complaining in an editorial:

> Just at present there is in the London camp of promoters an amount of friction that is a serious indictment against the honour and manhood of some of them.

The editor went on to cite 'contemptible methods of attack against their rivals' 'mean tactics', and even 'threats of violence'. Though never stated openly, it can safely be assumed that the eventual destruction of Wonderland by fire in August 1911 was a direct result of the battle, particularly when Jacobs opened up Premierland no more than a short walk from where Wonderland had stood, just four months after the 'mysterious' fire.

The rivalry, however, was not confined to these two men. Jack Callaghan, after a successful season at the Holborn Empire in early 1910, found that certain 'approaches' had been made to Lou Zeitland, manager of the Gibbons circuit of theatres of which Holborn formed a part, requesting that Callaghan's tenure of the theatre be terminated. Fortunately for Callaghan, Walter Gibbons and Zeitland refused to be intimidated.

The increasing tendency of promoters to engage in wars of attrition rather than simply co-operating was deplored by *Boxing* which by 1910 had taken upon itself, under editor John Murray, the role of unofficial watchdog and conscience of the sport. Murray warned that if they (boxing's administrators) did not get together: 'The axe is sure to fall; if not today or tomorrow, it will some day and the result will be a visitation of calamity to all. . . .'

The widespread abuse of rules and regulations, not to mention the increasingly bitter commercial rivalry was not, of course, the NSC's fault; but with the institution of the Lonsdale Belts, eyes increasingly turned towards 'Headquarters' for a constructive, authoritative lead. To make matters worse for the Club, it soon became clear that the Americans, by establishing the New York State Athletic Association in mid–1911, were taking the lead in organizing boxing.

The NSC, however, remained unmoved – content or condemned to being the nominal governing body, its control over the sport symbolic rather than practical, its grip over even the English championships tenuous, even haphazard at times. In fact, the early history of the welterweight title, first fought for in March 1910, illustrates just how much the Club and its belts were still at the mercy of commercial forces and individual champions' whims.

More than any other division, the welterweight class seemed to reflect at this time the varying fortunes of professional boxing. In 1910 the two men who had contested the British title back in 1907 – Curly Watson and the black South African Andrew Jeptha – were both in the news; Jeptha because he was almost blind and was about to receive a benefit from the NSC, and Watson because in March he never regained consciousness after being floored in the Wonderland ring by Frank Englis, a West Indian fighter.

The two men who entered the NSC ring that same month to contest the first welterweight Lonsdale Belt were notable for more than merely boxing prowess. Both were Jewish, evidence of the plethora of talent then emerging from among the first generation of English Jews born of parents who had arrived in Britain at the turn of the century from Russia and Eastern Europe.

Aschel Joseph (Young Joseph) was an East End hero and a Wonderland favourite. He was also, in 1910, at the heart of the newly formed Boxer's Union, and would be elected president in 1911. His involvement in the Union would lead him into some unlikely litigation after the championship match.

In 1908 Joseph had beaten Corporal Baker at the NSC to become welterweight champion and in an eventful career at featherweight and lightweight he had met champions such as Jim Kenrick, Owen Moran, Freddie Welsh, Pedlar Palmer and Seaman Hayes, among others.

Jack Goldswain, from Bermondsey, had been lightweight champion between 1906 and 1908 when he had beaten Johnny Summers, but in the period just prior to the title fight had apparently been inactive, preferring like so many prominent boxers before

BOXING, MARCH 26, 1910.
Vol. II.—No. 29.

# SPECIAL ISSUE. 32 Pages.

# BOXING

EVERY WEDNESDAY. ONE PENNY.
*The only Paper in the World solely devoted to Boxing.*

VOL. II.—No. 29. 26TH MARCH, 1910. Registered at the General Post Office as a Newspaper and for Canadian Magazine Post.

JACK GOLDSWAIN AND HARRY (YOUNG) JOSEPH

and since to work the music halls rather than take on serious opponents. It was to prove his undoing, as his weight had risen to well above the welterweight limit and the effort to reduce would render him weak and ineffectual.

Joseph, by contrast, had been trained to perfection by the ubiquitous Dai Dollings who would assist Tom Thomas to the middleweight title and play a significant role in Matt Wells's surprise victory over Freddie Welsh. Joseph was a fine athlete, described by the *Boxing* correspondent as, 'sleek, lithe, with the quick dash of an angry panther in his movements' – a box-fighter who won the majority of his contests on points.

Always active, he fought five times in the two months prior to the title fight, one of his victims being the doomed Curly Watson.

In the event, however, the first welterweight Lonsdale title fight was a great disappointment. Goldswain, from the very outset, looked weak, his punches were feeble and his main tactic appeared to be to hang on and hope to catch Joseph with a KO punch. He took regular, sustained two-handed punishment throughout the eleven rounds the fight lasted, principally uppercuts as the two men grappled. By the tenth he was being warned repeatedly, and in the eleventh, battered and bruised, he was disqualified for persistent holding. Joseph, by contrast, was unmarked when he left the ring to receive the belt.

The main talking point afterwards, however, was the decision of the NSC stewards to confiscate Goldswain's wages and training expenses, because the contract both men had signed prior to the fight had stipulated that, in the event of disqualification, no part of the purse would be paid.

Goldswain insisted on taking the Club to court and, in the case that followed, Young Joseph found himself giving evidence against the NSC, insisting that Goldswain had tried his hardest and should not be penalized financially.

Unfortunately for Goldswain, because of the existing contract he had signed, the judge at Westminster County Court decided there was no case to go before a jury and entered judgement for the NSC, with costs. Almost everyone, even friends of the Club, felt they had been unduly harsh.

Joseph himself proved something of a handful for the Club as champion – in fact, he would not defend the belt and it would be another two years or more of considerable confusion before the belt was once again on offer. The problem was that Joseph had too many irons in the fire and felt little loyalty towards the Club.

Within three months of winning the belt, he took on Harry Lewis at Wonderland for a version of the World title, losing in seven on a great East End occasion. By August he was considering a fight with Freddie Welsh for an alternative welterweight title (complete with belt) offered by Wonderland proprietor Jack Woolf. This did not materialize and so he took on and beat Battling Lacroix for the European title in Paris.

In January 1911 he met one of his main challengers for the English title – Arthur Evernden – but at the Ring, Blackfriars. Although he lost on a disqualification, he continued to claim both belt and title, claiming that the Evernden fight had not been under championship conditions. At this early stage in the belt history, the principle of returning the belt if defeated outside the Club premises and inside the championship limit had not been established – though this did not stop Evernden claiming that he was the welterweight champion.

In 1911 Joseph successfully defended his European title in May, but then lost it to Georges Carpentier in October, the fight ending in the tenth round, a considerable achievement when one considers the records of other British fighters against the glamorous Frenchman.

In April 1912, however, Joseph finally consented to put his English title on the line – but in Liverpool, against Johnny Summers. The two men had met four times before, all in 1904, when Joseph had won twice and

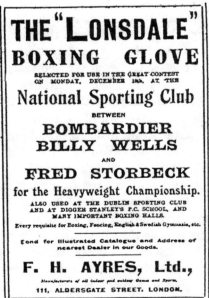

drawn once. This time, Summers proved the cleverer man, taking the title on points.

The belt, however, was now in no one's possession. Thus, in June 1912 the NSC persuaded Summers and the 'unofficial' champion, Evernden, to meet in what turned out to be an enthralling contest that had a dramatic conclusion.

Hard-hitting blacksmith Evernden, the younger, heavier man, was revealed by veteran Summers to have a weakness for body-shots. By the thirteenth, with both men tiring, they engaged in a tussle in one corner when Evernden broke away, staggered across the ring and onto the ropes. Summers followed him but Evernden had slithered to the canvas before further punches could be landed. Rising to his feet, Evernden staggered back across the ring, Summers throwing punches after him, only to fall again. He rose at the count of three, and was battered through the ropes, almost falling onto the ring apron, before coming to rest lying draped across the lower rope.

The NSC, contrary to all rules and tradition, was now in an uproar, as a consequence of which the referee, seated as was normal outside the ring, was unable to make himself heard. In the words of the *Boxing* reporter, chaos ensued:

> The excitement was rendered more tense than it would otherwise have been by the actions of Evernden's seconds. Apparently realizing that their man was now hopelessly beaten they had run round to his assistance and were pushing him up from the edge of the ring platform, while Arthur himself, still resolute to fight on while life lasted, grasped feebly but gallantly for the ropes.
>
> Summers naturally resented any illegal assistance being rendered to his opponent and fiercely struck at Harry Mansfield and the others who were doing their best to prevent an accident such as might have occurred had Evernden slipped off the edge of the platform onto his head. . . .

Although Evernden managed to regain his feet and the two even squared up, it was noticed, at last, that referee Douglas (still outside the ring!) was signalling that the bout was over.

When Summers made a successful defence against Sid Burns

at the NSC in December (in another enthralling bout in which the two fighters almost managed simultaneously to KO each other in the nineteenth round) it looked odds on that the Yorkshire-born veteran (he had been fighting since 1900, the Burns fight being his tenth championship contest) would secure a belt out-right. Instead, he succumbed to offers from the new Australian promotional king, Snowy Baker, who 'imported' a troupe of wel-terweights – Evernden, Burns, Tom McCormick, Matt Wells and Summers – for a series of welterweight title fights advertised as being for the British, Empire and even World titles.

Summers was defeated twice by Tom McCormick who in turn was beaten by Matt Wells, but although the latter then set off for America claiming to be World champion, the NSC simply refused to recognize the validity of any of the matches. Thus when Sum-mers returned to the UK in 1914 he found himself matched still as champion against up-and-coming Johnny Basham, who KO'd him in fourteen rounds.

The introduction of the belts – at least for the welterweight division – had thus signally failed to achieve a smooth succession of legitimate title bouts. In four years there had been nine welter-weight 'title' clashes and four champions, only two of whom were recognized by the Club and awarded a belt. The problem, inevitably, in a division boasting such attractive and popular fighters, was that rival promoters had been able to offer more attractive purses than the NSC.

However, even in a division lacking charismatic fighters, the problems remained of establishing continuity and coherence in title terms. The middleweights were a case in point.

In October 1909, Tom Thomas, recognized by most critics as the unofficial middleweight champion, issued a challenge to all-comers, and by November 'Peggy' Bettinson was negotiating with him to meet Charlie Wilson for £200 a side and a £400 purse, in addition to Lord Lonsdale's second championship belt.

Thomas, from Penygraig in Wales, was almost thirty years old and had been recognized as champion since 1906 when he had defeated Pat O'Keefe. Unbeaten as a senior professional in some forty contests, he was a hard puncher (88 per cent of his contests had ended in KO victories) but his career had been regularly interrupted by bouts of rheumatic fever. In fact, in the week prior

THE DEMON RABBIT

to the contest, his knee had given way in training and he had been taken home in a pony and trap.

Trainer Dai Dollings was employed to massage his joints after every sparring session, and it is no wonder that his career had been described as 'a record of victory gained by insurmountable perseverance and persistent ill-luck'.

Wilson, though a natural middleweight, had spent much of his career fighting at catchweight, some stone or so heavier. He was a fast, clever boxer; indeed, Bettinson had employed him to spar with Jack Johnson when the famous black champion had been in London preparing for an abortive championship contest at the Club against Tommy Burns.

In the event, the effort to get down to the middleweight limit, plus the undoubtedly harder punch of Thomas, proved decisive: a left hook, followed by a hard right which loosened three of Wilson's front teeth, ended a disappointing contest in only the second round.

Wilson later claimed that he had been poisoned, deliberately, by someone who had tampered with a rabbit pie he had eaten just prior to the contest! Thomas, however, set off on the obligatory music hall tour, toying all the while with a possible move up to heavyweight to challenge the then champion Iron Hague.

Despite numerous, often lucrative, offers, many of them scuppered by further bouts of rheumatics, Thomas was nevertheless matched with Jim Sullivan of Bermondsey in November 1910, in what turned out to be the first unsuccessful defence of a Lonsdale Belt.

Thomas had been his own worst enemy, for according to *Boxing's* correspondent:

> He entered into the match in careless fashion, and with the idea that the Bermondsey boxer would be his second victim for the belt, and so he rejected the services of his old trainer, Dai Dollings, the man who engineered the defeat of Fred Welsh from Matt Wells's corner. Tom actually did part of his training for the fight on horseback over the sand-hills of Port Talbot.
>
> The result was that he went up to London in flabby condition and was as slow as the proverbial cart-horse against the well-trained Sullivan. Nevertheless, no champion was ever battered as badly as Sullivan was; but Jim's boxing got him the points and the belt; which he was too ill to claim, as is usual, on the following day.

Thomas only had one more fight – an unofficial battle for the British light-heavyweight title in February 1911 at Wonderland under the auspices of Jack Woolf. He lost on a foul. There was talk of him meeting Billy Papke for a World middleweight title, but Papke withdrew. Within a month, Thomas was dead, having succumbed to pneumonia.

His successor, Jim Sullivan, seemed equally unlucky in cashing in on the belt. In May 1911 he too was matched with Billy Papke, who then claimed a version of the World middleweight title. The two met under the McIntosh promotional banner at the London Palladium, Sullivan being forced to retire in the ninth round. In February 1912 he met Georges Carpentier in Monte Carlo for the European middleweight title, only to be KO'd in two.

In May 1912 the NSC matched Sullivan with Jack Harrison in a title defence (at no small expense to himself, Sullivan complained) but illness eventually led to his having to hand the belt back without defending it – the first boxer to be compelled to do this.

Harrison was then matched with Irishman Pat McEnroy and produced a dull but determined performance to become the third holder of the belt in as many years.

# 3

## Peerless Jim and the East End Kid

Bettinson's hopes that the Lonsdale Belts would 'capture the boxers' minds, also the public's imagination and would leave the "dear bad old days" far behind', had been unfulfilled where the light, welter and middleweight divisions were concerned. However, in the three lightest categories – fly, bantam and feather – the first Lonsdale Belt decade was by any standards a great success, with almost every title match taking place within the NSC itself, featuring boxers of truly world quality: Jimmy Wilde, Tancy Lee, Sid Smith, Digger Stanley, Joe Fox, Owen Moran and the 'Peerless' Jim Driscoll.

If ever a boxer epitomized the ideals, the dreams – even the purpose – of the NSC, then that boxer was Jim Driscoll, said to be the only pugilist to have had his portrait hung on the walls of the old Covent Garden Club.

In fact, by the time the first featherweight belt was put up for challenge in February 1910 (the third belt in the series) Driscoll was twenty-nine years old and his greatest days were almost over. However, his career would reach a fitting climax: between 1910 and 1913 he would have five title fights at featherweight which would bring him a Lonsdale Belt outright, a European title and a World title.

The most popular, most natural contest for the first featherweight belt would have been Driscoll v Owen Moran. At that stage, both men could put forward strong claims to being World champion.

In early 1910, however, Moran was asking for too much money from the NSC for a Belt match with Driscoll, preferring instead to remain in the USA in pursuit of World champion Abe Attell; so Driscoll was matched, rather surprisingly, with a great Club favourite but certainly no world-class boxer, Seaman Arthur Hayes.

In fact, the contest was a gross mismatch with spectators calling for it to be stopped as early as the fourth round. Hayes was floored in the sixth which convinced referee Scott to call a halt.

Driscoll's preparations for the Hayes contest had been casual to the point of indifference: rising when he wanted, eating what he wanted, sparring with local lads including one Salam Sullivan, his regular music hall sparring partner. One suspects that the contest was arranged by the Club committee more as a warm-up for Driscoll who was, along with the Club, eyeing one if not two possible fistic gold-mines against Owen Moran and Freddie Welsh.

However, all this speculation concerning the famous Welsh trio had led to the very legitimate claims of Spike Robson being temporarily overlooked. On the domestic front, Robson, too, could claim to be English champion: he had defeated Johnny Summers back in 1906 prior to setting off for the USA where his impressive record included a win over 'Terrible' Terry McGovern. Thus, with negotiations stalled regarding Welsh and Moran, Driscoll and the Club felt that Robson's claims could no longer be ignored and, two months after the Hayes fight, the two men entered the NSC ring for what turned out to be a quite extraordinary, sensational contest.

Robson, realizing that Driscoll – the supreme stylist, cool and unruffled, always perfectly balanced – had to be knocked out of his stride, set out to unsettle and even unnerve him by being as outrageous as possible. And he succeeded to such an extent that many in the audience wondered quite what they were witnessing. 'Extraordinary', 'mysterious', 'amazing' were the words used in various reports to describe Robson's apparently suicidal tactics of inviting punishment, of deliberately planting his bullet-shaven head in Driscoll's line of fire, taking hooks, straight lefts, uppercuts, absorbing them all and then, smiling and laughing, coming back wildly, throwing punches from all angles. So effective were these antics that both the champion's eyes were soon closing and his composure seemed so shaken that there were moments when

THE FIGHT FOR THE FEATHER-WEIGHT CHAMPIONSHIP.

BOXING. APRIL 23, 1910.
Vol. II.—No. 33.

# BOXING

**EVERY WEDNESDAY.**     **ONE PENNY.**
*The only Paper in the World solely devoted to Boxing.*

VOL. II.—No. 33.      23RD APRIL, 1910.      Registered at the General Post Office as a Newspaper and for Canadian Magazine Post.

FRANK ("SPIKE") ROBSON AND JIM DRISCOLL.
*Who contested the Feather-Weight title last Monday at the N.S.C..*

he was missing with both lefts and rights, looking ungainly, puzzled, even rocky.

Unfortunately, Robson's madcap tactics eventually rebounded on him when, in the fifth round, he suffered a quite fearful accident. According to the *Boxing* correspondent, the bell sounded for the start of the round and Robson sped across the ring 'as though shot from a gun'. Driscoll had hardly risen when Robson was upon him. However:

> Jim whisked himself aside in time, but only just in time, or he must have been driven helplessly crashing onto his own chair which was just then being lifted out of the ring. And it was that chair that destroyed more than half of Spike's chances for he came plunging into it head down and met a corner with the top of his head. It was one of the most fearful crashes imaginable and an everlasting mystery about this astonishing contest was how Robson escaped going out there and then from concussion of the brain. The skin was split wide and deep, the blood gushing all over his shaken crown and down into his eyes.
>
> A gasp went up from the spectators and when we saw Robson dancing about with a broad smile on his face we could scarcely believe our eyes.

Robson, despite or perhaps because of the accident, continued to fight like a dervish for another ten rounds until the heavy punishment took its dramatic toll. In the last round he was hardly fighting back at all, simply rolling around the ring as Driscoll picked him off with rights and lefts. Then he paused momentarily to wipe the blood from his nose after a particularly sharp Driscoll straight left. The champion followed up with a stiff straight right that sent Robson almost through the ropes, mouth gaping. He struggled up at three, only to be floored again by another right. He staggered up once more before tottering across the ring to collapse in a heap, unconscious, a state in which he would remain for a full hour afterwards.

Driscoll claimed after the fight that he himself had been so badly hurt in the fourth round that it took him another four rounds to regain his vision. Again, according to *Boxing*: 'I fought by guesswork. I could not see him and it was only by a sort of instinct that I ducked and stepped for I could neither see him nor his blows coming.'

If we accept the conclusion of ringside experts that Robson must also have been concussed from the fifth round on, following the collision with the stool, then most of the drama and apparent lack of logic of much of the fight can be explained: neither man was fully conscious for long periods of it!

Early in the New Year of 1911 Driscoll was back in the NSC ring, in a return match against Robson. Ironically, their first sensational contest had been thinly attended; now the NSC was packed to the rafters for what turned out to be a much less exciting contest.

Driscoll was by this time aware of Robson's possible game-plan and acted accordingly – thus the surprise element was gone and Driscoll was in control from start to finish, Robson rarely troubling the Welshman.

Despite Robson's protest, referee Douglas had little option than to halt the fight in the eleventh round. Thus Driscoll took the first featherweight Lonsdale Belt home with him for keeps – in record time. It would be another two years before he defended his title.

In January 1912 he captured the European title from Jean Poesy (in a bout advertised for the latter's GB/IBU World title) and after flirting with the idea of retirement, was finally persuaded to put up all his titles against Owen Moran.

Moran had spent much of the intervening time in the States, unsuccessfully challenging Ad Wolgast for the World lightweight title in July 1911. The chance to take Driscoll's titles was too good to turn down, however, as, close to thirty years old himself, the prospect of retirement was looming for him as well.

Moran was probably one of the greatest British boxers never to win a Belt match – his commitment to big purse contests in the USA being the principal reason. He was no stranger to the NSC, however, having first fought there in 1901 for no more that £10 a side. Considered quick and elusive, good at the 'American' in-fighting style, he was admired by Bettinson and had appeared on the Club's famous 1907 fight bill featuring Sam Langford.

In fact, securing the Driscoll v Moran contest was quite a coup for the Club: it had been banned in 1911 and now 'it was necessary to ask for 3 gns for the lowest-priced seat, such was the widespread interest in the affair . . . and not long before the two men took the ring there was not even standing room. . . '.

Driscoll had trained hard for this, his last (or so he claimed) contest, and had included among his sparring partners a certain up-and-coming Jimmy Wilde. Much play was made concerning his long lay-off and a debilitating cold said to have weakened him considerably, but *Boxing* was inclined to regard this as a smokescreen.

The intriguing contest, a clash of two styles, proceeded very much as predicted, with Driscoll taking the first half of the contest by moving and jabbing, and Moran happy to pursue and work to the body, gradually wearing the older man down.

Driscoll was considered slower than when in his prime, his snappy left lacking in power, though his ducking, side-stepping and ability to slip away from trouble more than compensated.

'Like a deerstalker', *Boxing* described him, 'preserving his energy for the inevitable assault.'

Moran, gradually sensing that the contest was slipping away from him, began to step up the pace in the latter rounds, forcing himself into clinches where he was able to prise the tiring arms of Driscoll away in order to deliver uppercuts and work to the body. However, much of his work was marred by a gradual desperation – he was running out of time.

Only in the last round did victory for Moran look a possibility, with Driscoll, now grey-faced with fatigue, using all his skill and experience to keep himself on his feet. Though he took heavy right-hand punches that closed his left eye and had him staggering, clinging on, desperately weaving and swaying and flailing to keep the younger man away, it was still something of a surprise when referee Douglas declared the contest a draw.

Moran, however, leapt from his corner and raised his right arm in exultation, clearly relieved that he had not been beaten, before running across to Driscoll and embracing him.

Driscoll's career was now virtually over, although for some months in 1913 he and the NSC toyed with the idea of another defence of his title against one of a number of possible contenders – and there were plenty to choose from.

The featherweight division had become crowded at the top, with contenders such as Seaman Hayes (still plugging away), Tommy Mitchell, Darkey Haley, Joe Starmer, Nat Williams, Billy Marchant, Alec Lambert, Young Brooks and Ted Kid Lewis all clamouring for a shot at the title. The problem was that everyone seemed to be beating everyone else. As Ted Broadribb suggested in a revealing little article in *Boxing* in mid–1912, the confusion was due to poor handling and guidance. His boxers, he emphasized, 'usually have a good chance because I take good care to see that they have it'. A significant pointer for the future from a man who would soon become one of the most influential men in British boxing history.

However, by mid-1913 – with Driscoll having at last decided not to risk his reputation, and with Moran once again busy in the USA – the confusion had cleared to reveal Ted Kid Lewis and Alec Lambert as the nominated challengers for the vacant featherweight throne.

Ted Kid Lewis was a young man who, like many promising boxers of the period, was fighting almost every fortnight, exemplifying callous exploitation by managers and even, in Lewis's case, his own family. Driscoll, for instance, in an eighteen-year career had just over seventy official fights. By the tender age of seventeen, after only two years as a professional, Lewis had already exceeded that figure. And evidence of the mercenary outlook of his advisers came in a court case in 1914 when his manager – one Sam Shear – took him to court alleging breach of contract and loss of earnings after Lewis had decided to accept a contract with Harry Morris, then promoting at Premierland.

Lewis claimed in court, according to *Boxing*, that one week prior to the Lonsdale Belt contest with Lambert, 'the plaintiff, (Shear), had a conversation with him and told him he could get a lot of money by losing the contest. Witness declined to agree to the suggestion and said he meant to win the belt. . . .'

The Lewis v Lambert title fight revealed one of Broadribb's suspicions – that despite the apparent confusion at the top of the featherweight tree, there was really only one world-class fighter among them – to be correct. Although troubled by having to come down to featherweight (at seventeen years of age, Lewis was already much happier operating at lightweight), with the expert help of Dai Dollings he was too strong for Lambert, whose classic left-hand lead style, upright and correct, although keeping him in the contest until midway through, was not equipped to deal with a fighter like Lewis, whose heavier punch eventually took its toll. When Lambert was floored twice in the seventeenth, referee Douglas decided to call a halt.

Lewis, at this early point in his career, suffered by comparison with Driscoll. Only a youth, with a tendency to swing wildly at times, he looked raw (despite having had almost eighty fights) and was not as aesthetically pleasing to watch as Driscoll. Yet to those who looked carefully, it was clear that Lewis possessed a fighting intelligence superior to that of his peers – an ability to adapt his style and method according to circumstances. He needed little tactical guidance, and when asked during the Shear trial who was the best boxing manager around, he replied, 'I am.'

But his further involvement in Lonsdale Belt affairs would be mainly after the war. Following a ritual challenge to Owen Moran (who turned the chance down because the money was not sufficient) and an East End jamboree when winning the European crown at Premierland in February 1914, Lewis and his adviser/trainer Alec Goodman suddenly set off for Australia, leaving various promoters and potential challengers in the lurch. Australian promoter Snowy Baker had offered Lewis a series of fights with various globetrotting Americans in Sydney.

Although he took his Lonsdale Belt with him (to charm the ladies, including Ellen Terry, the actress who was also sailing to Sydney) it was clear that he would not be defending it. After fulfilling his contract in Australia (where he fought at catchweights well above featherweight) he travelled on to America in pursuit of Freddie Welsh and the latter's lightweight World title. By 1915 he was claiming the welterweight World title, which he was to contest with Jack Britton and others for the duration of the First World War.

By 1915, therefore, the NSC had declared the featherweight title vacant and had matched talented Llew Edwards with globetrotting Owen Moran – a move that presented Lewis with something of a problem.

Prior to the staging of the bout, Bettinson cabled Lewis for the return of the belt. Unfortunately, Lewis had managed, literally, to lose it. In early 1915 he had been struggling to obtain fights and had jumped at the opportunity to appear in a series of preliminary bouts staged to whet the appetite of customers for the forthcoming World heavyweight title fight between Jack Johnson and Jess Willard in Havana, Cuba.

Lewis took his belt along and placed it on display in a shop window in downtown Havana. When the historic and controversial bout finally took place, however, Lewis was still waiting to be paid for his own contest, and it soon became clear that the fight organizers were bankrupt. Realizing that enraged Cubans would soon be hunting down 'foreign' fight folk, Lewis decided to leave in a hurry – and in doing so apparently forgot about the precious belt.

Back in New York, he cabled a friend to collect it, only to be told that the belt had disappeared. It took another two months for police to trace the trophy – the thief attempted to pawn it and was arrested. Lewis had to borrow money to retrieve it, and years later could still recall the immense feeling of relief he felt at seeing it safe and sound once again. By the time the belt arrived back in the UK, however, the Edwards v Moran bout had ended – in much controversy.

This was to be thirty-year-old Moran's last opportunity to lay claim to a bona fide title. For Edwards, just twenty-one and a pro for two years (and almost forty contests) it was a dramatic step-up in class and yet, right up to the bell, he was the betting favourite.

Owen certainly did not look the veteran. As a *Boxing* correspondent described him:

> His skin bore that ruddy and bronzed hue which is always associated with the athlete in perfect condition. His sturdy, compact little frame looked a picture in its display of muscular development and which, nevertheless, was that of the boxer rather than of the strong man and wrestler.

On the other hand, the Welsh boy looked pale in comparison and so fine-drawn generally as to suggest that the making of 9 st will be a physical impossibility in the near future.

Once the bout began, however, Edwards's speed and ringcraft came into play. His seconds clearly feared that if Moran got too close, his tough brawling style would overwhelm their man; thus it was hit and move, taking no chances, forcing Moran to chase.

Moran was clearly an experienced, wily fighter as his dubious tactics revealed, but his various tricks ('heeling' with the rim of his gloves, holding Edwards's head) soon had the audience complaining. As *Boxing* continued:

The pair had got to close quarters when suddenly Moran pushed Edwards back and dropped to his knee. The Porth boy failed to grab the bait whereas Moran smiled grimly at the hoots of the crowd.

Moran sensed that body shots could retrieve what was clearly a losing position. Thus, in the next round:

Moran again commenced to rip away downstairs with both hands. So soon as he did so, the crowd yelled and booed but he persisted, apparently quite convinced in his own mind that what he was doing was quite in order. Edwards went down again, rose, and was felled by another body shot. Pandemonium reigned. The bell once again came to Edwards's rescue and, during the break, referee Douglas was seen to go to Moran's corner and expostulate with him earnestly. Moran appeared to nod in agreement and the bout continued, this time with Edwards able to keep his distance and recommence scoring at will.

However, towards the end of the tenth both men went into a clinch, Edwards crouched low and covered up. Moran struggled to rip his gloves away, even wrestled with the younger man and finally landed yet another low blow – upon which Douglas rose, waved the men apart and disqualified Moran.

Moran's response was immediate:

He jumped out of the ring and, following Mr Douglas to his seat, protested at the decision. The excitement amongst the members was intense and the building simply rung with the applause with which the decision was greeted. Moran, making himself heard above the din, claimed that he had not fouled Edwards.

'He was boxing all covered up,' said Moran, 'and was afraid of being hit in the body. I never fouled him at all. He is a quitter, that's why I went for the body.'

Mr Douglas refused to argue the point and simply said: 'I am sorry Moran but you only got what you deserved.' Moran allowed his seconds to lead him away but still protested loudly.

Moran thus left the British boxing scene in sad disgrace and gave up boxing in 1914. Llew Edwards also departed – to Australia, and once again he took the belt. At the end of the year he fought Jim Hill in Sydney for the Empire title but never again figured in a British title bout. Bettinson opined some years later: 'Whilst his pugilistic qualities are fully admired, we would rather he had stayed at home and done his share of soldiering', a sentiment increasingly prevalent in the later years of the war as the death toll mounted.

Of more immediate concern, however, was the belt. Like Lewis, Edwards was somewhat tardy in returning it. In fact, some two years later when Charlie Hardcastle was matched with Alf Wye for the vacant title, it was still abroad. And only in 1918 when Hardcastle had lost the title to Tancy Lee did it arrive back.

Hardcastle, a hard-hitting fighter from Sheffield, was a Club favourite and gained the title chance even though having been beaten by two close challengers. He was also considered fortunate to beat Alf Wye with a freak one-round KO. Bettinson remarked, however, that Hardcastle 'never looked up again after the death of Louis Hood following a contest he had with him at the Club'.

In fact, within five months, Hardcastle had lost his title to Tancy Lee.

# 4

# The Digger and the Bombardier

In October 1910 the following proclamation by Digger Stanley appeared in *Boxing*:

> I hereby give notice that I am ready to receive challenges from any British boxer at either 8 st 6 lb or 8 st for a substantial side-stake and purse and that, failing to receive such within three months or proving successful in such contests as might arise from this proclamation, it is my intention to assume the titles of bantamweight and flyweight champion of England.

Such a flamboyant declaration of intent was typical of Stanley, one of British boxing's most colourful and tragic figures. In 1910 he was well into his thirties, though no one – not even Stanley himself – knew his precise age.

Born in a gypsy caravan somewhere between Kingston-upon-Thames and Reading, he never learned to read or write and, though he possessed a gold watch, he could not tell the time. At fifteen years old he had been entrusted by his father into the care of one Billy Le Neve (or sold, according to Digger, for a gold sovereign and a pint of ale!), owner of a travelling boxing booth, from where he graduated to the professional ring.

He had achieved great success early in the century, defeating men like Owen Moran, Jim Kenrick, 'Cockney' Cohen, George Dixon and Jimmy Walsh; but in both Britain and the USA he had been overshadowed by Manchester-born Joe Bowker.

Bowker had won the British bantamweight title in 1902–03, defeating claimants Andrew Tokell and Harry Ware at the NSC.

However, following successful defences against Bill King and Owen Moran, the NSC decided Bowker was a featherweight, and brought Moran and Digger Stanley together in 1905 to contest the 'vacant' title. Moran won, but then also moved up to featherweight. Stanley, with victories over Ike Bradley in Liverpool and Sam Keller in London, claimed the title – although Bowker was still the 'popular' champ.

Much the same thing happened at world level. Bowker won the undisputed World bantamweight title in 1904 and defended it successfully in 1905 before relinquishing it. Digger Stanley was matched with American Jimmy Walsh to find a successor: once again, Stanley lost, but assumed the mantle (albeit the British version) when Walsh *also* moved up to featherweight!

Thus when the NSC responded to Stanley's challenge by arranging a match for the new bantamweight Lonsdale Belt with Bowker, it seemed a perfect way to settle what had become an unsatisfactory state of affairs. Oddly enough, despite Stanley's age, it was Bowker (though only twenty-seven) who was regarded as the veteran. And much doubt was expressed concerning his ability to make the bantamweight limit – understandable, considering that since 1906 most of his contests had taken place at featherweight, including two unsuccessful attempts to take Jim Driscoll's title.

When the fighters appeared in the ring, it was noted how drawn Bowker looked, and after the first round it was recorded in *Boxing*:

> Bowker's flesh showed a significant ruddy hue . . . this could only have been occasioned by a very close proximity of the blood vessels to the skin and intimated that Joe must have taken off a lot of flesh to enable him to get inside the weight limit. . . .

Both men were hard hitters, Stanley perhaps possessing the deadlier blow – though neither were KO specialists. Both were also acknowledged experts in ring tactics, at skilful footwork and speedy handwork. But Stanley was also inclined to employ somewhat ruthless, even border-line tactics on occasions.

He leaned on Bowker, held him round the neck with his left arm while working away to the ribs and stomach with his right, yet drew no admonition from the referee. He was also observed to thump Bowker with the butt and edge of his glove – again ignored by the referee. Yet the contest was by no means acrimonious: at one stage they both fell through the ropes; Stanley was up in a flash and, instead of attacking Bowker as the latter scrambled up, Stanley offered to help him up. They also exchanged humorous remarks – a speciality of Bowker's – and Stanley was frequently compelled to stop boxing in order to laugh.

The joking stopped in the eighth round. Bowker had, in the previous couple of rounds, been having great success, rendering Stanley groggy on occasions and leaving him badly shaken following a crisp left-wing combination. At the start of the eighth, Bowker continued to force the pace, driving Stanley back; both landed heavy blows before going into a clinch. Then it was Stanley's turn to demonstrate that he was by no means the weaker man, driving Bowker back across the ring and into the ropes, where he banged away at Bowker's kidneys again. Joe stooped almost double and Digger drove his left into his stomach. Bowker bent still more and then Stanley whipped his right under Joe's left and dug it hard to the mark.

Down went Bowker, clearly in agony as Stanley skipped away. Bowker, however, instead of taking a rest and preparing to rise, rolled over on his side and lay groaning as the count progressed. Suddenly, Stanley noticed that Bowker's seconds were throwing water on him from outside the ring. He dashed back, interposed his body, and protested – but was called away by his seconds. The count continued to the fatal 'Out!' with Bowker still prostrate and groaning.

There followed what the *Boxing* correspondent called, 'a lot of pantomime action', Bowker's seconds protesting to all and sundry while another 'pulled Joe's shorts out and seemed to peer within them. . . .' Several moments of confusion followed before it was announced that the result would stand – Stanley was the champion. In fact, triple champion, for not only had he won the British title but he would now claim European and World crowns.

Being the natural rover he was, Stanley then set off to exploit his new status and it was another two years before he returned to the NSC to defend the belt. Within two months of the Bowker fight he took on Londoner Johnny Condon at the Ring, Blackfriars, with all three titles at stake – and thus became the first belt-holder to risk his new status outside the NSC. After obtaining a close points decision, he set off for the USA – again, the first belt-holder to cash in on the belt's allure across the Atlantic.

But Stanley, though keen to earn money, lacked the cool, calculating financial brain of Freddie Welsh. Within no time at all, he was penniless again, having wasted his US earnings on the races and by August 1911 he was back in the ring taking on Ike Bradley at Liverpool, an opponent notable mainly for his extraordinary tattoos. He was adorned, apparently, with a bulldog on his chest, two snakes curling round his neck and a three-masted sailing ship just above his waistline. On his left arm was a horse and bridle, a wild man with horns, a Union Jack and a woman kneeling before a cross; and on his right arm a cobra and a ship's figure-head. None of which made the slightest impression on Stanley, who won comfortably on points.

He was now only British champion, however, and so in October 1912 he returned to the NSC to defend the title and belt against Scotsman Alex Lafferty.

Lafferty was a keen trainer anxious to build up his speed and stamina. But his raw enthusiasm, not to mention his undoubted awe at boxing in the NSC, were insufficient to counter the wiles and ringcraft of Digger Stanley. In a fight noted for its lack of excitement, the main cause for comment from one correspondent was the care with which one of Stanley's seconds rearranged the title holder's hair at the start of each round.

It now looked simply a matter of time before Stanley made the belt his own, but there would be a twist in the tale. In June 1913 he met Bill Benyon, a tough, durable little Welshman from Taibach who had also, like Lafferty, taken the contest at short notice. A pro for only three years, he had a mixed record, his most notable victory to date being over Curley Walker. But against Stanley he put up probably his best performance ever, matching the champion punch for punch, refusing to be overwhelmed by a clearly more skilful, experienced man and, in the end, receiving a close, though arguable decision.

It was suggested afterwards by way of explanation for the surprise result that the increasing number of admonitions Stanley received for foul play had aggravated and unsettled him. The rather tolerant attitude shown towards him in the past by the NSC was clearly changing.

Benyon made the most of his triumph: at Aberavon station he was greeted by a great crowd and was shouldered from the train to a waiting carriage; a procession began with a Welsh goat at its head, horns draped with a pair of boxing gloves, a band playing 'See The Conquering Hero Comes'. . . .

But it was a short-lived reign. In October he returned to the NSC and, in another hard-fought contest, was adjudged the marginal loser, Stanley this time doing just enough to convince the judges that he was worth the title.

The belt was now Stanley's for keeps, however, as well as the promised pension, due on his fiftieth birthday – if anyone was able to say with confidence exactly when that might be. . . . But Stanley was clearly no longer in any sort of physical condition to continue boxing at the highest level. In his next defence, against Curley Walker from Lambeth, he was up against a strong, determined young man, full of stamina and possessing a workmanlike right hand, but hardly world-class. Stanley tried all he could, including swinging his punches to avoid using his broken knuckles; but when the fight reached the thirteenth round, with Walker clearly the stronger man and hitting cleanly and hard, Digger transgressed once too often.

The referee stepped up to the ropes and disqualified Stanley – a decision greeted with loud applause, for he had been warned on numerous occasions during the fight and had taken little heed of the danger he was in. Stanley made no protest, as once he might have done.

Desperate times were to follow for the likeable but wayward Digger. His subsequent career was marred by ever-increasing disqualifications as he dragged his ailing form through fights made necessary by the fact that he was, as ever, destitute.

In 1917 he broke his thigh in a fall while training, and his health rapidly deteriorated. He died, aged – it was guessed – about forty-five in 1919, 'of want in a fourpenny lodging house in Notting Hill Gate'.

His much-prized belt, which he had hoped would bring him a pension, had long since found its way back to the NSC, whether retrieved from a pawn-shop or handed back by Stanley 'for safekeeping' is not known. Sadly, with no sense of history, the NSC later recycled the belt, scraping off poor Digger's name so that this classic little boxer has nothing to remind posterity of what he achieved.

Thus, by October 1910, almost a year since Welsh and Summers had contested the inaugural belt, five were in circulation, leaving only flyweight and heavyweight to be launched (light-heavy would only be recognized by the Club in 1913, the first belt being 'floated' in 1914).

In the heavyweight division, the problem for the NSC was that the general quality of the available contenders was so poor. In fact, in January 1910, when the idea of arranging eliminators for the new belt was being discussed, the eventual champion, Bombardier Wells, was more or less unknown.

Wells had won the army championship of India back in 1908, and on returning to England sought contests as a professional. He eventually found his way to referee Eugene Corri at the Wells Club who offered him a pound to box an exhibition with Gunner Mills of Woolwich Barracks. Corri then obtained for him bouts at Shoebury Garrison – his earnings now rising to £4 a bout – and, proving impressive, he was recommended to Harry Jacobs at Wonderland as a possible star attraction.

Jacobs paid Wells £8 to fight the 'house' favourite, Cpl Jackson, whom Wells KO'd in three rounds. Thus, when Hugh McIntosh, the Australian promoter, arrived in the UK on his quest to discover a 'White Hope' to challenge Jack Johnson, Corri was able to recommend Wells as a fresh new face. McIntosh immediately offered Wells four fights at £100 each, win, lose or draw. It would be via McIntosh's promotions, in fact, that Wells would come to the notice of the NSC.

The Club was chary of heavyweights. In April 1909, it had staged a heavyweight championship, when Iron Hague beat Gunner Moir in a one-round KO. Neither man was particularly popular at the Club, Moir being summed up by Bettinson in *The Home of Boxing* thus: 'Say that he was a big muscular man and you hit him off perfectly.' Iron Hague, meanwhile, was 'a big, rough fellow whose special joy was to eat, drink and leave the realities of life to others'. Corri, in his *Gloves and the Man*, added:

'Hague never had a cigarette out of his mouth except in the ring and when asleep. . . .' A stocky, often out-of-condition fighter, he was neither an attractive nor particularly 'busy' champion, preferring instead to spend time in boxing booths rather than pursuing international titles – possibly a sensible decision considering his humiliation at the hands of Sam Langford in 1909 when Hague had stood in at the NSC for the defaulting Johnson – a performance that had not endeared him to Club members.

By contrast, Wells's contract with McIntosh guaranteed him, after no more than a dozen contests, immediate top-of-the-bill status and in three contests at the King's Hall (McIntosh's base while Olympia was being completed) Wells disposed of contenders Sunshine, Voyles and Parsons. In January 1911, McIntosh matched Wells with Gunner Moir in the first of a series of heavyweight bouts billing the contest as for the heavyweight championship of Great Britain. Unfortunately, after almost winning the bout in the first round, Wells failed to capitalize and was KO'd by Moir, the principal damage being caused by body punches.

The ways of boxing promoters, however, are far from straightforward. The search for a 'White Hope' had always been more about symbolism than sheer boxing skills, as well as being a money-spinning soap-opera of sorts, and Bombardier Wells clearly remained a box-office draw despite the upset against Moir. He was tall, good-looking and of classical build, putting him, aesthetically at least, streets ahead of his tattooed, bulky, heavily sweating peers. The Moir defeat would, therefore, prove no more than a temporary blip in Wells's steady upward rise.

That is not to say that his closest challengers were not given opportunities to impress. P. O. Curran, considered by many the 'legitimate' champion, having beaten Iron Hague, followed Wells into the new Olympia to contest the Empire heavyweight title (plus a McIntosh belt) with Australian Bill Lang. Curran won – albeit on a bizarre 'foul': at the opening bell, Curran slipped and Lang struck him, only to find himself instantly disqualified! Unfortunately, the very next month Curran was himself disqualified for head-butting a US/Irish heavyweight called 'Porky' Flynn. When Wells defeated Flynn some weeks later in his 'comeback' contest, it was enough to relegate Curran to the back-benches in terms of a Lonsdale Belt match.

The NSC was now keen to jump aboard the 'White Hope' band-wagon and Wells was offered the opportunity to contest the first heavyweight Lonsdale Belt with Iron Hague. The latter's progress since his three defeats in 1909–10 had been encouraging. He had realized, perhaps, that there was much to be gained financially from becoming a key player in the McIntosh 'circus' and had made great efforts to get into shape, intriguingly joining Freddie Welsh's camp where the little Welshman put him on a diet of nuts and vegetables, something of a culture-shock for the bucolic Yorkshireman.

However, the true status of the contestants was perhaps reflected in the fact that the purse at stake was one of the lowest ever for a Belt contest, smaller even than that awarded for the bantamweight title, and less in total than the money posted as side-stakes.

For once, Wells did not succumb to the pressures of the expectations placed upon him; as Bettinson drily put it: 'Wells remembered to box.' Which was just as well, because in Hague he was fighting a man who had brought himself closer to maximum fitness than at any time in his ponderous career. Wells was even confident enough to shrug off the effects of a heavy right-hand shot that momentarily staggered him. Instead, he kept Hague at bay with his long left jab and the final KO – a right-hand shot – was clean and decisive enough for all present to feel sufficiently confident in hailing a worthy champion, even though doubts were considerable as to his ability to go much further.

Following the Hague match, the publicity machine was cranked up to full volume and the hapless Bombardier (described by Bettinson in *The Home of Boxing* as 'a pleasing young man . . . yet completely and hopelessly out of court in any crucial contest. . . .') was propelled onto the international stage where Jimmy White – speculator and gambler – set up a World title fight with Jack Johnson. This ultimately foundered on the rocks of moral indignation and official government concern, (not to mention Lord Lonsdale who had been opposed to the fight because it was so obviously a mismatch. Wells, he considered, had no chance at all).

Undeterred, however, and following an uncertain victory over Fred Storbeck of South Africa for the Empire title, Wells set off for the USA in pursuit of Johnson, only to be flattened in quick succession by Al Palzer and Gunboat Smith. Much chastened, he returned home and ended the year by retaining his Empire title against George Rodel, an ex-sparring partner.

The year 1913 would prove even more of a disaster for him. In June he was KO'd by light-heavy Georges Carpentier in Ghent in a challenge for the European title. Nevertheless, he re-entered the NSC ring for the first time since the Hague victory to register a victory over 'Packy' Mahoney – his second notch on the Lonsdale Belt (which had more or less been forgotten amid all the drama!). This was followed by wins outside the Club over light-heavyweight Pat O'Keefe and Gunner Moir before he returned to the NSC for the return with Carpentier in December 1913.

The result of this bout – a KO inside a minute for Carpentier – was a shattering blow for British boxing, already in 1913 at something of a low ebb. Yet it did not succeed in ending Wells's career. Indeed, probably in a perverse way, it sealed his popularity with the British public. As Trevor Wignall wrote in *Ringside*:

Wells had the gift of drama. We knew whenever he ducked under the ropes that he would either send us bounding to the heights, or sink us in depression. We realized also that he had neither the temperament nor the hardihood for his craft. He had too kindly a heart, as was often shown by the distress on his face when he had an opponent rocking. The night in London when he was smacked down by Carpentier in a little over a minute, there were few cheers for the winner, but there were sighs of sympathy for the loser that resembled a gusty wind blowing over grass. . . .

As regards the Lonsdale Belt, his two victories in 1911 and 1913 were deemed sufficient for the Club to offer him the trophy to keep. By the outbreak of the war he had held the title for three years – the required time limit – and had defeated all credible opponents. Wells, to his credit, insisted that he win the belt *inside* the ring; thus, in December 1916 he was matched with Irishman Dan Voyles whom he stopped in two rounds.

Joe Wilson, with Wally Pickard acting as second

Although the flyweight division introduced by the Club in 1911 was by no means a new one, the decision by the NSC committee to set a limit of 112 lb certainly tidied up a complicated situation: prior to this, anyone below the bantamweight limit of 188 lb could call himself a flyweight.

The first flyweight championship Belt match was held in December 1911 and the two men selected to battle for the honour were Sid Smith and Joe Wilson. Smith was the generally acknowledged champion, having won recognition earlier in the year when defeating Stoker Hoskyn at the Ring, Blackfriars and defending a month later at Liverpool Stadium against Louis Ruddick.

Wilson was a tough little fighter with a KO right hand; Smith, by contrast, was stylish and fast on his feet and would win the majority of his career total of ninety-two wins on points. The two men were the first to contest a Belt match in the newly refurbished Covent Garden Club. During the 1911 close season there had been an extensive rebuilding programme undertaken in response to commercial pressure which more than doubled the original capacity; and the inaugural contest produced an exciting, skilful encounter entirely appropriate for the occasion.

It was a match that turned on a complete contrast in styles. As *Boxing* put it: 'Sid was dancing lightly around like a gnat at sunset with that curious hunched shoulder pose so characteristic of him. Wilson's stand was a much stiffer one and at times absolutely stationary while, when he did dance about, he seemed to do rather more so in imitation of his rival than for any useful purpose.'

Wilson succeeded in staggering Smith in the fourth: 'He tottered and Joe, following his advantage up with a quick left hook dropped his man in a heap on the deck. There was a sharp intake of breath throughout the theatre, while shouts of excitement went up.'

Smith rose at nine, was put down again for another count of eight – but Wilson could not finish it. Smith gradually regained control of the fight and continued to 'nick' rounds with faster hand-work until the twelfth, when he was caught again, 'suddenly, by a straight right-hander in the mouth, which sent him down with a thud'.

He was quickly up, then down again, but once again Wilson demonstrated his inexperience by allowing Smith to recover and the little Londoner proceeded to dance away with the decision, and the belt.

He then set off for the USA in January 1912 in search of financial rewards, but was back again in March, his promised series of engagements not having materialized. With purse offers forthcoming from the NSC he returned to the Ring, Blackfriars, beat Curley Walker and in April 1913 defeated Eugene Criqui in Paris to take the European and World flyweight titles.

At this point, the NSC requested that he defend his belt against Johnny Hughes of Wales. Smith considered the purse derisory and returned the belt, preferring to take up an offer from Ring promoter Dick Burge to fight Bill Ladbury in a contest advertised for the 'World' title. Ladbury, from Greenwich, stood just 5 ft 2 in and liked to do his fighting at close range where he could bang away with hooks from either hand and, in a shock result, he put poor Sid down some eighteen times during the contest to lose his title. It was Smith's last title fight.

Some six months later, Ladbury accepted the purse Smith had

XING, Oct. 6, 1915.
Vol. XII.—No. 318.

A THUMPING COLONEL.

# BOXING

PUBLISHED EVERY TUESDAY, IN LONDON: EVERY WEDNESDAY IN THE PROVINCES. | ONE PENNY.

THE ONLY PAPER IN THE WORLD SOLELY DEVOTED TO BOXING.

VOL. XII.—No. 318.          OCTOBER 6TH, 1915.          Registered at the General Post Office as a Newspaper and for Canadian Magazine Post.

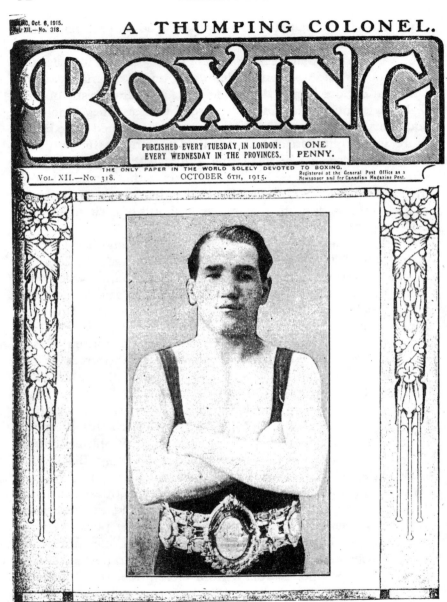

**SID SMITH,**

Ex-Fly-weight Champion of the World, who is taking a well-earned benefit at the Bermondsey Town Hall on October 7th.

The Pride of Wales: Freddie Welsh, Tom Thomas and Jim Driscoll *c* 1910.

Belt winners in uniform. *Back row*: Bombardier Billy Wells, Pat O'Keefe, Johnny Basham, Dick Smith. *Front row*: Jimmy Wilde, Capt. Bruce Logan, Jim Driscoll. 'The Sportsman's Battalion' *c* 1917.

Lew Harris    Jim Driscoll    J. Armitage.    Joe Beckett    Bombardier    Dick Smith    H. Morton    Thomas McQueen    Major
George Cook    Albert Lloyd    Jimmy Wilde    Billy Wells    Stephen Donoghue    Kid Lewis    Arnold Wilson
   Eugene Corri    Jim Higgins

A benefit night for Eugene Corri, referee at the NSC, c 1920.

A. F. 'Peggy' Bettinson, co-founder
and manager of the NSC.

'Digger' Stanley *c* 1912.

Joe Symonds *c* 1915.

Mike Honeyman *c* 1920.

THE THREE LANCASHIRE BOXING CHAMPIONS, 1932-3.
JOHNNY KING (British Bantam-weight), HARRY FLEMING (Manager),
JACKIE BROWN (World's Fly-weight), and JOCK McAVOY (British Middle-weight)

Tommy Farr training for Ben Foord,
March 1937.

'The Pride of Manchester'.

Nel Tarleton receives his belt from the Mayor of Liverpool while Johnny
Cuthbert looks on, October 1931.

White City, June 1952. Randolph
Turpin v Don Cockell.

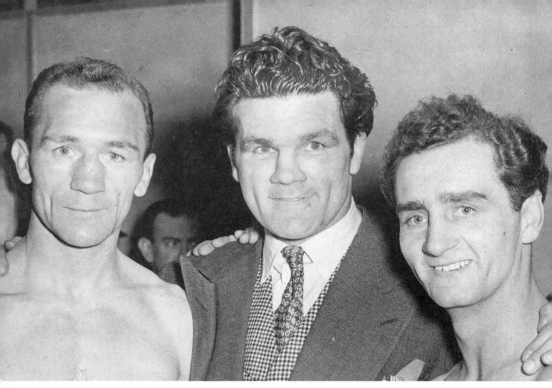

Freddie Mills between Tommy Barnham and Frank Johnson, May 1952.

## *Promoters in Solomons's Shadow*

Jack Cappall between Danny O'Sullivan and Ronnie Clayton (Benny Huntman looks on), November 1951.

David Braitman and Ronnie Ezra.

Charles Donmall, General Secretary
BBBC 1929–49.

Cecil Nichols, fifty years a timekeeper, at the NSC *c* 1950.

E. J. 'Teddy' Waltham, General Secretary BBBC 1950–72 with Onslow
Fane, Board Chairman, March 1950.

Ronnie Clayton and his dog 'Dinky'
at the Swan Hotel, 1959.

Johnny Frankham's son John at a
horse fair, 1975. (*Sport & General*)

## *Belts on Display*

Joe Lucy hangs up his belt at the Thomas A'Beckett, 1956.

snubbed from the NSC to defend his World crown and fight for the vacant British title and Lonsdale Belt against Percy Jones of Wales, only to lose on points over twenty hard rounds.

The contest with Jones had been placed in some jeopardy by the latter's inability to get inside the limit by the two o'clock deadline. According to *Boxing*:

> Ladbury volunteered to allow him till 9 pm to remove that weight but Jim Driscoll [Jones's trainer] is too old a bird to be caught by any chaff of that description. To have weighed in at 8 st only an hour or so before entering the ring would have done Percy no good and so he was promptly taken out for a spin round the houses. The exercise combined with a little skipping did the necessary work, but as anyone can understand, Jones wasn't any the fresher for his exercise.

The fight itself was described by observers as 'sensational'; it began in a manner that summed up the two men's approaches:

> Jones's advance was caution personified. Crouching low with both gloves well up for protection, he stole out to meet Ladbury whose advance was only a shade more determined. Bill didn't crouch. He never does. He looked at Percy and then lashed out a left hook. Jones ducked it. Ladbury looked amazed, fancied he saw another opening and hooked again. Three of these followed in succession and Jones ducked them all.

Jones scored with a fine straight left, however, time and again and gradually built up a commanding lead. Both men had moments when they could have ended it, particularly Ladbury, who put the weakened Jones down in the nineteenth round, but Jones survived and at the end of twenty rounds he received a close verdict.

Yet Jones was forever struggling against nature to make the flyweight limit. Only twenty-two, he ought to have been fighting at featherweight; his handlers, who also controlled 'The Mighty Atom' Jimmy Wilde, thought otherwise, and the consequences were probably inevitable.

Jones was eventually tempted to go to Plymouth and meet local favourite Joe Symonds over the championship course and was forced to retire in the eighteenth round. Symonds claimed the World title but the NSC ignored the result and called upon Jones to defend his belt against Jimmy Berry from Newcastle. At the weigh-in, however, the challenger failed to put in an appearance. (Also unable to make the weight, he had simply walked out of his training-camp and returned home without telling anyone.) Thus, Jones was matched four months later with Tancy Lee from Edinburgh.

By now, not even the expertise of trainer Jim Driscoll could manage to get Jones inside the flyweight limit. He paid three successive visits to a Turkish Baths and even then could not pass the scales. The title fight was called off and they fought at catchweights with the weakened Welshman retiring after fourteen rounds of cruel punishment. *Boxing* was scathing in its criticism:

> It is by no means sure, by the way, that the attempt to melt the little Welsh miner down to 112 lb may not have ruined his career as a fighting man. This weight-making against all the rules of physiology is becoming a farce. Nay more – a crime. Percy Jones is a growing youth . . . but one supposes that they must have felt that a belt in the hand is worth any number of backers in the air. It is perhaps a common policy but it would be unfair to say that it was either wise or humane. . . .

Jones, in fact, never fought again, although it was not weight-making that ended his career. Two months after fighting Lee he returned the belt, and joined the Royal Welsh Fusiliers, the war being two months old. In France, in 1915, Jones suffered from trench fever and poison gas and by 1918, having gone through thirty operations and a leg amputation, was so broken in health that he had to be taken about in a wheelchair.

When he attended a charity show at the Cardiff Empire in 1922 he was reduced to a pitiful 4 st 2 lb, yet still had a sense of humour. 'If you are short of an exhibition bout,' he told Jim Driscoll, 'I'll take you on just to show I haven't forgotten what you taught me.' He died on Christmas Day that year, aged thirty.

Ironically, the man Jones had beaten to become flyweight champ also came to grief in the trenches. Bill Ladbury, who had joined the Royal West Kents in 1914, was sent to France in June 1917 and was killed in action. Blown to pieces by a bomb, there was nothing left of him to bury and his name was inscribed upon the Menin Gate. Many years later, the belt he had been given by friends to commemorate his 'World' title win over Sid Smith could be seen on display at the Royal Six Bells at Colliers Wood, South London, the public house his son bought from the proceeds of a collection raised among boxing people by his manager, Harry Williams.

# 5

## A Golden Era

The system of Lonsdale Belts had been in operation for some five years when the First World War broke out – an event that was to have profound effects on the sport of pro-boxing.

The wartime restrictions and the wholesale regimentation of men created a situation that, from an administrative point of view, suited some NSC committeemen. With the advent of war, they were presented (due to their close alliance with the Imperial Services Boxing Association) with the opportunity to help 'run' and regulate boxing in exactly the way some of them had always dreamed of.

Boxing had always been closely linked to patriotism by the Club; the desire to regulate the championships had been in part a desire to see British fighters regain the ascendancy they once enjoyed. With a war on, that patriotism could be focused even more narrowly. Championship belt-holders – especially if they happened to be serving men – were symbols of their country in a dual sense: not only representing the best of British manhood in terms of courage, skill, fair play etc., they could also be shining examples to the thousands of young men needed in the trenches.

Many of the men concerned responded appropriately. Pat O'Keefe, who would win the middleweight belt outright in 1918, did a lot of recruiting. Fred Dartnell, manager/trainer, recalled his regular cry: 'Join the army and you'll be a champion like me!' Boxing, O'Keefe recognized, kept the population entertained: 'Give the public plenty of boxing and you'll have no Bolshevism!'

Bombardier Wells, of course, being an ex-regular, made the perfect recruitment symbol and travelled the country exhorting men to rally to the flag, while Dick Smith, his regular opponent

BOXING, August 29, 1914
Vol. X.—No. 260

# Why Fred Welsh Has Gone Away.

# BOXING

PUBLISHED EVERY TUESDAY IN LONDON: | ONE
EVERY WEDNESDAY IN THE PROVINCES. | PENNY.

THE ONLY PAPER IN THE WORLD SOLELY DEVOTED TO BOXING.

Vol. X.—No. 260.     AUGUST 29TH, 1914.     Registered at the General Post Office as a Newspaper and for Canadian Magazine Post.

DICK SMITH (CRUISER-WT. CHAMPION) PREPARES FOR
STERNER FIGHTING.

in title fights during these years, was pictured prominently, bayonet at the ready.

Johnny Basham and Jim Driscoll served in France together and regaled fans with tales of the trenches and the camaraderie 'over there', while Tom McCormick wrote letters to *Boxing* until meeting his death on the Somme. Dick Burge, meanwhile, though no longer a fighter, used his position as promoter at the Ring to cajole men to join. He threatened an embargo on boxers not wearing khaki.

By happy chance, therefore, the Lonsdale Belts could be seen to serve as both reward and compensation to 'patriotic' boxers for, while championship contenders who remained in the country found chances to earn big money rare – unlike certain of their colleagues such as Owen Moran, Ted Kid Lewis, Llew Edwards, etc., who stayed in the USA and earned tidy sums – the opportunities to win a Lonsdale Belt outright were considerably enhanced.

Prior to the war, champions crowned at the Club and presented with their belt had been free to weigh up offers from competing promoters and, as we have seen, quite often what the NSC had to offer was not considered good enough to induce them to a return and defence. With the closing down of alternatives, champions found themselves *having* to fight at the Club – indeed, were grateful for the opportunity, their bruised financial egos assuaged somewhat by the prospect of a pension if they won the belt outright.

Certainly the number of championship contests held outside the Club dropped almost to nil, while the number of belts won outright increased dramatically. Between 1909 and the outbreak of war, excluding the heavyweight division, there were thirty-four British/English title fights, ten of which were staged outside the Club by 'commercial' promoters, while just two men – Jim Driscoll and Digger Stanley – won belts to keep.

Between 1914 and 1919, there were twenty-five title fights – only two of which took place outside the Club – one of which 'Peggy' Bettinson promoted outdoors at Kensal Rise, ostensibly to give the populace at large the opportunity to see Jimmy Wilde perform, the second being a Dick Burge promotion, theoretically to raise money for the troops.

During that period, Jimmy Wilde, Joe Fox, Johnny Basham,

Pat O'Keefe, Dick Smith and Bombardier Wells won belts out-right, closely followed by Tancy Lee in 1919. What with having to purchase a new lightweight belt in June 1919 to replace the one Freddie Welsh was clearly not going to return, the Club found itself purchasing eight gold belts in no less than three years – an expensive business. . . .

Whether or not this represented a 'golden age' in terms of boxing quality is another matter; some champions were clearly talented fighters who would have risen to the top, war or not, while others could perhaps regard themselves as fortunate to have been in the right place at the right time. The first wartime belt winner, however, was a boxer of skill and courage and certainly one of the all-time greats – Johnny Basham.

Basham was brought together with veteran Johnny Summers in December 1914 to contest the 'vacant' welterweight title. Sum-mers had taken the crown in 1912 but, after two successful defences, had gone to Australia where, in a tripartite tourney with Tom McCormick and Matt Wells, Wells had emerged vic-torious. The Club had never recognized Wells's claim to be British champion and so Summers and Basham were theoretically con-testing a 'vacant' title, although if Summers won, he would take the belt outright. Now a veteran of thirty-one, with over 170 contests behind him, he was both form and sentimental favourite.

Basham, however, just twenty-four, Newport-born but fighting out of Liverpool, was to spring a surprise. He had been fighting since he was sixteen and, after graduating from boxing booths in South Wales, had broken through at Liverpool Stadium, since when he had beaten quality opposition such as the Belgian Quen-dreaux, Eddie Beattie, Young Ahern, as well as Gus Platts in an eliminator.

By 1914 Basham was a regular soldier, a private (later sergeant) with the 3rd Battalion Welsh Fusiliers, having spent some six years as an army reservist. Unlike most of his contemporaries, he had not taken the 'yankee dollar' as a fighter (nor for that matter the Australian pound), even though in 1912 he had been wooed by American manager Charlie Harvey in New York.

Two years on and Basham's decision to ply home waters had paid off, though Summers clearly felt that Basham's relative inex-perience would let him down. Despite entering the ring some 5 lb lighter than Basham (who scaled 10 st 5 lb), Summers waded in from the outset and succeeded in putting Basham down in the second round. Basham, the quicker, more mobile fighter, had been expected to use his younger legs to keep out of trouble but, by allowing Summers to achieve such early success, ('Summers walked after his man as though he was walking to breakfast. . . .') he gave the impression that he was overawed.

However, as the bout progressed and Summers expended a great deal of energy (while taking considerable punishment in the process) Basham gradually took control, hitting and moving until, in the fourteenth round, he caught Summers with a series of combinations that put the Yorkshireman down and out.

It was a sad blow to Summers, a man whose immense championship pedigree should surely have yielded him a belt to keep.

Basham, however, was now well launched; despite losing a European title fight the following April, he followed this up with his first title defence against Tom McCormick in May, the first time a belt match had been made between serving soldiers.

McCormick, though giving no weight away, and seemingly as fit as the army could make him, was observed to be 'more or less muscle-bound'. Unlike Basham, whose entry into the regular army had considerably toughened and strengthened him, McCormick had stiffened up – principally because, though physically fit, he had not been able to take a professional fight for almost a year.

Thus, a normally fluent, vicious left-hooking fighter was rendered slow and uncertain, while his famous defence seemed strangely easy to breach. Basham's ability to box on the retreat left McCormick floundering and out of range, and three knockdowns in the thirteenth round ended the fight.

McCormick's poor luck would continue; Basham, though having to wait a year before the army granted him leave to defend his title, took on Eddie Beattie at the NSC, confident that he could make the first Lonsdale Belt at welterweight his very own.

Beattie was a tremendously strong, tough fighter, who could take a great deal of punishment as well as dish it out; but absorbing punishment was by now becoming a forte of Basham's, despite his tall, slight, deceptively frail-looking frame. In one of the fastest, most fiercely contested, hardest-hitting bouts seen at the Club for many years, Basham's superior technique saw him gradually wear Beattie down until, in the nineteenth round, the latter was floored by a right-left hook combination. Up at eight, he staggered down again, rose, was floored again – at which point referee Douglas decided the end was nigh. Basham was thus the proud possessor of a belt that had caused its fair share of controversy and heartbreak. As a postscript to the struggle for its possession, within weeks of cabling his congratulations to Basham, Tom McCormick was killed by a shell in a big 'push' on the Western Front: 'joking to the last,' as his close friend and boxing companion Cpl Jim Winspear later wrote.

The next belt to be awarded – aside from the one offered to Bombardier Wells – was at bantamweight, to a clever little fighter from Leeds called Joe Fox. Following Curley Walker's victory over Digger Stanley, the Lambeth man found weight-making problems insurmountable. His prevarications and demands regarding possible defences eventually convinced the NSC committee that he should hand the belt back and, in November 1915, Fox was matched with the official challenger, Jimmy Berry of Northumbria. As was by now the rule, both men were serving soldiers and both would experience great difficulty in making the weight, though Fox was fortunate enough to be able to avail himself of the services of famous trainer Jack Goodwin to assist him. He needed him: it is said when they first met and Joe stood on the scales that Goodwin whistled and said, 'I thought you said you were fighting for the bantamweight title? You sure you ain't made a mistake and mean lightweight? You'll want both legs off to make the poundage!'

'Peggy' Bettinson, in his autobiography, commented:

Fox was a rare money-match winner, an irritating as distinct from clever boxer. There is, it is true, little that is engaging in his ways but at his weight he was a difficult man to beat. For he had the rare gift of making his opponent fight his own way.

The first challenge for the title bore that judgement out. In a tedious contest, watched by a critical and impatient Digger

Stanley, Fox gradually wore Berry down who, tough ex-miner as he was, conceded on his stool at the end of sixteen rounds.

His next contest, against Tommy Harrison – the 'Pet of the Potteries' – was no more compelling to the Covent Garden cognoscenti, something of a grind, notable mainly for a great deal of holding and illegal use of the glove. Nevertheless, Fox took the fight on points.

Fourteen months later he met hard-punching ex-flyweight champion Joe Symonds, then serving in the Royal Navy, and this time he had a real fight on his hands. Symonds attacked Fox to the body and Fox suffered some anxious moments, but in the seventeenth Symonds had exhausted himself. He collapsed to the canvas and, though he rose, he was immediately floored again. The referee decided Fox had done enough, and the belt was his for keeps.

It would not be misusing an overworked term to call Jimmy Wilde a phenomenon of the ring. Ex-miner, ex-booth fighter, he never weighed more than 100 lb throughout his career and rarely seemed troubled with making the flyweight limit – a limit that, as we have seen, seemed to crucify many of his challengers. Yet, though so small, he was built, according to contemporary observers, on the same lines as heavyweight Bob Fitzsimmons: broad shoulders and thin, spindly legs and arms.

He had been trained originally by a Welsh mountain fighter called Dai Davies and boxing writer Denzil Batchelor was particularly taken by Wilde's style, describing him thus in *British Boxing*: 'He could box like a Driscoll or stand toe-to-toe and trade punches like one of the primitive pit-fighters from whose ranks he had won his way to the pinnacles, but his special genius lay in fighting in retreat, a shadowy, spindly starveling, noiselessly sliding out of range of great bombardments to pinpoint his counter attack with exquisite shrewdness and finality. . . .'

His wonderful punching power came from those broad shoulders, and his ability to knock opponents out – men to whom he was often giving away a stone or so – was part of his magnetic appeal. He was not, however, a superman, and the decision of the Welsh camp to enter Wilde for a title fight with Tancy Lee in January 1915, for which he had to concede almost a stone and which he lost, was heavily criticized.

Tancy Lee held the title for just nine months. In October 1915 he took on Joe Symonds and the two men put on a terrific match. Symonds eventually forced Lee out of his rhythm, weakening him until he fell from sheer weariness in the twelfth and fourteenth rounds, and in the sixteenth 'went to pieces like a cathedral which had been hit by a German bomb'.

Thus, when Wilde met Symonds some four months later, in February 1916, he had to be at his best. Symonds was a tough, relentless, not to say stubborn fighter, who carried the fight to Wilde just as he had to Lee, rushing and crowding the Welshman, forcing him to employ his amazing ability to duck and dive. Eventually, it was Symonds who ran out of steam and Wilde ruthlessly finished him off. A ripping left to the body caused Symonds to gasp, 'whereupon Wilde steadied him up some more with three rights to the jaw. Joe's defence collapsed, and Wilde drove him back with lefts and rights planted everywhere. Driven into a neutral corner, Symonds stood helplessly and with his hand half held out. But Jimmy meant to make sure and sending three vicious lefts to the body, plus three simultaneous rights to the jaw, finally beat Symonds down to one knee. Symonds rose only, however, to hold out his hand in token of acknowledged defeat.'

Wilde followed this up some two months later by defeating Johnny Rosner in defence of the World title that had come attached to the British one – a title he would hold until 1923 when Pancho Villa defeated him in New York. Two months after the Rosner fight came a second defence of his Lonsdale Belt, against Tancy Lee, who really had no business fighting at flyweight (within a year he would take the featherweight title and go on to clinch that belt outright). Nevertheless, he put up a great battle, trading punch for punch until, in the tenth, Wilde's power told. Lee was floored by a right and though he beat the count and went on to survive until the eleventh, Wilde soon finished him off.

Wilde was now British boxing's sensation and capable of filling arenas many times larger than Covent Garden. 'Peggy' Bettinson thus set up an unofficial title fight for him against Johnny Hughes at Kensal Rise, which Wilde won in the tenth.

Another successful World title defence followed, against the American Zulu Kid; then, a month later in March 1917, he

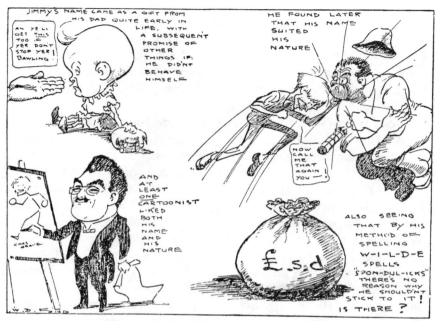

How boxers gain their names – Jimmy Wilde

overwhelmed another Bermondsey boy, George Clark, inside four rounds to make the belt his own. From then on, apart from a fund-raising tourney at the NSC which involved no belt, Wilde would concentrate on 'money' matches.

Part of Wilde's attraction must have been the prospect of seeing him beaten: so often the betting appeared to favour the other man simply because of the vast differential in weight. However, in over 150 professional contests, he was defeated on just six occasions. As Denzil Batchelor put it in *British Boxing*: 'He was never approached let alone mastered on equal terms.'

Pat O'Keefe, who would take the middleweight belt outright a year after Wilde's flyweight triumph, could not claim such domination and invincibility, but was, nevertheless, one of the great characters of British boxing. Despite the Irish-sounding name, he was born a Cockney in the East End in 1883 where he fought bare-knuckle as a youth before taking up the gloved game. By 1903 he was good enough to win a welterweight competition at Olympia, and in 1906 he won, successfully defended and then lost (to Tom Thomas) the middleweight title in the space of six months.

The following year he went to France where he beat Charlie Allum to claim the French title (no residential qualifications apparently necessary in those days!) and in 1908 he began to globetrot. He was in Australia for the great Johnson v Burns World title fight – indeed, he sparred with Burns and was in his corner during the actual contest.

Returning to England in 1911, he racked up a string of victories before taking on Bombardier Wells for the British heavyweight title in 1913. Wells KO'd him, but it took him fifteen rounds. Five months later, O'Keefe travelled to France to fight Georges Carpentier for the European middleweight title, and was again KO'd, this time in five.

For some time he had been in line for a shot at the English middleweight title and Lonsdale Belt, and when Jim Harrison forfeited, O'Keefe was matched with Harry Reeve in February 1914 at the NSC. Reeve was then only twenty-one with a long career ahead of him (an enormous career, in fact, which would not end until 1934!); O'Keefe was by now twenty-seven and approaching veteran stage. He proved too wily for Reeve, and took the title on points.

As was his way, he wasted no time in getting back into the ring and successfully defended his title at Premierland against Nicol Simpson just eight weeks after the NSC fight. O'Keefe's points victory, needless to say, was a popular one.

A month later, he took on old rival, Jim Sullivan. Sullivan, who had taken the title back in 1910, was on the comeback trail but O'Keefe had no trouble in jabbing his way to a comfortable points victory. The two men would meet again some two years later in a controversial contest staged by Dick Burge at Golders Green Hippodrome. Fighting at catchweights, the two produced a bloody encounter that led General Haig to issue a ban on big money fights involving serving soldiers.

Three months later, in May 1916, O'Keefe lost his title at the NSC on points to Bandsman Jack Blake, whom O'Keefe had KO'd a year earlier in a catchweight match.

Blake danced round the champion at a speed that left Pat standing. He stabbed O'Keefe with a fast left and hooked him savagely to the body with his right. Old Pat plodded on, falling further behind with each round, patiently waiting for the right opening for the winning punch. He staggered Blake in both the tenth and seventeenth rounds but was unable to finish him off. In the nineteenth, however, he whipped in a vicious left hook to Blake's jaw, then banged over his right.

Blake hit the floor with a crash as the audience watched spellbound. One of Blake's seconds darted into the ring, thinking it was all over, saw that Jack was moving, so darted out again. It was a flagrant breach of the rules but the referee was busy watching the timekeeper beat out the count.

The Bandsman dragged himself off the canvas at seven; he was badly shaken but possessed enough fighting instinct to duck and dodge and make O'Keefe miss as he chased in for the kill. Pat strove his utmost to put over a winner but it was beyond him. The final bell rang – and Blake's hand was the one raised.

The army and the war then dominated both men's lives for the next two years; in February 1918, however, they were brought together at the NSC during an air-raid. Blake was by then a much weaker man – having been injured at Mons, he was probably neither physically nor psychologically very fit – and in the event the fight lasted no more than two rounds, Blake suffering a KO.

O'Keefe, who won a Lonsdale Belt outright when defeating Blake, was quoted before the fight as saying: 'If I get home safely tonight I don't think I will fight again.' He reached home unharmed as the raid continued, and he never did fight again.

Dick Smith, winner of the inaugural light-heavyweight (then called the cruiserweight) belt launched in April 1914 was, by any standards – but particularly those of his day – almost a part-time fighter. His was a curious career consisting of some twenty-one bouts, ten of those being title fights, seven of which he lost, six by KO!

A former policeman from Woolwich, he turned pro at the veteran age of twenty-seven with two ABA heavyweight titles to his credit. Indeed, he fought most of his pro fights at heavyweight but with little success. He lacked a sufficiently powerful 'dig' to succeed at the premier weight; he was also prone to being KO'd, suffering this fate at the hands of Georges Carpentier, Bombardier

BOXING. July 12, 1916.
Vol. XIV.—No. 358.

# Why Wolgast Fouled Welsh.

# BOXING

PUBLISHED EVERY WEDNESDAY | ONE PENNY.

THE ONLY PAPER IN THE WORLD SOLELY DEVOTED TO BOXING.

VOL. XIV.—No. 358. JULY 12TH, 1916. Registered at the General Post Office as a Newspaper and for Canadian Magazine Post.

## BANDSMAN JACK BLAKE,

Displaying both his belts—the upper one being that formerly won by Jem Mace, and presented to Blake after his victory over the Dixie Kid, and the other the Lonsdale Middle-weight trophy.

Wells (three times), Joe Beckett (twice), Frank Goddard and Jack Bloomfield.

However, it says much for the dearth of top-line light-heavies in 1914 that he should have been given a shot at the title after just *two* professional fights, and one of those being a points defeat. This first title fight, against his points conqueror Dennis Haugh, was, by all accounts, something of a farce, *Boxing* commenting:

> If only the broth of a boy from Tipperary could gather in some boxing brains from somewhere – we are not so anxious that he should learn to box because that would be but a pious aspiration for the impossible – but we would like to see him able to fight as intelligently as he undoubtedly does on heroic lines.

Haugh possessed guts and determination, but was simply not a boxer. Add to that the fact that he broke his left forearm in the ninth round, and Smith's victory is understandable. And yet with so much going against him, Haugh still managed to wobble Smith with one or two wild swings and after the first rounds, during which he served as little more than a chopping block, he almost took the fight over, chasing and thumping the weary Smith all over the ring.

Following two KO defeats at the hands of Bombardier Wells in 1915 and early 1916, Smith then met Harry Curzon, considered a good bet to steal the title. But it proved a dull contest, dominated by clinches and admonitions from the referee to 'break'. Smith simply outlasted Curzon to gain a second victory. In fact, 1916 would prove an extremely busy year for Smith: four fights. Following a third futile attempt to take Wells's title, he came up against Harry Reeve, who had already failed in an attempt to take the middleweight title from Pat O'Keefe.

Stepney-born Reeve, although he did not produce much form to take Smith's title away, was a more accomplished, skilful boxer, and during the twenty-round contest – though it was considered slow and boring to watch – he completely outthought and outboxed Smith, whose career now looked more or less over.

However, fate – or more specifically, the war – took over. Reeve went to France and was badly wounded, so badly it was thought he might never box again. He took too long to recover for the

Club's liking, however, and they asked for the belt back. Almost immediately, Smith was matched with up-and-coming Joe Beckett, a chance the thirty-four-year-old could never have imagined would come his way.

Beckett, a future heavyweight champion of England, was an ex-booth fighter who carried a powerful left hook with which he had dispatched his last four opponents. Victims included Harry Curzon (three times), Harry Reeve and Dan Flynn, and at twenty-six he was approaching his physical peak.

Smith, however, produced the best performance of his short career, using the ring while he scored with his reliable left hand, taking the best his two-fisted opponent could offer on his arms, shoulders and elbows. Smith was on the retreat for much of the second half of the fight but, as Beckett tired, he asserted his authority and dominated the point-scoring so that the result, well received as it was, upset no one.

Beckett would gain his revenge, of course, KO'ing Smith in 1920 and 1923 in heavyweight title matches as the remarkable Londoner continued his unlikely career – a career that would see him take on Georges Carpentier in Paris in 1919 for the European heavyweight title and go down to a KO defeat in eight rounds.

The final outright winner of a Lonsdale Belt during the war years – James Tancy Lee – was, by any standards, a marvel of the professional ring. Born in 1882, his pro-boxing career, officially at least, started late, in 1910, following his ABA triumph at bantamweight – a triumph ruined when he was stripped of the title and had to return the cup because of breaches of amateur rules. Life had a tendency to play such tricks on Tancy.

By 1915, when he embarked upon a series of four championship bouts for the British flyweight title, he was already considered a veteran, though having had just twenty pro bouts. His first 'title' shot had been against Percy Jones. Lee won, but it transpired that Jones had breached championship conditions by failing to make the weight and the title was declared vacant. Lee proceeded to inflict upon Jimmy Wilde the little man's first pro defeat, then lost the title to Joe Symonds. A year later, and Wilde took his revenge, stopping Lee in eleven rounds.

Tancy then challenged Joe Fox for the bantamweight title. On at least two occasions all seemed set, terms were agreed, but each time Fox cried off through illness. Eventually, aged 35 and having moved up to featherweight, he took on Charlie Hardcastle, the incumbent champion, KO'ing the Barnsley man in four rounds. By now Joe Fox was operating at featherweight and Lee prepared to defend his title, anxious to rack up three wins and secure a pension. But the jinx struck again: first the military would not allow Fox to fight, refusing to grant him leave. When finally they relented, Fox went down with flu. Welshman Billy Fry was next in line but again the army intervened – twice, in fact.

Finally, in October 1918, a worthy opponent was found in Joe Conn, an instrument-maker from London and considered by many as a future World champion. Conn had been involved some two months earlier in a controversial contest with Jimmy Wilde – a mammoth promotion at Stamford Bridge – and his subsequent defeat left him eager to re-establish himself.

Conn was thus odds-on favourite. A good defensive boxer, young and strong, he tended to finish contests inside the distance: thirty-three KOs featured on his record. By contrast, Lee's fights usually became tests of endurance: in eight title fights, only one had ended before the tenth round, the rest continuing until the sixteenth or seventeenth rounds when either he or his opponent succumbed through exhaustion and pain.

For Lee, stamina was the key. If he threw caution to the wind and went for an early KO – and failed – then he would be vulnerable to the younger, stronger man. Thus, he set out to lure Conn into expending useless energy. As one correspondent put it, for Lee it was a matter of matching the pace of his duck against the speed of Conn's punch.

As it happened, Conn's advisers had told him to move swiftly onto the offensive. Thus it was to hit or be hit – and for seventeen rounds both men fought all out, damaging their hands in the process. Conn, in fact, broke his right hand as early as the sixth, almost stopping Lee in the process. Even with one serviceable hand he almost succeeded in stopping Lee in the twelfth but Lee, true to form, shook his head, came on and by the fourteenth was reaping the benefit of his endurance.

Conn, unable to respond in kind (both hands had by now been broken) was weakening. Floored at the end of the sixteenth, he was put down twice at the start of the seventeenth with hard right swings before the final right ended the affair.

Lee was now anxious to secure that third notch, his main challengers being two Welshmen: Billy Fry from Tylorstown and Danny Morgan of Tirphil, both of whom had beaten Lee earlier at catchweights. After a series of matchmaking mishaps, which saw Fry withdraw at the eleventh hour, Morgan stepped up to challenge Lee. The young man seemed supremely confident, as *Boxing* commented, 'standing some two inches taller and looking all the more than his seventeen years younger, Morgan seemed almost indifferent in his confidence, whereas the stockier little Scot looked somewhat grimmer than usual. . . .'

The fight started slowly, Lee forcing but by no means on top, Morgan clever and tough, taking Lee's best shots and coming back with his own; gradually the ringside betting moved towards Morgan, especially from the fifth round on. Morgan held a lot, trying to nullify Lee's determined attacks close in and he also slipped many of Lee's swings; there was also a great deal of head-to-head banging, but in the eleventh Morgan was still strong enough to start boxing at distance, jabbing away at Lee with speed and accuracy.

Lee rallied in the twelfth and thirteenth, and had some success, but from then on it appeared to most observers that Morgan was in control; with Lee's legs tiring rapidly, all the serious point-scoring looked to have been done by Morgan. According to *Boxing*:

As the last gong sounded, the two men shook hands and Tancy Lee returned wearily to his corner to listen to the consolations of his seconds. We rose to leave, full of regrets that poor old Lee could not have met the active Welshman some two years back when the match between them was first suggested, when, that is to say, Tancy was that much younger and Morgan by that much less experienced.

Yet when Mr Bettinson climbed up to the ring to announce the verdict, well, we could scarcely believe our eyes. There had been a happy ending after all – for Tancy that is – even if everything else had been outraged to secure it. . . .

# 6

## Cochrane's Heavyweight Follies

In June 1918 it was announced from the premises of the NSC in Covent Garden that a British Boxing Board of Control (BBBC) had been established which would henceforth serve as sole governing body for the professional sport. Its officially stated aims were 'to encourage boxing in general, to raise the standards of pro-boxing, to control and regulate the sport and to act as a central board of control'.

In fact, unbeknownst to many, the Board had been established as long ago as 1914 but had been put 'on ice' during the hostilities. Then, as now, the composition of the Board had been heavily weighted with NSC members (ten in all) but had also involved a number of military men – members of the Imperial Services Boxing Association.

The reason for the close involvement with the military was the NSC's desire to see boxing recognized and accepted at the very highest levels, and the Club's hard work during the war in raising money for military ambulances, not to mention organizing huge popular tournaments involving American and French forces stationed in the UK, certainly helped establish boxing as the number one military sport.

But with the war approaching its end, there were fears of the ISBA continuing to run the game in a manner that even the most conservative of Club members might think unduly restrictive. For though men like Bettinson and Douglas felt that the military emphasis on tight organizational control and individual discipline might be useful in helping 'cleanse' the pro-game of its more seedy and undesirable tendencies (not to mention curb its ram-

72

pant commercialism), there was also the danger that too much regimentation could ruin it as an entertainment.

All of which helps explain the rather sudden, unheralded appearance of the Board even before hostilities had ceased. By establishing it without consulting the ISBA – most of whose members were still engaged on active service – and by packing it with NSC members, the Club had avoided what might have become an awkward and protracted series of negotiations. As John Murray, editor of *Boxing*, wrote at the time: 'We can guess at the motives which actuated them and may even suspect that circumstances conspired to force their hand.'

As it happened, the idea of an all-embracing body to control every level of the sport, both professional and amateur, which the military clearly favoured and which the Club did not, was shelved. A Cmdr Walcott RN was deputed by the new Board to pursue the idea but within a year or so it had been quietly dropped. And by the time the ISBA came to consider its permanent involvement on the Board, the fact that the latter was dealing exclusively with professional boxing caused the military men to think again. 'The time was not propitious,' they eventually announced,' for full membership of the new body.' Instead, representatives were appointed (usually NSC members with military connections) to ensure the ISBA's voice and views would be heard.

The Club's *fait accompli*, as it were, may have saved boxing from becoming a creature of the military establishment, but the composition of the new Board was fatally flawed from the start. John Murray – who would be one of its harshest critics throughout the inter-war period – called it 'the narrowest oligarchy known for some centuries . . .' and indeed, the confusion and bitterness of the 1920s and 1930s might have been avoided had the new body been conceived along more democratic lines.

As it was, it would be regarded by many within pro-boxing as merely an extension of the NSC, a creature designed to ensure the old Club remained the dominant force in British boxing. Which was ironic because ever since the NSC had instituted the belt system, many people within the sport – John Murray and *Boxing* in particular – had been urging it to go further and take responsibility for all aspects of the game. Now it had taken the plunge, neither it, nor its creation, would receive a great deal by way of thanks.

The new Board (which apart from ten NSC members also included two ISBA reps and two 'commercial' non-metropolitan promoters to provide some 'balance') did attempt early on to broaden the membership base by deciding to include professional boxers on the governing committee, although the method chosen to select them did little to persuade critics that the NSC was not behind everything the Board did. A 'voting college' of all past and present holders of the Lonsdale Belt was given the task of selecting three representatives. Thus Bombardier Wells, Jim Driscoll and Pat O'Keefe became the first professionals to serve on the new Board of Control. Soon after this, a Professional Boxer's Benevolent Fund was established, its aim being to help ex-pros fallen on hard times, and the three boxer-reps were given a certain responsibility for administering it.

As for activities within the ring, the Board was swift in taking decisive action. In July 1918 Alf Mansfield had the dubious distinction of becoming the first boxer to be suspended by the Board following what was described merely as 'misconduct' in a contest with Lewis Williams. In July the following year, when Alf Mansfield was reported again, this time by promoter Billy Ames for his conduct in a contest at the Ring, Blackfriars, the Board imposed a hefty three years' suspension on him. In December 1919 Mansfield appealed to the Board for clemency and permission to fight Billy Enyon at the Ring. When he was turned down, he became abusive and threatened to take legal action, backed, he claimed, by the Ring management. In the event, Enyon decided not to risk his career in court and declared that he would not meet Mansfield – a significant victory for the new Board. Mansfield duly apologized and his sentence was cut, while Enyon went on to fight for the British bantamweight title in 1920. Sadly for Mansfield, within a few years he was blind and applying to the Board again – this time for help from the Benevolent Fund.

For the NSC, shorn of its quasi-official 'governing body' role, life would become gradually more difficult. A succession of big-time promoters was to vie for supremacy in London while in the provinces men like Nat Dresner, Billy Ames and Jack Smith would lay the foundations for a new 'geography' of British championships.

The Club's monopoly of the Lonsdale Belts would prove insufficient to prevent its grip on championship contests slipping. In fact, where three divisions were concerned – middle, welter and heavyweight – the belts rapidly lost any significance whatsoever. Between the years 1919 and 1924, there were to be twenty-two championship contests involving the three weights, only five of which were for a belt and only two of which would take place inside Covent Garden.

There were two principal reasons for this: the heavyweight division was traditionally the most glamorous and prestigious in terms of pure entertainment and thus the most difficult for the Club to compete for with tempting purse offers: second, the arrival back in England of Ted Kid Lewis, probably Britain's greatest ever boxer and a massive box-office draw – again, generally too expensive for the Club to bid for.

The heavyweights had never been a favourite division with the Club, partly because of the palpable lack of real talent down the years but also, more significantly, because the heavies were 'popular', and the Club was traditionally suspicious of what Norman Clark, in *All in the Game,* called 'the fly-by-night patrons, seeking temporary excitement and to be in the show but with little sustained interest in the sport as a sport. . . . They wanted big crowds at the Albert Hall, plenty of light and noise. . . .'

All of which C. B. Cochrane, showman and theatre entrepreneur, was keen to provide. Immediately before the war he had staged glamorous shows at Olympia (credited with making boxing fashionable): Bombardier Wells v Colin Bell, Freddie Welsh v Willie Ritchie, etc. By 1919 he was busy booking Olympia – as well as taking out a lease on the Holborn Stadium – and was aiming to stage a World heavyweight title fight, every promoter's dream. The scheme involved a triangular tourney between Bombardier Wells, Frank Goddard and Joe Beckett, the ultimate winner to fight Georges Carpentier for the right to meet Jack Dempsey.

Although Wells had fought only three times at the NSC, Cochrane's decision more or less to annex the title for his own promotional use (rather as Hugh McIntosh had done before the war) clearly irritated the NSC management. Thus, when Beckett beat

Wells at Holborn Stadium, the Club declared the title vacant – a matter which was really for the new BBBC to determine – and matched Frank Goddard with Jack Curphey for a new belt.

To all intents and purposes Beckett had been deposed, because, in the popular mind, whoever held the belt was champion. In the past, if a champion belt-holder had been beaten outside the Club, the belt had been returned but the new champion's right to the *title* had been respected. The belt had simply been held in abeyance.

There was more than a touch of pique, however, about the move. Wells had originally been asked by Bettinson to make a defence of his title against Goddard at the Club and a generous purse of £3,000 had been put up. Goddard had been happy to accept but Wells had refused, declaring somewhat nobly that he wanted to 'earn' the right to meet Goddard by first beating those men whom Goddard had beaten – one of them being Beckett. Wells had even accepted a much lower fee to fight Beckett – £1,000. Thus, the last heavyweight title about to be fought at the old Club (and only the fourth Belt fight at the weight since 1911) went ahead under a cloud of promotional wrangling and backbiting.

It resulted in a champion – Frank Goddard – for whom almost no one had a kind word. He was, in fact, an NSC-nurtured fighter. Committee member Col. Middleton had been so enthusiastic about his potential he had bought him a farm, even built him a gymnasium; and Goddard had initially repaid that investment with wins over Beckett, Voyles, Dennis Haugh, Tom Gummer and Dick Smith.

But he would flatter to deceive. As Bettinson unkindly commented in *The Home of Boxing*: 'Was there ever a more imposing physical specimen, a man who so closely approximated mahogany; was there ever a champion with ability so severely limited?'

Goddard was ponderous and easy to hit; he was also a poor trainer, inclined to indolence. As experienced Harry Reeve noted when in training camp with him:

He is a lot younger than his years in many ways . . . and it is the boy in him which makes him so keen about his pet animals. He had three canaries when I was down there and a Shetland pony as well as rabbits and dogs and I may say that he took a lot more interest in his pets than he did in his coming fight for the championship and belt even!

His fight with Curphey summed up his strengths and his weaknesses: he could absorb punishment and he could use his strength to stop opponents (of his forty career wins, thirty-four came inside the distance; of his fifteen defeats, only six were by KO). But to survive at the very top he needed more than strength and endurance. As Reeve put it: 'He will have to learn how to stop punches with something else than his face.'

Against Curphey he took any number of long-range shots to the jaw, jabs and hooks with the left, slamming rights – in fact, he was outboxed for much of the time. But in the tenth he had worn down his opponent sufficiently to knock him out. Neither man, however, had looked particularly attractive 'Like two cart-horses at a Russian ballet,' as one *Boxing* critic put it.

From Cochrane's point of view, however, the Goddard win was perfect. The NSC's belt holder was thus matched with the 'pretender' Beckett, who duly KO'd him in two rounds. Unfortunately, six months later Beckett himself would be KO'd by Carpentier and, though Cochrane still had a contractual option on the Carpentier v Dempsey fight, the great showman's dream of matching a British heavyweight for the World title was over. So, too, though he did not know it then, was his promotional career in Great Britain.

In an important sense, Bettinson and the NSC were to have the last, albeit bitter, laugh on Cochrane. They had long warned that promoters such as Cochrane were a menace to the sport: the massive purses they put up simply inflated the market along with boxers' egos. Life was made difficult for everyone and everyone was doomed to disappointment. What appeared as just sour grapes was now revealed as prophecy.

Quite suddenly Cochrane announced in a letter to *Sporting Life* in September 1920 that he was giving up the boxing side of his affairs, 'because in my capacity as a showman I must keep faith with the public. . . .' In other spheres of his business life, he explained: 'I have always treated with people who regarded a contract as a pledge, as something by which they would stand.

Unfortunately this has not been the case in some of my boxing enterprises.'

Ostensibly the failure of American Pete Herman to fulfil various terms of an agreement to fight Jimmy Wilde had been the last straw. But it emerged that Joe Beckett's behaviour had also been instrumental. Beckett had signed a contract after the Carpentier affair to meet Bombardier Wells again (for the 'unofficial' British title). The contract stipulated that, if successful, he would meet one of a number of named men, including contender Frank Moran.

The terms were generous: £3,000 win, lose or draw for the Wells fight and £2,000 for the follow-up. Beckett beat Wells, and Cochrane announced that Moran would be his next opponent. Beckett suddenly got cold feet, however, particularly when he saw Moran dispose of Frank Goddard. He complained of the money that he had been offered and claimed he had not realized he might have to meet Moran.

After much wrangling, Cochrane tied down Beckett to his contract but had clearly been disgusted by the latter's attitude. Thus he responded in print (*Sporting Life*), detailing exactly how generous he had been in the past, how he had helped Beckett rise from obscurity to his present position, and concluding: 'In addition I have made him several presentations not included in my contracts as well as a costly championship belt, also no part of any contract.'

The reference to the belt (for Beckett's unofficial heavyweight title) must have caused some hollow laughter at the NSC. And within the game in general and the BBBC in particular, Cochrane received little sympathy.

Beckett, despite finding little favour with the NSC committee (a feeling mutually shared) did manage one Belt contest – against Dick Smith in 1923 at the Holland Park Rink – soon after which he retired, not surprisingly a rich man.

Goddard retained the title but not the belt against Joe Bloom-field at the Albert Hall in 1923 and was succeeded by Phil Scott in 1926, but it would not be until 1932, with the arrival of Jack Peterson, that a British heavyweight title holder would don a Lonsdale Belt.

★

# OLYMPIA

## KENSINGTON, LONDON, W.

Under the Management of CHARLES B. COCHRAN.

FRANK GODDARD (Queen's Bays.)
(Lord Lonsdale Belt Holder.)

## TUESDAY JUNE 17,
### —1919.—

# Heavy Weight Championship of Gt. Britain.

## Great 20 Round Contest
### Of 3 minutes each.

JOE BECKETT
(Champion of Gt. Britain.)

*PRICES (inc. Tax)*—5/9, 11/6, £1 4s., £2 7s., £3 10s., £5 5s., £10 10s.

## Seats may now be booked at HOLBORN STADIUM.
### Telephone: HOLBORN 526.

If the NSC thought it had the field to itself with Cochrane's sudden departure from promoting, it was to be disappointed. In fact, Cochrane merely passed his commitments and contracts on to Major Arnold Wilson who had been acting as his right-hand man at Holborn Stadium.

Wilson, finding Olympia too expensive, turned to the Albert Hall as the venue for big contests and during the next four or five years would stage a series of fights at the heavier weights that would continue to leave the NSC in the shade.

Wilson's principal 'draw' was Ted Kid Lewis, once the British featherweight champion, now destined to cut a swathe through welter, middle and even light-heavyweight ranks. During the years 1920–24 Lewis would contest nine of thirteen British championship battles at welter and middleweight – the majority promoted by Wilson.

Lewis had won the World welterweight title during his wartime sojourn in the States. When he was defeated by Jack Britton in 1919 he decided the time was right to return home to the UK and 'clean up'. His arrival stirred up lurking resentment.

Early in 1920, just after Lewis's first fight back in the UK, a letter was read out at a BBBC meeting from Col. R. B. Campbell regarding 'unpatriotic conduct of certain leading British boxers', with a suggestion that the Board 'boycott' these men. The Board, however, 'could not see their way to take active action in the matter'.

Thus Lewis began his campaign back in England fighting Matt Wells at the Albert Hall – the first time the building had been used for a professional contest (and a financial flop).

Between January and May 1920 he beat middleweight contenders Frank Moody, Jerry Shea and Gus Platts before taking on Johnny Bee at Holborn – his first fight under the Cochrane/Wilson banner. The bout was advertised as for the 'vacant' middleweight title, Pat O'Keefe having retired. Lewis KO'd Bee in four rounds to claim the title; three weeks later, however, the NSC matched Tommy Gummer and Jim Sullivan for the middleweight Lonsdale Belt. Gummer won, the BBBC dithered, and confusion had begun.

In June, Lewis moved down to welterweight and at Olympia under Cochrane he beat Johnny Basham, the official belt-holder and European and Empire champion. Lewis now claimed two British titles and, after a short trip to the States, he returned to the Albert Hall in November 1920, where, now under Wilson, he beat Basham for a second time.

As he set off for the States again (Lewis was never one to let the grass grow under his feet) the arguments intensified as to exactly which title he held. The debate was fuelled by suspicions that the BBBC was discriminating against Lewis by apparently refusing to recognize him as champion at *any* weight. Doubts as to his war record were the principal reasons for this and much was made of Lewis's claim to have served in the US army in late 1918. To do so, it was argued, would have meant him taking out US naturalization papers. The fact that he had been billed for a fight in Liverpool as from the United States only increased the confusion. In fact, Lewis had remained a British citizen (though his son and wife were both Americans), but the debate opened up old wounds – in particular his avoidance of the call-up. There were letters written to various newspapers that accused him and others of cowardice. This provoked a shoal of letters in defence of Lewis which exhibited a definite desire to forget the war and all its horrors.

Such arguments had little effect on Lewis – nor, as we have seen, did they affect the attitude of the BBBC. Lewis was British and could fight for British titles: the problem was, which one? And who would decide which one?

In March 1921 Gus Platts beat the 'official' middleweight champion and belt-holder Tommy Gummer in Sheffield. Under existing regulations, the belt was returned to the Club and Platts recognized (despite Lewis's earlier claim) by the BBBC as champion. The NSC then invited Platts to put his title up against Joe Bloomfield – the winner to receive the Club's belt – but Platts decided to decline the offer, preferring instead to meet Johnny Basham at the Albert Hall.

The Club thus decided to do what it had done two years previously when Bombardier Wells had turned down an offer to defend his title. It simply offered the belt opportunity (and by implication, the title) to someone else, in this case Ted Kid Lewis! In effect, as reported in *Boxing*, it deposed Platts just as it deposed

Joe Beckett, a decision, if we are to believe promoter Wilson, not entirely endorsed by Lord Lonsdale:

> When his Lordship presented these belts I am sure he did not mean to give any monopoly as to where championships should be decided and in a conversation with me on the night of the Platts/Basham fight he was of the opinion that the competition for Lonsdale Belts should be broadened. I think the game would be healthier if it were so. . . .

However, in the case of Wells v Beckett, the decision had been motivated to some extent by annoyance and hurt pride. This time the reasons had been more blatantly commercial. The Club had taken out a lease on Holland Park Skating Rink – a sizeable venue in West London holding some 6,000–10,000 paying spectators. To fill such a venue, they needed a compelling star name battling for a title and having failed to secure Frank Goddard, Bettinson considered Ted Kid Lewis was the only British fighter below heavyweight who could draw crowds in sufficient numbers to make such a venture worthwhile.

When the Club had been limited to its Covent Garden premises there had been no need nor compunction to appeal to paying customers. Now that it had decided to step out into the market-place, as it were, the niceties of tradition and precedent were jettisoned.

In the event, Basham beat Platts at the Albert Hall in May 1921 and Lewis beat Bloomfield in June at Holland Park. In October Arnold Wilson brought the two 'title claimants' together at the Albert Hall and Lewis prevailed again. Everyone now agreed that Lewis was the middleweight champion, but with no thanks to the NSC.

But what of his claim to be welterweight champion as well? No one held the belt because the title holder and outright belt-winner Basham had been beaten twice by Lewis in 1920 at Olympia and the Albert Hall. Lewis was clearly the champion and yet, when the BBBC issued its official list of title-holders, the welterweight division was deliberately left vacant. The reason? The Board had simply adopted the NSC rule that insisted no one could hold more than one belt at a time. The Board went further and attempted to match Basham with Ted Moore for the 'vacant' title – a decision that only earned it yet more ridicule and criticism.

Lewis, however, was not finished yet. In November 1921 he took on 'Boy' McCormick, the British light-heavyweight champion (and belt-holder) by way of a warm-up for his World title fight with Georges Carpentier. Though Major Wilson disclaimed any intention of billing the fight as for the British title (both men would be coming into the ring well below the light-heavyweight limit) Lewis's fourteen-round victory saw many proclaiming him a *triple* British champion!

Wilson, whose promotions were 'to blame' for creating such confusion, was adamant that the real villain was the NSC for imposing its belt conditions on British championships:

> The belt is a private gift from that great sportsman the Earl of Lonsdale to a man who wins his championship *at the NSC* and is not necessary to a championship, as proved by the fact that Beckett and Harrison (heavy and bantamweight champions respectively) are included in the BBBC's championship list. If the belt is not necessary to a championship, *neither are the conditions attached thereto.*

This implied criticism of the Board was given more point when the latter turned down an application from Wilson to join it as a promoters' representative – a refusal that Wilson saw as yet more evidence of the NSC's undue influence on the governing body.

Lewis's tendency always to go for the cash rather than the glory would ultimately cause him unexpected anguish. In November at Holland Park he defeated Roland Todd's challenge for his middleweight title and belt and was thus poised to win the trophy outright. Typically, however, he chose to meet Todd in a return in February 1923 at the Albert Hall for a bigger purse than the NSC was able to offer at the time – and Todd beat him.

According to Lewis's son and biographer Morton, the ex-champ was somewhat shocked to discover that his defeat meant his having to return the belt to the Club. An NSC representative called at the Lewis household some days after the Todd defeat and, with Lewis absent, persuaded his wife Elsie to hand the trophy over 'for cleaning'. Lewis was indignant and even con-·

sidered charging the Club with larceny ... convinced that he could only lose the belt under Club auspices, thus ignoring more than a decade's traditions as well as overlooking the fact that the belt was the Club's property anyway. (Lewis would have to be content with the belt presented to him by Max Darewski – a famous theatrical star of the day – at Premierland in 1922).

A rematch with Todd and a Lewis victory under the Club's promotional banner would certainly have secured him the Lonsdale Belt outright, but Lewis was no longer the fighter he had been. Music hall tours, film-work, running a night-club, endless travelling to and from the USA had sapped him of a great deal of his fighting energy – although his long and distinguished career was not quite over.

In July 1924, in one of Arnold Wilson's last promotions at the Albert Hall, he beat Hamilton Johnny Brown in a defence of his still 'unofficial' welterweight title; four months later, in Edinburgh, he met defeat at the hands of Tommy Milligan.

Lewis was, by any standards, a phenomenal fighter. Bettinson described him thus when still in his prime:

His ways are not engaging: they tell of an especially hard, relentless merciless school; of the blood and fire of the ring; of a viciously practical fellow. . . .

And A. G. Hales wrote in 1921:

He has the cunning of some primitive animal. He can wait and wait and never grow flurried when points are being piled up against him, and when his enemy makes one bad mistake he is on top of him like a cobra striking its prey and when he does land either hand he makes the best and gamest of them go sick. . . . For he is a savage punisher when he thinks the moment has arrived for him to open up his batteries and the way he hurls his punches into body and head of an opponent is a caution to see. . . .

That he never won a Lonsdale Belt outright after winning three successive championship bouts at both welterweight and middleweight may seem, in retrospect, unjust, yet not unique:

Johnny Summers, Sid Smith and Joe Beckett all racked up successive victories, but secured no belt.

It was merely the consequence of a situation in which a highly symbolic trophy – although only fifteen years old already a national institution – was awarded by a body growing ever more unsure as to its role and purpose.

# 7

# Not So Roaring Twenties

Although events had conspired in the immediate post-war years virtually to remove title matches at the heavier weights from the NSC's control, the position was almost reversed for title fights below welterweight. Between 1919 and 1924 there were nineteen British championship contests at light, feather, bantam and fly-weight, fifteen involving Lonsdale Belts, fourteen at Covent Garden. Thus for these divisions, titles and belts would appear to have been almost synonymous.

The figures, however, are deceptive. In the flyweight division, once Jimmy Wilde stepped down in 1918 there would only be one Belt/title contest in six years: Elky Clarke beating Kid Kelly in 1924.

In the featherweight division, although new champion Mike Honeyman defended the title three times at the Club in 1920 and 1921, once Joe Fox had secured the crown he set off for America and remained there for three years during which time the title was in abeyance.

As for the lightweights, Ernie Rice – champion and belt holder in 1921 – lost his title in Liverpool in 1922, and the Club would not stage another Belt contest until 1924.

A principal reason for the erratic progress of the belts was, as ever, economic. After an initial boom in interest in the sport, riding on a general economic upsurge following the Armistice, there came a slump. In 1922, for instance, there were just four title fights, only two of them in London. Champions and contenders found attractive purses at lighter weights few and far between – while America offered much better pickings.

The situation became so bad that in 1924 *Sporting Life* made

Bantamweight champion Tommy Noble and wife, 1919

a suggestion that Belt rules be altered so that any champion leaving Britain should first deposit the belt with the Club and if, after two months, he was still abroad, the belt should be put up for competition again. If the champ returned within a year, he could box for it against the 'resident' champ. At that point there were only six British title holders anyway, only three of whom, all of them abroad, possessed a belt.

A good example of the lure of the USA having a detrimental effect on the domestic game was Johnny Brown, who won the bantamweight championship in 1923. Brown's real name was Phil Hickman. Born into a Jewish family in the St George's district of Whitechapel in 1902, he began to box as an amateur when aged thirteen and turned pro two years later with Joe Morris, a prolific manager either side of the First World War.

The necessity to help his widowed mother was the ostensible reason for his taking up prizefighting, an occupation for which Brown was not temperamentally suited – though his courage and stamina, not to mention his hard punching (twenty-six KO wins in fifty-one career victories) made him, ultimately, an extremely

prosperous man. He scrapped away in relative obscurity for two
or three years at venues such as the Ring, Premierland and the
Manor Hall, Hackney, before, aged eighteen, he received an invitation to box in the USA. Managed by Charlie Harvey, he
embarked upon an eighteen-bout stint that honed his skills sufficiently to enable him to challenge Bugler Lake, British bantamweight champion, to a non-title fight in Plymouth in late 1922.
Lake defeated him, and Brown returned to the States but, in late
1923, he was matched a second time with Lake, this time at the
NSC and for the latter's British title. He triumphed, and a busy
year followed: ten wins in twelve months before he battered Harry
Corbett to defeat in sixteen hard rounds to register a second
notch on the belt. Eight months later it was the turn of Mick Hill
to be subjected to the hard hands of Johnny Brown, although the
challenger had Brown down in the penultimate round in what
proved to be a punishing battle from start to finish.

Thus Johnny Brown had won a Lonsdale Belt outright in less
than two years – a win notable for two reasons. Brown would be
the only Jewish fighter to win a belt outright. And the one he was
presented with turned out to be Digger Stanley's old belt, with
the little gypsy's name erased. . . .

However, although just twenty-three years old, Brown's top-
line career was now more or less over. Anxious to cash in on his
status, there being little by way of lucrative opportunities in the
UK, he hurried back to the USA where, in a disastrous campaign
(six straight losses in a year), he failed to obtain a World title
chance and clearly lost much of his enthusiasm for the profession.
Like Teddy Baldock and Jim Higgins, Brown's anxiety to earn
money in a hurry – particularly on the American treadmill –
would lead to 'burn-out.'

With regard to British championships, Brown's absence and
subsequent disillusion meant a three-year gap between title fights.
When finally the NSC offered him a challenge – against Alf Kid
Pattenden – Brown turned it down, preferring instead to meet
the box-office star Teddy Baldock in an unofficial title fight at
Clapton Stadium. Baldock, then only twenty-one, KO'd Johnny
Brown in just two rounds.

The NSC took much of the criticism for the increasing tendency of champs like Brown not to defend the titles they possessed,

but with no hard and fast rules governing Belt defences, and with the new Board of Control having devised none of its own, whenever the Club *did* try to force the issue, its motives were impugned and it was roundly criticized by everyone concerned. The paucity of pure offers was often cited by reluctant champions for refusing to defend but in the 1920s the NSC, as a going concern, was itself struggling.

Norman Clark, BBBC Secretary in those years, recalled, in *All in the Game*: 'After the war, club life in London . . . was giving way to jazz-band rendezvous, cheap restaurants or (for those people who could afford it) nightly circuits of anything and everything that was going. . . .' The Club, in effect, was no longer fashionable.

The Covent Garden premises had always been too small to attract an audience large enough to enable the management to offer big purses to British title holders and, though the Holland Park Rink had been secured in order to allow the Club to mount attractive promotions, it would be sparingly used. Hopes of 20,000 crowds had been dashed from the outset when LCC safety regulations reduced the capacity to a third. Thus never more than one British title fight per year took place there during the six years of the Club's lease. Quite simply, there were too few British fighters attractive enough to fill even so reduced a stadium in London.

Sadly for 'Peggy' Bettinson and the Club, top boxers knew this and refused to be inveigled into fights unless they were *guaranteed* a substantial lump sum in advance. The following account of an attempted deal involving Bettinson, Charlie Rose (a boxing manager) and heavyweight Frank Goddard illustrates the problem:

'Now boys,' said Bettinson. 'I have secured premises at Holland Park large enough to hold 20,000 people. Now I propose to give you chaps 50 per cent of the "gate" provided you do not ask for any guarantee.

'As you know, this is contrary to the Club's general procedure which insists on a 60–40 division and I am breaking this rule only to give the new annex a good start. What do you say?'

Rose, looking at Goddard said, 'That seems a fair propo-
sition, Frank. I should accept it if I were you.'

Goddard, meanwhile, slapping his breeches with his whip,
hereupon asked 'Peggy', 'How much money do you think I
should get, guv'ner?'

'At Club prices your cut should run into about £4,000,
Goddard,' was the reply.

'Farmer Frank's reply struck us all dumb. 'Guv'nor, £4,000
is too much money to pull down in one lump. You give me
£2,000 and you can have the other for yourself.'

I can see Bettinson as plain as if it were today. He had refilled
his glass, rising from his chair to do so, but instead of drinking
it he dashed it to the floor and wrathfully exclaiming, 'Damn
you Goddard', walked from the room, banging the door behind
him.

'What have *I* done?' cried Goddard, wearing a look of
injured innocence. Retorted Charlie Rose with an admiring
smile, 'And everybody tells me you are nothing but a dumb
cluck, Frank.'

'Peggy' Bettinson, according to his autobiography, was equally
unsuccessful with 'international' stars:

I was assured that Jack Britton was disposed to come this way
to defend his title against Kid Lewis. I inquired for Britton's
terms and learned that he would fight here, if he were paid
round about £8,000. Can you imagine anything more impossible? To stage a contest between Britton and Lewis on those
figures would eat up little short of £16,000. For the life of me
I cannot understand the mind of present champions.

The Club was not disposed to gamble: it left that to 'entrepreneurs' like Cochrane and Wilson, and Wilson's spectacular
'crash' in 1924 (he bankrupted himself by booking Wembley
Stadium for a Jack Bloomfield v Tommy Gibbons contest which
flopped) merely confirmed Bettinson's opinion that so flamboyant
an approach was foolhardy.

The Club's relative inactivity did, however, provide provincial
promoters with opportunities. The first of them to make a sig-

THE

# GREATEST BOXING PROGRAMME

## EVER OFFERED TO THE SPORTING PUBLIC,

### AT THE STADIUM, LIVERPOOL. 'PHONE ROYAL 647.

On MONDAY, JUNE 26th, at 7.30 p.m.

**BILLY AMES and NORMAN HURST present**

THE BANTAM-WEIGHT CHAMPIONSHIP OF GREAT BRITAIN

# JIM HIGGINS v. TOMMY HARRISON

(HAMILTON)
Bantam Champion of Great Britain and Winner outright of the Earl of Lonsdale's Championship Challenge Belt.

(HANLEY)
Ex-Bantam Champion of Europe.

Under strict Championship Conditions for £100 a side. In the Ring at 9 o'clock prompt.

| THE WORLD'S CHAMPION BURLESQUE (To a Finish). | SPECIAL FIFTEEN (3-MIN.) ROUNDS MIDDLEWEIGHT CONTEST. |
|---|---|
| **WALLY PICKARD v. JOE BOWKER** | **PETER JACKSON v. IKE CLARKE** |
| (The Boxer, Jockey, Humorist) (Ex-World's Champion) | (Liverpool) (Birkenhead) |

EXTRA SPECIAL TWENTY (3-MIN.) ROUNDS HEAVYWEIGHT CONTEST.

**ALBERT LLOYD.** v. **ARTHUR TOWNLEY**
(Cruiserweight Champion of Australia) (Birkenhead)

ADMISSION : 3/6, 5/9, 11/6, 22/6, 33/6, Tax included. LADIES SPECIALLY INVITED

nificant post-war impact was Billy Ames, manager of Billy March-ant and Tom Moody, among others. Along with manager Norman Hurst, Ames lured European bantamweight champion Charles Ledoux to the Palais de Dance, Hanley in October 1921 where local man Tommy Harrison caused a sensation by winning the title on points.

Unfortunately, the BBBC – a member of whose original com-mittee Ames had once been – refused to extend its recognition to Harrison. The Board had affiliated to the IBU – an organiz-ation formed in France in 1920 – whose rules insisted that a European title could only be won by a national title-holder, which Harrison was not. It was a tactless decision by the Board, one which smacked a little of sour grapes. Ledoux had been European champion since defeating Digger Stanley in 1912. He had then beaten NSC all-time favourite Jim Driscoll in 1919 as well as KO'd the official bantamweight title/belt holder Jim Higgins.

Higgins, meanwhile, had been giving Harrison the run-around by refusing to defend his title against him despite generous purse offers from Ames and Hurst (reputed to be well over £1,000).

Eventually, however, they succeeded in luring Higgins to Liverpool where Harrison – a veteran of thirty who had been fighting since 1909 – KO'd Higgins in thirteen rounds.

Ames had decided views on the undue influence of the NSC and its symbol of authority, the Lonsdale Belt, declaring:

> The belt, while ornamental and desirable (is) not the *sine qua non* to a championship. . . . They are a recent innovation, and in my opinion they have no bearing on the issue. The NSC is a monopoly. I have argued for many years that it would be good for boxing if legitimate championships were distributed throughout the provinces. The provincial public and provincial boxers are the very backbone of boxing: given a champion and his most logical challenger in a match organized by a promoter of repute . . . then I say that a bout must be considered a championship whether decided in London, in Liverpool or elsewhere. . . .

A sentiment no doubt echoed across the border in Scotland where, almost simultaneously, Nat Dresner, a young pawnbroker-cum-entrepreneur was setting out to blaze a brief promotional trail from the unlikely base of Edinburgh. Like Ames, Dresner was briefly a member of the BBBC. He was also a manager of exciting young talent and in July 1922 he featured both Alex Ireland and George McKenzie (future British champs) on his debut tourney at Waverley Market – the success of which encouraged him to set up Scotland's first ever British title match between Seaman James Hall of Peebles and Johnny Brown of Hamilton for the latter's lightweight title.

Dresner's combination of Ames's regional know-how (matching local men with huge followings and allowing in the unemployed at reduced prices) with Cochrane's showman style (he employed programme sellers immaculately dressed in white woollen jumpers with 'Nat Dresner' inscribed back to front in bold green letters) produced record attendences. Some 12,000 packed into the Industrial Hall for the Brown v Hall fight; 21,000 squeezed into the same venue the following year to see Ted Kid Lewis take on Tommy Milligan for the British welterweight title; while 10,000 watched Milligan go down to Dresner's own Alex Ireland

BOXING, FEBRUARY 9, 1921.
Vol. XXII. No. 597.

**BENNY McNEILL v. JOHNNY BROWN.**

# BOXING

### Three Pence Every Wednesday.

Vol. XXII.
No. 597.

*The Only Paper in the World solely devoted to Boxing.*
FEBRUARY 9, 1921.

Registered at the G.P.O.
as a Newspaper and for
Canadian Magazine Post.

JIM      HIGGINS
Record Outright Winner of a Lonsdale Belt.

for the British middleweight title in 1928 – the year, incidentally, of Dresner's untimely death aged just forty-six.

Both Dresner and Ames demonstrated the growing strength of regional boxing – and the untapped potential for audiences, particularly where title fights were involved. The London monopoly of such events – whether it be by the NSC or the Cochrane/ Wilson spectacles at Olympia and the Albert Hall – obscured the fact that British boxers, especially champions, could draw upon strong local support.

The reluctance of the NSC and others in the capital to promote regular title fights was blamed on the lack of 'attractive' champs and contenders. What they failed to appreciate was that the days of pre-war greats such as Wilde, Lewis, Lee, Welsh and even Wells were over. British boxing, like British society in general, was settling into a long, introverted period when genuine world-class fighters would be rare, but when areas such as Manchester, Liverpool, Glasgow and Belfast would produce hundreds of local heroes.

London itself was very much a city of localities – Premierland in the East End, the Ring, Blackfriars, south of the river: these were as fiercely partisan as Scousers and Geordies. And it would be to these specific audiences that promoters, including the NSC, would eventually find themselves appealing.

The fortunes of the lightweight title and belt demonstrate this 'regional' effect for, apart from Seaman Hall's two victories – the first for Ames in Liverpool, the second for Dresner in Edinburgh – the division would be dominated in the Twenties by Londoners with specific local constituencies: Ernie Rice, Ernie Izzard, Harry Mason, Sam Steward and Fred Webster, fighting at venues such as the Albert Hall, Holland Park Rink, the Ring and the NSC itself.

Rice, Izzard and Mason in fact were 'characters' and thus self-publicists, which helped to make up for their lack of genuine international class. Rice was from Hounslow, of Italian extraction and a cousin of Bandsman Rice. His career, like so many inter-war boxers, began in the boxing booths in 1912 and took off in 1920 when he won a Ring competition and belt. Within the space of a month he was matched with Devonian Ben Callicott at the

Ernie Rice, Light-weight Champion of England.

NSC (Callicott being an experienced fighter managed by Harry Jenkins, the Plymouth Cosmo promoter and BBBC committee member) and Rice's heavier punch settled matters in the seventh round.

His nickname, 'Elbows', referring to his unorthodox stance and elbow cover, is said to have been bestowed upon him in the USA. Bettinson, predictably, considered him ungainly and awkward although at the same time acknowledging his 'heart' and perseverance. Eugene Corri, in *Gloves and the Man*, was more appreciative:

> A very aggressive fighter, he walks right into his man with pantherine cunning and prowls after him without a moment's pause, punching hard with both hands all the time, keeping his chin down and covering up with his arms and elbows, Ernie is very difficult to hit.

He was also difficult to 'read', feinting, as he often did, with both shoulders and fists. He was also something of an extrovert, encouraged perhaps by one of his trainers, the Welsh ex-middleweight contender Fred Dyer who, in his fighting days, would regale the audience with 'Thora, my darling', usually through swollen and battered lips. Rice's own 'dialogue' with the ringside patrons earned him a rebuke in 1919 from the fledgling BBBC: he was carpeted for having appealed to the crowd after a dubious decision (not to mention having arranged with his opponent to go 'halves' on the purse).

He was also ambitious: following his Belt success he set off for the USA in search of Benny Leonard, the World champion at lightweight, but was badly beaten by a certain 'Sailor' Abe Friedman – a defeat that caused Rice to take a prolonged lay-off due to cut eyes.

He returned to the UK and threw down a challenge to Ted Kid Lewis, expressing supreme confidence that he could KO the great man, but finally took up Billy Ames's offer of a defence against Seaman Hall at Liverpool in September 1922, which he lost on points. Enter Ernie Izzard and Harry Mason, and the start of a period of title confusion.

Mason took the title from Seaman Hall at Olympia in May 1923, and, following a successful defence against Rice in November, set off for the USA. While there, the IBU ordered him to defend his European lightweight title, but he refused, pleading a busy schedule. The IBU promptly deposed him.

At this point, the NSC decided to 'float' the lightweight belt which had not been contested since 1921. The Club committee appeared to ignore the champion Mason, and matched Izzard against Jack Kirk from Doncaster – the finalists in a lightweight competition the Club had been running.

The decision dismayed many commentators; the editor of *Boxing* wrote:

> As events will now apparently work out, we shall find ourselves quarrelling over the claims of two lightweight champions – one national and one NSC. In other words, we shall be back in a position from which the Lonsdale Belts were first instituted in order to rescue us. . . .

The evidence suggests, however, that the Club had offered the chance to Mason to win the trophy but that he had demanded too much money. Following Izzard's Belt victory over Kirk in November, the BBBC minutes note that Mason was then offered a 'title' match with Izzard, refusal of which would result in Mason 'being deprived of the championship'. Mason did refuse, Izzard was confirmed as champion in the December ratings and was matched with Teddy Baker for the belt and title the following April.

Izzard, from Herne Hill, was, like Ernie Rice, noted for his peculiar stance and build. The 'Human Hairpin', although a comfortable lightweight 9 st 9 lb, was almost 6 ft tall and thus looked painfully thin. The story goes that during a hard fight at the Ring his father, who acted as second, took a lump of ice from a bucket and applied it to the back of Izzard's neck, at which point a wag shouted, 'What's the use of ice to 'im? Why don't you give 'im a good beefsteak?'

Izzard had started out in life as a messenger at Throgmorton Street in the City and was remembered as such by Eugene Corri, NSC referee and member, but also a stockbroker – a stark illustration of the social divisions reflected in pro-boxing. As a boxer, Izzard was a fine stylist rather than a hard puncher, able to exploit his long reach with deft footwork and, in a fifteen-year career, he racked up over 100 wins while suffering just nineteen defeats.

In 1924, when aged nineteen, on a trip to the USA, he caught the eye of Benny Leonard, who offered him a sparring partner's job. Izzard, however, turned the offer down, hurrying home instead for a proposed Belt match at featherweight with Danny Frush. The fight fell through and he found himself fighting for the lightweight belt instead.

In fact, he would be extremely unlucky not to take the belt outright: his three title fights spanned just seven months but, following the second victory over Teddy Baker, he came up against none other than Harry Mason, now back from the USA and anxious to re-establish himself.

The match was staged at the Holland Park Rink, providing the Club with enough money with which to meet Mason's considerable demands. As it turned out, it was a sensational bout with a controversial ending.

For eight rounds it was a keenly fought contest with Mason on the receiving end of some heavy punishment, including a hard right that put him on the floor in the fifth. But, gradually, Mason began to find his range and in the eighth he caught Izzard with a left-right combination that put him down and almost out of the ring. From that point on, confusion reigned, due largely to the fact that the referee, as per NSC rules, was outside the ring.

With the crowd in an uproar, Izzard struggled to rise, while Mason hovered over him. Mason, however, claimed in *The Jockey* that he could not hear the timekeeper. His account of what happened next is interesting:

> I counted the seconds to myself and at what I thought was a good ten I ran across to him, piloted him to his corner where his seconds appeared dumbfounded by the swift change in the tide of war. Turning to go to my corner, I saw the referee gesticulating wildly with wide-open mouth. What he was saying I couldn't hear as the whole house was on its hind legs by this time and shouting at the top of its collective voice. But I sensed what he meant and, though I hated to do it, I turned and charged down fiercely on poor defenceless Ernie. Of course it didn't take me long to floor him again, and yet again.

*Allsports Weekly*, March 1926

The fight was now a farce, the noise deafening, women at ringside apparently fainting at the one-sided carnage. Yet, amazingly, Izzard was still on his feet when the round ended. By now the referee had clambered into the ring, and during a long delay, while the seconds worked feverishly on Izzard, the various officials consulted one another on what to do.

Eventually, Mason's seconds became impatient with the moments ticking away – allowing Izzard more and more time to pull himself together – and Alec Goodman shouted to the timekeeper to start the next round. The bell rang, Mason rushed across to Izzard's corner, only to be pushed away by Izzard's seconds, who claimed they hadn't heard the bell. Izzard was promptly – mercifully – disqualified!

Such uproar and confusion seemed to follow Mason around. One of boxing's more unusual, even extraordinary, figures, he was born in Leeds in 1903 and grew up in London's Jewish East End. He made regular appearances at Manor Hall and steadily built up a reputation, so that when Premierland reopened in splendour in early 1922, Mason was featured on the first night bill.

Indeed, as Kid Lewis's career drew to a close, Mason saw himself as the great man's successor. He was a true product of the jazz age: a dancer, singer and amateur musician, he conducted dance-bands, dressed in a top hat and tails and frequented fashionable, risqué night-spots. He was the 'Admirable Crichton of the ring' according to Eugene Corri, or the 'Fighting Fiddler' to the more mundane fight cognoscenti.

He was also a great believer in publicity, particularly of the negative kind, and revelled in provoking both the crowd and his opponents. Although from the East End, he made the Ring, Blackfriars, his 'home' venue – an odd choice for a Jewish boy, for the Ring crowd, being predominantly South London, were not noted for their racial tolerance. Wearing the Star of David on his trunks – a fashion for Jewish boxers in the inter-war years – did not help matters, just as enlisting as a special constable during the General Strike and riding around on a horse was hardly calculated to endear him to local dockers.

The dapper 'Star of the East' really came into his own in 1925. Mason's victory over Izzard in June that year was the beginning of a twelve-month period during which he had no fewer than seven British title fights at light and welterweight – three involving Lonsdale Belts, the rest fought under the promotional banner of Harry Jacobs at the Albert Hall.

Jacobs, once promoter at Wonderland and founder of Premierland, had gone bankrupt in 1914, a victim of his own gambling obsession. Now, as matchmaker for a new syndicate that had stepped into the gap left by Major Wilson, he could make the Albert Hall his new stage – and Mason would be one of his star turns. They suited one another – Jacobs, like Mason, knowing a thing or two about publicity and no stranger to controversy. In fact, the first welterweight title fight against Hamilton Johnny Brown (for the 'vacant' title but not for a Lonsdale Belt) ended in uproar when referee Moss de Yong awarded the fight to Brown. Jacobs got up into the ring to condemn the result and the referee, and a month later Mason won the rematch on points. He then defended his lightweight title successfully against Ernie Rice (the latter being goaded into fouling Mason and suffering a much disputed disqualification) before defending the welterweight title against Len Harvey – a poor fight that ended in a draw.

Until now, Mason's controversial performances had generally been resolved in his favour. The tide was about to turn. At long last the NSC decided to 'float' a new welterweight belt – incredibly, the first since Johnny Basham's outright winning sequence ended in 1916. Since then, Kid Lewis, Tommy Milligan, Johnny Brown and Mason had held the title but none had fought for a belt. Now the Club tempted Mason into a match with Jack Hood, a bright prospect from Birmingham, then just twenty-four with over thirty wins to his credit.

Hood would prove to be the supreme British welterweight during the Twenties and early Thirties. However, in this, his first title fight, he was awarded a verdict that almost no one, including Lord Lonsdale himself, felt he deserved.

'Jack had been outpaced, outboxed, outgeneralled and outfought... and... save a few fleeting occasions, Hood was never really in the picture at all,' the *Boxing* correspondent wrote. Hood did succeed in flooring Mason in the third round for a count of seven but generally Mason's ability to avoid Hood's punches while jabbing left after left into the younger man's face appeared to have gained him a runaway verdict.

However, Hood agreed to a return with Mason some two months later and this time the result – a second points victory for Hood – was unanimous. In a somewhat lack-lustre fight, Hood did all the pressing while Mason appeared unable to generate much energy or enthusiasm. The points verdict for Hood surprised nobody.

Although Mason's career would continue well into the 1930s and although he would regain the welterweight title in 1934 for a brief period, he never fought for a Lonsdale Belt again. In many ways, his career typified the era where the belts were concerned: in eleven championship fights which included six victories, he secured just one notch on a belt – the controversial Izzard fight. As such, he was following in the footsteps of his hero Kid Lewis, another great Jewish fighter who, despite dominating various divisions, failed to secure a belt outright.

By contrast, Jack Hood hardly ever had a championship contest where a belt was *not* at stake: in seven contests for the welter and

# NATIONAL SPORTING CLUB

## MONDAY 31st MAY 1926 at 7.30 p.m. at

# HOLLAND PARK HALL

### HOLLAND PARK AVENUE, W.11.

### 20 ROUND CONTEST

For the Welter Weight Championship of Great Britain and the Lonsdale Championship Challenge Belt.

## FOR £250 ASIDE AND PURSE.

 *v*

### JACK HOOD
(Birmingham)

### HARRY MASON
(Leeds)

**12 ROUND CONTEST AT 10st. 4lbs.**

## ALF MANCINI *v* SONNY BIRD
(Shepherds Bush)　　　　　　　　(Chelsea)

### 6 ROUND CONTESTS AND OTHER BOXING.

**PRICES (including Tax): 8/6, 12/-, £1 4/-, £2 7/-, £3 10/-,**
**All Seats Reserved.**

### TICKETS

may be obtained at N.S.C., Covent Garden (Gerrard 2905, 2017, 2045), at Holland Park Hall, W.11 (Park 4874, 4875). Keith Prowse & Co. & Alfred Hayes, Agents.

Holland Park Hall is easily accessible from all parts of London.—by Tube (C.L.R.) Holland Park, Shepherds Bush and Uxbridge Road Station. 'BUSES 32, 49, 49ᴬ, 88, 112, 184, 185 & 286 PASS THE DOOR.

Shocks and Surprises at Holland Park Rink.

Hood *v* Mason, *Boxing*, June 1926

middleweight titles, five were under NSC auspices while a sixth
was scheduled for Holland Park but was cancelled in controversial
circumstances. Hood won the rearranged fight and was then given
the welterweight belt by way of compensation.

Hood was certainly a boxer in a class above his contemporaries.
That he only added the European title to his British laurels was
due mainly to brittle hands which deprived him of a KO punch
– a vital asset if one wanted to succeed in the USA. He made
gallant attempts in the early Thirties to take the middleweight
title from Len Harvey, but he was clearly not heavy enough to
operate comfortably among the harder hitters such as Harvey and
McAvoy. Nevertheless, in Lonsdale Belt terms, he was one of
those men the Club seemed to smile upon, increasing the resentment felt among those boxers who did not possess the skills and
charisma of a Hood or a Harvey.

More typical perhaps were the experiences of featherweight
contenders Mike Honeyman and Billy Marchant who met in 1920
to contest a new featherweight belt. Marchant was an interesting
character; one of four fighting brothers from Salford, managed

by Billy Ames, he had run away from home in 1905 aged fifteen to join a boxing booth. A year later his father sent him down to London where Manchester exile Joe Bowker had a gym and, not long afterwards, Billy began his full-time boxing career.

Within two years, in 1907, he had amassed seventy-eight contests and manager Ames, along with Manchester promoter Jack Smith, used him to help develop the burgeoning Manchester boxing scene which would produce so many fine champions in the coming decades. Billy himself always seemed a trifle unlucky. In 1912 he went to the USA with flyweight champion Sid Smith and made a good impression. On his return he became a regular top-liner all over the country and a contender for the featherweight title, but was squeezed out in a very competitive series that eventually saw Ted Kid Lewis take the crown in 1913.

During the war, in 1918, Billy was badly wounded but was back in the ring a year later and finally earned the right to meet Honeyman for the featherweight title.

Honeyman, from Woolwich, had begun his career in 1913 and would eventually amass a total of 167 fights. At that point in January 1920, aged twenty-five, he could boast an impressive record – just nineteen losses in over one hundred contests, including a points victory over Marchant the previous year. Honeyman was a fast, elusive boxer without a strong punch, able to move swiftly out of danger and rarely KO'd (just seven times in a thirteen-year career). Marchant certainly found him hard to hit and chased him for a full twenty rounds: indeed, he appeared to have done more work than Honeyman (Jim Driscoll is said to have left early, whispering into Billy's brother's ear that 'your kid's won this fight hands down'.) But the judges thought otherwise and, to some amazement, awarded the title to Honeyman.

The result confirmed the conviction of Mancunians that the NSC was biased against Marchant – a point hard to prove. Certainly the Club did not boycott Billy, who earned good money over the years through his NSC appearances, often at the top of the bill. Like his brothers, Marchant was a quality performer in a period when men fought so regularly and often neglected to plan for top honours in any systematic way. Thus they took on more contests than were necessary and, with such a work-load, were bound to lose occasionally. Unfortunately, the losses sometimes occurred when a championship was at stake. Marchant was one of those fighters, a man too willing to take each and every contest arranged for him by his manager.

Honeyman's next opponent was that other ring phenomenon – Tancy Lee. Lee was now thirty-eight years old and approaching the end of his long and successful career. Nevertheless, he lasted until the nineteenth round when the referee intervened, Honeyman having 'put more sting, more bite into his punches; he was less of a running, racing, prancing boxer than usual.'

However, his third opponent could not have been more of a test – bantamweight belt-holder, Joe Fox. Fox was yet another hardy veteran and an accomplished box-fighter. Honeyman's tactical limitations were exposed by Fox whose ability to tie up and frustrate opponents was well known. In fact, Honeyman made a crucial mistake in eschewing his normal boxing style to embark upon a tactic of infighting. He lost on points – and thus failed to secure the third notch that would have made the belt his own. Indeed, Honeyman's experience of missing out on the crucial third notch would become almost the norm for featherweights during the next decade: George McKenzie, Johnny Curly and Harry Corbett would all win two and lose the third, the sequence finally (and only just) broken by Johnny Cuthbert in 1930.

But possibly the unlikeliest of boxers *not* to win a belt, given that he was clearly in a class above the average, was Scotsman Elky Clark. Clark shared with Harry Mason a musical talent: indeed, Clark was a semi-professional and, according to Eugene Corri (in *Gloves and the Man*) could play the piano, organ and guitar: 'Clark likes best to play Scottish melodies with patriotic fervour, whether it be a plaintive piece like the "Flowers of the Forest" or a Scottish reel that sets everyone dancing.'

His distinctive appearance – red hair standing up straight like wire – earned him the soubriquet 'Red Granite', but he was no natural showman: indeed, he was incredibly shy. Many years later trainer Joe Aitcheson recalled that, when on road-work, Clark would stop the moment he saw anyone coming, take out an old pipe and make as though he was just sitting having a quiet smoke!

Clark was a correct, almost faultless stylist, a wonderful judge of distance, possessing skilful footwork and great stamina. The latter was perhaps his key attribute – over shorter distances he was liable to have the occasional decision stolen from him.

His comparatively short career – just forty-five bouts in all – was ended by injury, but for a time he held out the promise of becoming a World champion. In 1924 he stopped Kid Kelly to take the British flyweight title and belt, and over the next few months he added the Empire and European titles. In 1926 he defended his British title at the NSC against Kid Socks (real name Harry Stockings), a fighter who had come through the hard Manor Hall school, a tough little battler who had shocked Clark by 'pinching' a twelve-round decision from him in 1925.

In 1927 Clark went to New York to take on Fidel la Barba for the World flyweight title but was beaten over twelve rounds, being badly 'thumbed' in the first round – an eye injury that would end his career as well as lose him his eye. For his pains, he would earn a mere £500 from that contest after managers and agents had taken their considerable shares.

Although Clark struggled for some time to regain fitness, the NSC became impatient to get its belt back and insisted that Clark return it, once it looked unlikely that his eye injury would allow him to fight again. It was a callous, thoughtless gesture by the Club – particularly when one considers that he had held the belt for almost three years and had defended it twice. What was good for Jack Hood was apparently not good enough for Elky Clark.

By contrast, the fighting fraternity continued to hold Clark in the highest esteem. Johnny Hill, the fighter who took his place in the next Belt fight against Alf Barber, insisted that Elky first give his permission before he took the fight.

Rather touchingly, Clark opened a pub on his retirement called the Lonsdale Bar – an undeserved tribute to an institution whose lack of heart was gradually helping to devalue its precious trophy.

# 8

# Boxing Politics and the Colour-Bar

The symbiotic relationship between the NSC and the BBBC is often cited as the reason for the relative anarchy of British boxing during the 1920s. Rival promoters felt that they were placed at a disadvantage when dealing with the NSC as a competitor because of the latter's overwhelming influence on the Board of Control which the NSC had founded more or less single-handed.

But the problems of the Twenties were more complicated: the motives of those involved more commercial than altruistic. Pro-boxing was a business and cynicism was an essential lubricant helping to oil the wheels. Thus, a great deal of the 'outrage' expressed by promoters, managers and boxers at alleged inadequacies and shortcomings of the Board were more the result of thwarted ambition and narrow sectional interests than any concern for the health of the sport in general. Moreover, accusations that the Club and the Board worked hand in glove for the Club's benefit were not strictly true. On occasions, the Club was to show more willingness to abide by decisions that adversely affected it than many of its loudest detractors.

Additionally, there was an important divergence of opinion between Club and Board concerning boxing's 'legal' status.

At its very first meeting in 1919, certain Board members expressed the desire for some kind of official status to be granted from the Home Office. This wish ran counter to the natural instincts of the NSC – in particular those of Lonsdale and Bettinson. In October 1921, when the Board intimated its intention to seek 'charter' status similar to that granted to the British Medical Association, Lonsdale voiced his opposition and suggested the

107

government would not agree. *His* idea was to request that the Home Office grant the Board advisory committee status, allowing it to grant licences to promoters, referees, etc. Lonsdale suggested that he was the person to achieve this via his friends in high places and the Board acquiesced.

Nothing transpired, however, and the issue appeared to have died – which was perhaps Lonsdale's intention. However, in 1923 and 1925 there were moves by individual MP's to introduce bills into Parliament to establish a legal basis for the Board and boxing; and in April 1925, with Cmdr Kenworthy's Bill looking likely to proceed, the Under Secretary of State for the Home Office requested advice from the Board as to certain specific details. This brought Lonsdale and Bettinson back to the Board's offices to state, rather impatiently, that in their view boxing already *was* legal – as long as it was carried out under NSC rules – and they cited various legal cases in which the NSC had been involved at the turn of the century. The Bill, Lonsdale felt, was irrelevant and superfluous, and his original idea of the Board issuing licences with Home Office approval was insisted upon. Kenworthy's Bill failed, however, and the Board was no better placed than before. (In fact, British boxing, unlike the American sport, has never been granted legal status.) The resulting power vacuum was thus perpetuated – to the detriment of the Board's authority.

This is not to suggest that Lord Lonsdale thought the Board a bad idea – on occasions he even baled it out financially when funds were low, as they perpetually were in the early years when there was little by way of income to draw upon.

There was, nevertheless, an awkward relationship between Lord Lonsdale, the NSC and the Board, only exacerbated by the endless saga of the belts. Though regularly derided, ignored and scoffed at by promoters, managers and even boxers, they remained an obsession, while the Club, struggling to survive economically during the Twenties, was understandably jealous of this symbol of its authority. Thus, whenever there were disputes about who should or should not fight for a belt, when and for how much, the Board very often found itself waiting upon the Club's decision, giving the impression at times of being ineffectual and very much the junior partner.

This was perfectly illustrated in 1926 with the sensational

announcement that Lord Lonsdale had been in consultation with American authorities discussing the possibility of floating the belts as symbols of World championships, an idea current before the First World War. Whether or not there was much in the story, Lonsdale was happy to play along, neither confirming nor denying, while the Board's authority to deal with international matters again looked compromised.

In boxing 'politics' 1926 would in fact be a crucial year particularly as it brought the death, after a long illness, of 'Peggy' Bettinson. One of the most powerful men in British boxing since the turn of the century, he had been a fixed point in a turning world and his departure heralded the end of the NSC as a major force in the game.

Within two years of Bettinson's death, the Club's tenure on the Covent Garden building where it had been situated since 1891 would end, and it was to become a transient, though still influential, commercial operation, guided by Bettinson's son, Lionel.

The year 1926 would also see the start of a life and death struggle for the Boxing Board, sparked off by a controversial decision – the suspension of senior referee Joe Palmer. In March, Palmer was refereeing a fight between Johnny Sullivan and Len Harvey at the Ring, Blackfriars. At the end of the bout, Palmer adjudged Sullivan to be the narrow winner on points – to the amazement of many and the consternation of promoter (and manager of Harvey) Dan Sullivan.

Following much press criticism of the verdict (only one of nine defeats that Harvey would suffer in a 142-fight career) Palmer was asked to appear before the Board to explain himself.

Unfortunately, he could produce no record book, and witnesses called by Sullivan (who was a Board member) simply expressed their opinion that the decision was wrong. Whilst assuring him that they were not calling his honesty into question, the Board decided to take his licence away. Palmer was disgusted but dismissive. As he wrote in *Recollections of a Boxing Referee*: 'I was not concerned about the loss of the certificate . . . as a matter of fact I have not the least use for the Board's certificate . . . promoters engage referees on their known worth and reputation, not on the evidence of a piece of paper.'

The Board's arch-critic, John Murray at *Boxing*, was predictably

scathing: 'Mr Palmer has every justification for holding himself to have been one of the most ill-used men who have ever sat in the chair of a referee. . . .'

Thus, when the Board did act, it received no thanks for its troubles; when it did nothing, there were criticisms that it was a moribund body. As *Boxing* put it when calling for its disbandment: 'It has ever been an unwieldy, inchoate mass, lacking any real power, also the means to exercise any had it possessed such. . . .'

The response by certain London managers was to attempt to replace the Board with an organization of their own: in June 1926, at the Anderton Hotel in Fleet Street, the Boxing Managers' Union, later retitled the British Boxing Alliance, was formed; among those present at the inaugural meeting were Harry Levene, Alec Goodman, Andrew Newton, Joe Morris and Charlie Rose.

Bill Evans reported in the *Star* that the Alliance aimed to take over from the Board or that, at the very least, proposed 'to regularize relations between boxing promoters and managers' and to be a 'power for good in the boxing world'. By August the organization could boast some sixty London members and to have control of the majority of London boxers. There were badges for its boxers to wear and directives issued that appeared to ban them from fighting non-member boxers. In September it held a fund-raising tourney at the Manor Hall, Harry Abrahams promoting, the boxers involved including Kid Berg, Phil Scott, Johnny Curly, Tom Berry and Harry Corbett, with exhibitions boxed by Johnny Sharpe and Ted Kid Lewis.

By August 1927 the Alliance had drawn up draft agreements to be used between managers and boxers (priced 6d) and had issued a list of champions and challengers – not so very different from the Board's list although it did include Len Johnson as challenger to Tommy Milligan in the middleweight division – of which more later.

The Alliance also issued a full statement as to its intentions and its position, making a point of deriding the Board's complaint that, without legal authority, no one could hope to govern boxing. The Alliance cited the FA, the MCC, and continued: 'No one of the other ruling bodies . . . wield or pretend to possess any authority other than that entrusted or conceded to them by the general consent of the members subscribing to the respective Associations.' The Board had failed, it continued, because it was self-appointed and had secured no agreement from those inside the sport. The BBA's authority, by contrast, would rest on consent and agreement and the myriad problems of promoters, boxers and managers would, it claimed, be settled by common consent.

It was all very impressive, but the suspicion lingered that men such as Ted Broadribb – one of the prime movers in the BBA – were motivated more by short-term gain than by any concern for long-term 'democracy'. Even some of the BBA's most fervent champions, such as Sydney Ackland of *Boxing* who was to serve as the organization's first secretary, seemed no wiser as to how *any* self-appointed organization could, overnight, transform itself into a body respected and, more important, obeyed by all.

With so much suspicion, envy, greed and desperation involved, co-operation in British boxing was clearly an impossible dream. No surprise, therefore, when an autocrat suddenly appeared on the scene, metaphorically to bang heads together and assume some kind of grip on things. In April 1926, the name of Charles Donmall appeared in both the minutes of the BBBC and reports of the BBA.

At that time Donmall was a manager of boxers in a small way as well as proprietor of an engineering supplies company struggling somewhat under the impact of recession and slump. He was listed as chairman of the BBA and was active in drawing up plans of action relating to 'model' contracts and disciplinary codes. At the same time, perhaps unbeknown to the Alliance, he was gradually taking up more responsibility for work that the Board of Control secretary Norman Clark was unable to perform.

Appointed as honorary secretary in 1924, Clark had been forced to move to Birmingham in search of work – his salary so small it was often outstripped by his expenses claims. However, he found travelling to and from the Midlands irksome and, during his increasingly prolonged absences (he was also involved with the MCC and international tours), Donmall took on more and more of Clark's duties. Donmall, however, was not a mere secretary: he was a keen administrator, anxious that the Board start drawing lines of demarcation between managers, promoters and referees and that it send representatives to all major contests.

During 1927 his involvement grew as Board meetings often

struggled to obtain a quorum; but at exactly what point he decided to throw in his lot with the Board and abandon the Alliance is not known. That his departure was resented is certain: Ackland at *Boxing* made a coded reference to it in November 1929 when he talked of the Board having 'recruited its present secretary from the BBA', adding acidly, 'recruited is such a nice word. . . .'

By mid-1928 Donmall had, in fact, completely taken over from Clark while ostensibly acting as the latter's deputy. When Clark returned from a long period of absence he found that radical plans to reorganize the Board had been drawn up by Donmall. Clark duly resigned, the impression being that his departure was hardly cordial. Donmall thus took office as Board secretary in mid-1928: in fact, the 'new' Board set up residence in Donmall's firm's offices following its departure from Covent Garden (after the NSC vacated the premises). From now on, the Board's staff were actually Donmall's, doubling up on their duties – typist, office secretary, etc. – and drawing their additional salaries from the Board's funds.

The first radical reorganization of the Board would come to fruition at the start of 1929. During 1928, however, as Donmall began to flex his muscles as secretary, the battle between Board and Alliance was joined in earnest, and the boxing world in general experienced for the first time the distinctive Donmall style.

The first controversy came in April when Board referee J. W. H. T. Douglas (son of the NSC founder C. H. Douglas) disqualified Jack Hood and Joe Bloomfield in a catchweight bout at the club for 'not trying'. The Board suspended both boxers for two months until 25 May.

The repercussions were to cause an uproar. Hood had already signed a contract with the NSC to fight Alf Mancini at the Holland Park Rink for a £3,000 purse and the welterweight Lonsdale Belt. The fight was thus cancelled with heavy losses incurred by everyone, in particular Ted Broadribb who, as manager of both men, stood to lose two commissions. There were loud complaints in the press but what irked most critics of the Board was the NSC's meek acquiescence in the Board's decision ('The boxing public are surprised that it has accepted this blow in the face without a whimper . . .' said an editorial in *Boxing*).

Ted Broadribb, however, smelled a rat. In his autobiography, *Fighting Is My Life* (written decades after the event, it must be said) he suggests that the Club already knew that the title fight could not take place as planned because the Club's lease had run out at Holland Park and the new proprietors (a car-hire firm) were anxious to move in. The 'convenient' suspension of Hood meant that the Club was saved from having to pay an estimated £1,000 to Broadribb by way of forfeit in the event of the fight being cancelled for any other reason than, say, the suspension of one of the principal boxers.

Broadribb made none of this public at the time: perhaps he only suspected the truth and could prove nothing. There was much talk of taking the Board to court (particularly by Mancini who had lost the chance, or so it seemed, of earning a healthy purse through no fault of his own). There was also a great deal of comment on the Board's methods – the fact that the hearing had been held 'in camera', that no reasons for the suspension had been published, along with much huffing and puffing concerning the Board's 'arbitrary powers'. *Boxing* declared: 'It behoves the Board to walk warily, to govern, if it proposes to govern, with the consent of the governed.'

The BBA, now styling itself as the alternative governing body, instituted its own enquiry and, not surprisingly, declared the ban unwarranted, recommending that it be 'ignored by everyone interested in the game'.

But the ban was not ignored, and no one took the Board to court. The Hood v Mancini fight, being an attractive one, was snapped up by two independent promoters in Birmingham and took place at Perry Bar Greyhound Track – in the pouring rain before some 20,000 spectators.

Within a month of the Hood v Mancini affair, the Board again entered controversial territory by overruling the NSC's choice as to who should contest a championship and thus a Lonsdale Belt.

The bantamweight title had been in abeyance for some two years ever since Johnny Brown had won the belt outright in 1925. Since then Teddy Baldock, the 'uncrowned' bantamweight champion, had won and lost the British version of the World title within the space of five months in 1927. With his manager Joe Morris claiming that, since the second title fight had been an overweight match, Baldock was still champion, the idea that he should risk all in a contest for the British title was of little interest, particularly from a financial viewpoint. So the Club announced that the new belt would be contested by Mick Hill and Kid Nicholson. A few weeks later, however, the Board declared that the title should be contested by Alf Kid Pattenden and Young Johnny Brown, and that if the latter was unable to fight by 15 June (he had a South African trip planned) then Nicholson could take his place.

*Boxing* commented sarcastically that the Board's ruling constituted 'red revolution'. The Club, in the person of Lionel Bettinson, announced that *it* alone decided where belts should go – but, once again, the Board's decision stood. Brown went to South Africa and Pattenden defeated Nicholson at the NSC to become the first holder of the fifth bantamweight belt.

Once again, the BBA attempted to exert influence and insisted on putting its weight behind Mick Hill as the challenger; but when Pattenden eventually defended his title it was against the Board nominee, Young Johnny Brown, whom Pattenden defeated to earn a second notch on the belt.

Although there were more accusations that such decisions by the Board were prompted by favouritism towards managers who were sitting on the Board itself, it was clear that the BBBC, with Donmall at the helm, was exerting itself in a way that it had never done before and that people were choosing to obey.

The BBA, in fact, was beginning to look a trifle desperate. In October, the Board considered the case of Young Stanley, who had struck referee Jack Hart during a bout at Premierland, and suspended the boxer for six months. The BBA also investigated the case and declared that it was sending its findings to the IBU to which it had affiliated in August. But this proved to be the BBA's last significant gesture of defiance.

The Board, which had withdrawn from the IBU back in 1924, wrote to the European body and stated that the Alliance 'was not and never had been a governing body of boxing in Great Britain', a statement accepted by the IBU. Within a couple of months, the new, reformed BBBC would have been ratified and the BBA would rapidly fade away.

The determination of certain boxing managers and promoters

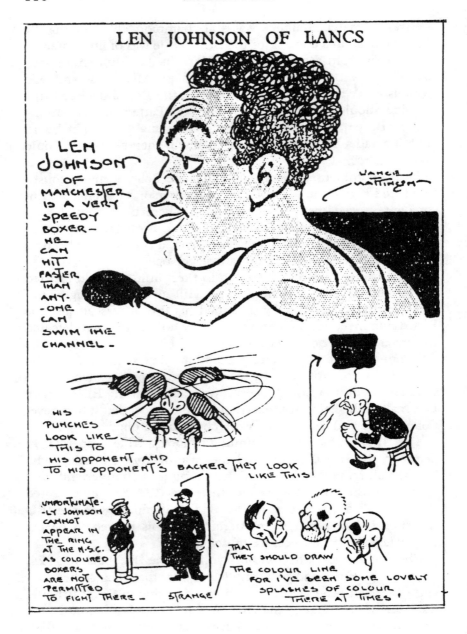

to dispute the Board's decisions and authority might be viewed as positive, demonstrating a concern for the game's 'health', a desire for a fairer, properly run sport, democratic and open. Unfortunately, for all the talk of rights and freedom, the general, almost supine, acceptance of the Board's decision not to allow Len Johnson to fight for a British title and thus a Lonsdale Belt simply because he was coloured suggests that justice and freedom really only applied to matters commercial.

Len Johnson was, without a doubt, one of Britain's finest boxers during the late Twenties and early Thirties. His ability to defeat men regarded either as contenders or champions proved a continual embarrassment to boxing's authorities who would, one guesses, have preferred not to have had to spell out their policy if for no other reason than there appeared to be no logical justification for it.

After the war, in Europe, coloured fighters held both national and European titles; in the USA coloured men fought for titles at all levels – except the heavyweight title, a legacy of Jack Johnson's tenure before the war. And it is that which provides, perhaps, a clue to the British stance.

Jack Johnson's cavalier treatment of the NSC in 1908–09 when he reneged on an agreement to defend his title at the Club (and maybe even a financial debt to 'Peggy' Bettinson) appears to have resulted in the Club's determination never to allow a coloured man to hold a Lonsdale Belt. Indeed, coloured fighters in general appeared very rarely at the Club after the Johnson incident. Add to that the Home Secretary's decision to ban the Wells v Johnson World title fight in 1911, as well as placing pressure on promoter Charles Cochrane to drop plans to match 'Gunboat' Smith ('White' World champion) against Sam Longford in 1914 – in both cases because the fight might cause unrest in the Colonies – and one can see how the Club's stance could be regarded as having official (government) approval.

But in the post-First World War period such reasoning looked increasingly flawed, particularly in Len Johnson's case. Johnson was English-born, in Manchester, of mixed parentage: his mother was a Manchester girl, his father a West African seaman who had served in the British army during the war.

Johnson himself did not flaunt his colour (in contrast, perhaps, to Jack Johnson). He was no flamboyant showman; indeed, he was a model sportsman and his general demeanour inside and outside the ring was exemplary (more than could be said of someone like Harry Mason!). There was thus no possible excuse to object to him as many did to his American namesake; yet it was clear from the very moment he emerged as a contender for both welterweight and middleweight titles in 1925 that his way to the top would be stubbornly resisted.

A single defeat at the hands of Jack Hood in 1925 was enough to eliminate him from the welterweight series then being staged at the Albert Hall and Holland Park, but two victories in the same year over Roland Todd – then middleweight champ but about to be deposed – were not enough to earn him a contender's spot in the series to determine Todd's successor.

Tommy Milligan, George West, Ted Moore, Frank Moody and Todd himself were to be involved in four title fights at the Albert Hall and Holland Park in 1926–7; and it was in these years that reference began to be made openly to the 'colour-bar'. The fact that Johnson had defeated West three times, Moore once and Todd twice raised the obvious question as to why he was being 'overlooked' by promoters while these lesser men had been given their chance against Milligan.

*Boxing* commented lamely that 'coloured boxers are not permitted at the Albert Hall', and that while there did not appear to be a specific rule on the matter at the NSC, 'no coloured fighters had actually appeared there in recent years'. The *Daily Herald*, however, in 1926 had stated the opposite – that there *was* a colour-bar at the Club, yet had reduced the issue to the level of a joke.

Johnson was extremely popular, especially at the Ring, Blackfriars where in 1927 he scored yet another triumph when he defeated the British 'Golden Boy' Len Harvey – a result that prompted the BBA to install Johnson as their official contender for Milligan's title. But still nobody defied the 'unwritten' rule and put him up for a title shot.

In 1929, unable to obtain meaningful bouts with top middleweights, Johnson moved into the cruiserweight bracket and defeated Gypsy Daniels. Daniels had won the light-heavyweight title in 1927 but, although he remained undefeated, had been stripped of the title for refusing to accept a reasonable offer to defend it. Once again, the BBBC was placed on the spot, especially as the new cruiser champion, Frank Moody, had secured the title by defeating Ted Moore – yet another Johnson victim.

Ignored by his country, Johnson decided to take on Leone Jacovacci, the Italian coloured middleweight European champion. Jacovacci (who intriguingly had appeared in England some years earlier billing himself as 'Jack Walker' and claiming British nationality) had beaten Johnson in 1927 in Milan but now Johnson reversed the result and claimed the European title. The British Board refused to recognize him, however, stating that in order to challenge for a European title, a boxer had to be a national champion.

Matters came to a head in 1929. Jack Smith, Manchester promoter and BBBC committee man, was keen to promote Johnson in a World title fight against Mickey Walker, and Smith's persistence appears to have forced the issue. In February the Board's minutes make reference to the words 'of white parents' respecting qualification for a British title fight. Previously the rule had only stated 'of British nationality'. The revised regulation (No. 24, paragraph 27) appeared to close the issue, especially as Lord Lonsdale himself was said to have approved the new wording.

In late 1929 mention is made in the minutes of Johnson being granted a personal interview by the Board in order that it explain the rule to him. No record exists of Johnson's reactions, but *Boxing* at long last appeared highly critical of the Board's stance and printed indignant letters from boxing fans disgusted at Johnson's treatment.

The whole sorry episode was made the shabbier by the tendency among boxing folk to blame somebody else. The Board, in particular, claimed it was 'impossible' for it to recognize Johnson as a contender, implying that it was only enforcing a decision made at government level – a judgement accepted by Johnson's home town newspaper, the *Manchester Evening News*:

Those behind the scenes know that the BBBC is not to blame for the rule that debars British-born coloured fighters from boxing for a British championship. It is a great pity but everyone finds that things are not always plain sailing for them, especially in these days. We all sympathize with Johnson, particularly here in Manchester, but the rule stands and little more can be done about it.

Whether the ban really was Home Office-approved is debatable: the Board was extremely keen in these troubled years to be seen as an arm of government, implementing and interpreting various rules and regulations passed in Parliament. But, as will be seen in the Jeff Dickson case, the Board was often mistaken in its interpretations of sensitive rules regarding 'alien' boxers.

In fact, it would be the American promoter, Jeff Dickson, having operated successfully in Paris for several years, who would eventually stick his neck out and promote a Johnson fight as a British championship contest, when he matched Johnson with Len Harvey in 1932 (although the contest still does not appear in boxing record books as a title fight, while many other more dubious matches are included).

Making retrospective judgements on people and institutions in matters cultural is often a meaningless enterprise. In Johnson's case, however, it must be said that, by denying him his rightfully earned (hard-earned) opportunity to contest a Lonsdale Belt, the prize was devalued. (There is an irony here in that the first-ever boxing belt fought for in Great Britain involved Tom Molyneux, a black American ex-slave.)

Boxers, especially champions, need few excuses to avoid dangerous opponents and the suspicion lingers that men such as Milligan and Harvey could have made a stronger stand to see justice done for a fellow professional. After all, authority was continually under challenge in the inter-war period, with an abundance of unofficial, i.e. non-Lonsdale Belt-holding champions. Harvey himself was no 'yes-man', playing an important part in the Boxer's Union that flourished in the late Thirties. And managers such as Harry Levene were quick to assert and defend the rights of Jewish fighters when the occasion arose, not to mention 'the principles of natural justice' he and others felt should apply whenever the Board dealt with *them*.

## JEFF DICKSON'S NEWS REEL. No. 6.

*I* HAVE pleasure in announcing that at the Royal Albert Hall next Wednesday I shall be privileged to stage a match between Len Harvey, who has for so long held the British Middle-weight Title, and Len Johnson, of Manchester.

Because of his colour the British Boxing Board of Control refuse to accept Johnson as a logical contender. Public opinion, however, is quite decided that he approaches more closely to the standard by which Harvey is judged than any 11st. 6lb. man in the country.

I am presenting this fight in response to and at the earnest request of my patrons.

Harvey and Johnson will fight at the strict middle-weight limit so that a vast public will have proved to them who is the better man, and so have settled a question much debated throughout the British Isles.

# ROYAL ALBERT HALL

Manager ... ... C. B. COCHRAN.

## WEDNESDAY, MAY 11th, 1932, AT 8 p.m.

### MIDDLE-WEIGHT CHAMPIONSHIP OF GREAT BRITAIN

(Not recognised by the British Boxing Board of Control) 15 (3-min.) ROUNDS

# LEN HARVEY

(BARNSBURY), Middle-weight Champion of Great Britain, Winner Outright of Lord Lonsdale's Belt.

v.

# LEN JOHNSON

(MANCHESTER), the Outstanding Contender and Challenger for a World's Title.

## A Sensational Supporting Card

EIGHT (3-min.) ROUNDS CONTESTS

| | | |
|---|---|---|
| **DEL FONTAINE** (CANADA) | v. | **ARCHIE SEXTEN** (BETHNAL GREEN) |
| **WILLIE UNWIN** (CAPE TOWN) | v. | **EDDIE ROBINSON** (BIRMINGHAM) |

SIX (3-min.) ROUNDS CONTESTS

| | | |
|---|---|---|
| **MOE MOSS** (ALDGATE) | v. | **LEO PHILLIPS** (BIRMINGHAM) |
| **KID FARLO** (WHITECHAPEL) | v. | **PETER NOLAN** (WALSALL) |
| **JOHNNY QUILL** (CUBITT TOWN) | v. | **HARRY JENKINS** (KENTISH TOWN) |

| PRICES OF ADMISSION *including Tax* | Gallery | Balcony | Boxes & Up. Orch. | Mid. Orch. | Lower Orch. | Stalls & Loggias | Ringside |
|---|---|---|---|---|---|---|---|
| | 8/6 | 12/6 | 18/- | 21/- | 24/- | 30/- | £2-2 & £2-8 |

Seats can be booked at the Royal Albert Hall, and at Messrs. Keith Prowse, Alfred Hays, District Messengers, Webster & Waddington, Webster & Girling, all Agencies; Jeff Dickson's Offices, 8 & 10, Cecil Court, Charing Cross Road, W.C.2 (Temple Bar 5523 & 8922). BIRMINGHAM: Jim Murphy, Farcroft Hotel, Rookery Road, Handsworth (Northern 0957).

No one, it seemed, was prepared to demand as much for Len Johnson.

# 9

## Dickson's Yankee Invasion

In January 1929, at a meeting of members, stewards, licence-holders and other interested parties at Australia House in the Strand, plans drawn up by Charles Donmall the previous May for a complete reorganization of the BBBC were endorsed, although formal agreement was only secured by Lord Lonsdale giving all present a stark choice: either agree to the new Board or lose him as the figurehead of pro-boxing.

The new Board included six non-financially interested stewards and two vice-presidents, although *Boxing*, the eternal critic, pointed out that the stewards' powers were limited. Commercial promoters had three voting representatives and, when combined with the referee' votes, could secure a majority. Thus the way was open, *Boxing*'s editor claimed, for men with a financial interest in the sport to continue to wield ultimate control.

Once again, the NSC's members were prominently involved in various capacities and this, the critics continued, would mean the boxers finding themselves outnumbered and at the mercy of men who either knew little of their professional lives or men who were, in effect, their employers.

'This is a scheme,' *Boxing* thundered, 'for placing the boxers where they (the Board) feel they belong – in kennels.'

Nevertheless, the new rules and regulations of the BBBC were published and by June 1929 notices were appearing in the press calling on all promoters, managers, referees and boxers to take out licences.

Boxing managers in general – the core of the BBA – met some days after the Australia House meeting at Fred Dyer's gym and agreed to give the new Board a year's trial. But the worries of

123

**NATIONAL SPORTING CLUB**

# ☛ AT OLYMPIA ☛

### On Thursday, 16th May, 1929, at 8 p.m.

## 3 CHAMPIONSHIP BELT CONTESTS

15-ROUND CONTEST at 11st. 6lb.
for the Middleweight Championship of Great Britain
and Europe and the Lonsdale Championship Challenge
Belt.

## ALEX IRELAND *v.* LEN HARVEY

(EDINBURGH)
Middleweight Champion of Great Britain and Europe.

(LONDON, late of PLYMOUTH)

15-ROUND CONTEST at 9st.
for the Featherweight Championship of Great Britain
and the Lonsdale Championship Challenge Belt

### HARRY CORBETT

(BETHNAL GREEN)
Featherweight Champion and Holder of Belt,

*v.*

### JOHNNIE CUTHBERT

(SHEFFIELD)
Ex-Featherweight Champion and Ex-Holder of Belt.

15-ROUND CONTEST at 8st. 6lb.
for the Bantamweight Championship of Great Britain
and the Lonsdale Championship Challenge Belt

### KID PATTENDEN

(BETHNAL GREEN)
Bantamweight Champion and Holder of Belt,

*v.*

### TEDDY BALDOCK

(POPLAR).

**AND OTHER BOXING (time permitting).**

### Prices of Seats : 8s. 6d., 12s., £1 4s., £2 7s., & £3 10s.

(ALL PRICES INCLUDE TAX.)

TICKETS can be obtained at The National Sporting Club, Covent Garden, W.C.2 (Gerrard 2905, 2017, 2045); The Ring, Blackfriars Road, S.E.1 (Hop 3966, 5697) ; Premierland, Aldgate, E.1 (Royal 4993); Messrs. Keith Prowse, 159, New Bond Street, W.1 (Regent 6000); Ashton and Mitchell, 33, Old Bond Street, W.1 (Gerrard 7980); Alfred Hays Ltd., 26, Old Bond Street, W.1 (Regent 2400); Webster and Girling, 43, Upper Baker Street, N.W.1. (Welbeck 6666); and usual Booking Agencies.

some concerning the Board's close links with the NSC would now prove prophetic. 1929 saw the Covent Garden Club close its doors for the last time. With 'Peggy' dead, his son Lionel now controlled Club affairs and domestic boxing for the next few years would be dominated by his efforts to create a powerful promotional organization closely allied with the new BBBC – and with the Lonsdale Belts once again the symbol of authority.

Dramatic evidence of the new BBBC/NSC link-up came in May 1929 when the Club took out a lease on Olympia and staged a giant British championship/Lonsdale Belt show featuring three title fights: Alf Kid Pattenden defending his bantamweight crown against Teddy Baldock; Harry Corbett putting up his feather-weight title against Johnny Cuthbert and Alex Ireland taking on Len Harvey for the middleweight belt.

All three champions lost and, in an historic move, the belts were presented in the ring by Lord Lonsdale himself. Johnny Cuthbert thus became the first man to receive his belt in such a manner – indeed, Cuthbert would become the first man to win a Lonsdale Belt outright at venues outside the old Club.

The Club was clearly fired with ambition and in the years to come the dream of constructing a magnificent new club/arena in central London would be pursued enthusiastically. In January 1930 it opened new offices in 21 Soho Square; and in April shares were issued and a new venue decided upon – in Hertford Street, Mayfair.

But the Club was not totally obsessed by the metropolis. It had listened to critics who felt that the provinces should be given a fair crack of the whip where British championships were concerned and, by late 1929, the Club had teamed up with promoters Jack Smith in Manchester and Johnny Best in Liverpool. Thus in October 1930 Al Foreman took on George Rose at Belle Vue Stadium for the lightweight title and a Lonsdale Belt – the first time a belt had been competed for outside London. A month later, in November 1930, Johnny Cuthbert and Nel Tarleton met to decide the featherweight title at Liverpool Stadium and, in time, Newcastle, Leicester and Birmingham would stage NSC-sponsored title fights. The Lonsdale Belts had gone 'on tour'. . . .

The new syndicate, however, would leave no stone unturned, and in 1931 the Board's and Club's harshest critic – *Boxing* – was actually taken over by parties sympathetic to the powers-that-be. John Murray, proprietor and former editor, was deposed, a new editor was installed and the magazine immediately announced its support for the new Board.

Such support, however, was going to be necessary because from the very outset the new 'cartel' would find itself challenged vigorously. A month after the new BBBC was endorsed, Harry Jacobs died. The Albert Hall lease that he had held with his brothers was now open to offers, providing an opening for someone with both ambition and financial muscle. It soon transpired that Jeff Dickson, the Paris-based American impresario, was keen to secure an option on the venue. Within weeks, via various British connections, and with the help of the Albert Hall general manager, C. B. Cochrane, he had succeeded.

Dickson was a flamboyant showman/promoter, very much in the Cochrane mould. At the Cirque de Paris, he had staged bull-fights, wrestling, cycling, circuses – and boxing: anything, in fact that could be presented with spectacle and colour. The Albert Hall appeared the perfect venue for him to begin a British promotional career, with a promise to bring American World champions to Britain – something British promoters had signally failed to do.

Almost from the first, however, the BBBC set out to oppose Dickson's UK operation. When he applied for a licence, he was turned down flat, at first without explanation. In all, he would make some six applications in the course of six months and would be interviewed on a number of occasions – but to no avail.

In June 1929 the Board quietly inserted a rule into the regulations that stated that only British-born, British-domiciled individuals could hold a promoter's licence – a rule clearly devised for Dickson alone (shades here of the Len Johnson saga).

The decision to bar Dickson polarized opinion in British boxing. Those on the 'inside', such as Jack Smith and Lionel Bettinson, favoured the ban; some, like Harry Levene, kept quiet and attempted to have it both ways; but others, in particular Ted Broadribb, were very much opposed to the Board's stance.

Ted Broadribb's managerial career must rank as the most successful in Lonsdale Belt history. Born in East Street, Walworth in 1888, the son of a bricklayer, 'Young' Snowball, as he was called during his boxing days, succeeded in stopping a sixteen-year-old Georges Carpentier but soon realized that managing boxers was more his forte.

Johnny Matthieson – the 'Flying Scot' – was one of his first charges, but much of his title success was to be achieved with men from his own Bermondsey area, a part of the world renowned for producing fighters of the highest quality. Sid Smith, winner of the first flyweight belt, Curley Walker, Tommy Noble, Bob Marriott, Jim Sullivan – all had Broadribb either as manager or second.

Throughout his long career Broadribb would guide champions to Lonsdale Belts at every traditional weight: Sid Smith at fly; Dick Corbett at bantam; Harry Corbett and Nel Tarleton at featherweight; James Seaman Hall at lightweight; Jack Hood at welterweight; Gus Platts at middleweight; Freddie Mills at light-heavy and Tommy Farr and Johnny Williams at heavyweight.

Hood, Tarleton and Dick Corbett all won belts outright during the Thirties, the period when Broadribb was at his peak, promoting, matchmaking and handling a 'stable' of boxers distinguished by the letter S (for Snowball) on their trunks.

In 1928, on the occasion of the Hood v Mancini title fight, Broadribb's many talents were demonstrated: he helped the promotion by selling tickets as the spectators filed in; he acted as steward directing them to their seats; he seconded one of his boxers in a preliminary bout; and he refereed the first contest when the official was late in arriving. Finally, he sat back at ringside to watch the principal bout, unable to serve in either corner as he was manager to both men!

Although later to be criticized for his handling of Freddie Mills and considered somewhat harsh and ruthless in general, he would remain a force in British boxing throughout its 'modern' history.

Broadribb had found himself at odds with the new Board almost from the first. In January 1929, the BBA, very much a Broadribb project, had more or less collapsed as managers decided to throw their weight behind the newly constituted Board. In April 1929, Broadribb had arranged a featherweight title fight for his boxer, Harry Corbett, against Scottish champion Johnny McMillan. The Board, however, announced that Corbett must fight Johnny Cuthbert on or before 3 May for the title – despite Broadribb's claim that the McMillan fight had been arranged first.

Broadribb, it is certain, would have defied the Board but the Scottish promoter backed off. That Cuthbert won, the fight being featured on the NSC's 'super-tourney' at Olympia, must only have rubbed salt into Broadribb's wound.

Broadribb then found his business affairs further complicated and disrupted by the Board's decision in July that his application for a manager's licence be turned down. The new rules insisted that a promoter/matchmaker could not manage more than four boxers. Broadribb's matchmaking activities for British Sporting Promotions – which ran big outdoor shows at Clapton Dog Track – thus rendered him ineligible, despite the fact that he had one of the biggest boxing 'stables' in Britain.

Broadribb, predictably outraged, threatened to give up boxing altogether and accused certain northern manager/promoters sitting on the Board of holding dual licences. (This was the first hint at the problems the Board would face when trying to enforce its rules whilst omitting to ensure that its own executive was abiding by them.)

Thus, at the same time as Dickson was experiencing his problems with the Board, Broadribb was in the mood to cause trouble. No wonder, then, that he was soon chief agent and fix-it man for the enterprising American. And with Broadribb advising him and smoothing his path, Dickson conducted a carefully organized publicity campaign, meeting with the sporting press on a number of occasions to put his case with skill and charm.

He announced that he had offered to form a British company and employ British staff to operate it; he claimed that despite scurrilous rumours to the contrary, propagated by various Board members, he had broken no rules or regulations laid down by various governing bodies in Europe. At the same time, he made it clear that he understood the real reason behind his debarment: the NSC feared a sizeable opponent in the capital's promotional stakes and was leaning on the BBBC to do its bidding and keep Dickson out. *Boxing* observed:

> For boxing to live and prosper there must be a board or organization empowered to control promoters, managers and boxers. But like a judge, it should be above and outside the turmoil and in a position to render impartial decisions and to enforce respect. . . .

Clearly, the BBBC – linked so closely with the NSC as it was – could not guarantee that respect. Neither could it ensure the loyalty of its own members, a fact made clear when it sought to exploit its licensing role to threaten and cajole boxers and managers upon whom Dickson would have to rely if his promotions were to succeed.

Dickson was confident the law was on his side:

> If boxers who appear for me are handicapped in securing engagements in England I will pay the expenses of a test case in court to prove that the BBBC have no right to keep an Englishman from making his living in his own country as a professional boxer.

Abandoning hopes of coming to an amicable agreement with the Board, Dickson set up the first of his British promotions at the Albert Hall – Scotsman Johnny Hill, British flyweight champion, versus Frankie Genaro for the latter's IBU/NBA World flyweight title – the latest in a series of World title bouts involving Hill, Genaro and Frenchman Emile Pladner, all of whom were under contract to Dickson.

Hill had already won a version of the World title, defeating Newsboy Brown at Clapton Stadium in August 1928 but had subsequently relinquished it following defeat by Pladner in February 1929 in Paris. Genaro had then defeated Pladner in Paris to claim the crown.

The Board, realizing that it could not prevent Dickson from staging the tournament, now turned its attention to blocking Genaro, claiming that, as an alien, he needed a work-permit and he could only obtain *that* if the Board granted him a licence. The Board's confidence was boosted by the fact that, since June 1929, the Ministry of Labour had consulted it whenever foreign boxers sought entry to the UK to fight.

But it was soon made clear in Parliament that the arrangement only applied where boxers were 'of no repute', and where the Home Office needed the Board's expertise to help determine whether the boxer had anything to offer that a British fighter could not. Where a boxer was of international repute, as Genaro clearly was, the ministry acted independently.

Thus, as Genaro stepped onto British soil in early September, he was greeted not, as the Board had predicted, by a Ministry of Labour official brandishing an exclusion order, but by Jeff Dickson and Ted Broadribb welcoming him with open arms.

The Board was now losing battles and steadily losing face. Its claims that Genaro was under suspension by the NYAC for breaches of regulations committed by his manager fell apart when it was revealed that the NYAC had lifted the suspension days before the fight without consulting the Board. And even when tragedy – in the form of the sudden death of challenger Hill in training – appeared to have scuppered Dickson's plans, he merely substituted Ernie Jarvis for Hill and pressed on.

The introduction of Jarvis brought the whole affair to a head. Jarvis was managed by Harry Levene, a Board member. Amid

acrimonious scenes, Levene was suspended and the Board proceeded to issue an edict on the eve of the fight threatening anyone
who took part with similar punishment.

But Dickson's tournament went ahead, involving not only Jarvis
but also boxers Johnny Cuthbert and Johnny Peters, as well as
referee Matt Wells – all of whom were suspended by the Board.
However, the Board had bitten off more than it could chew.
Levene issued a writ against the Board claiming restraint of trade
and denial of natural justice. Worse still, he publicly revealed the
extent to which the Board's licence system was a farce and was
being flouted by just about everyone.

How, he claimed, could the Board withdraw his licence when
he had never taken one out in the first place? He went further,
alleging that very few people actually serving on the Board had
licences either – certainly not Dan Sullivan, manager of the Ring,
Blackfriars and of boxer Len Harvey. Thus Lionel Bettinson –
Board member and secretary of the NSC – had broken regulations
by hiring Harvey, as had the Board's star referee, Eugene Corri, by
officiating at the Ring, not to mention other 'unlicenced' venues.

He also accused Board members Joe Morris and Jack Smith of
breaking the Board rule that prohibited promoters from managing
boxers and finished up by claiming that Board secretary Charles
Donmall had 'issued threats on his own responsibility which made
him appear to be a dictator and head and front of the BBBC
instead of its paid servant. . .'.

In early November the Board realized it had no choice but
to back down and rescind the suspensions. In January 1930 it
approached Dickson after the World title fight at the Albert Hall
involving Jack Kid Berg, and asked him to take out a licence,
stipulating only that he should form a British company to run his
affairs – something Dickson had offered to do anyway. The company was duly formed, with Ted Broadribb holding the majority
of the shares. Dickson was thus free to operate in the UK and
Broadribb had won a significant victory over his old enemies.

For a few years, the NSC/BBBC syndicate, though chastened
and badly bruised after its tangle with Dickson, managed to
remain in charge of British championships. After the relative
confusion of the middle-to-late Twenties when the Lonsdale Belt
system had almost fallen into complete disuse, the early Thirties

Ted Broadribb *c* 1931

saw a complete reversal: between October 1929 and December 1933, of thirty-one title fights, only four were not promoted by the NSC and thus did not carry a belt.

Len Harvey won a middleweight belt outright, the first since Pat O'Keefe; Johnny Cuthbert won a featherweight belt outright, Jack Peterson went a considerable way towards lifting the first heavyweight belt outright since Bombardier Wells, while Jackie Brown took the first flyweight belt outright since Wilde. Dick Corbett put two notches on a bantamweight belt (which he would later be awarded for keeps).

The new regional policy of the Board and Club was also a great success, with nine championship Belt matches being held at Belle Vue, while Johnny Best at Liverpool staged three title fights.

Dickson, meanwhile, at first pursued a more eclectic course, searching for heavyweights who might excite the crowds. But, according to Broadribb, success was some time in coming: 'Life was not anything like as smooth as we anticipated'; and Dickson often found himself spending large sums of money with little to show for it. In 1940, in *Topical Times*, he outlined some of the

Advertisement in *Boxing*, c 1933

purses he paid Britain's top boxers during his period as Britain's principal independent fight promoter:

> In 1930 I paid Len Harvey £1,000 to box Dave Shade. In the next three and a half years up until he boxed Jack Peterson on 4 June 1934 I paid our Leonard £13,197. This represented ten fights.
>
> In sixteen months I paid Jack Peterson £11,330 for five fights . . . Jack Doyle took £5,759 from me within sixteen months for four bouts while George Cook earned £1,762 for four clashes.
>
> In just over a year Jack Hood boxed five times for me. He didn't win a single fight but lost two and drew three.
>
> Yet he collected cheques with my signature on them for £5,051 in all. . . .
>
> Those figures are pretty interesting from many points of view but the figure that interests me is one of over £200,000 or about a million dollars which the British boxing fans laid on

the line for tickets to my shows while I promoted in England. I wonder where it's all gone to?

Very often, however, the crowds simply refused to turn up even when fighters like Len Harvey were involved. When Harvey fought Marcel Thil for the World middleweight title in July 1932, Dickson planned for a gate of 50,000 at White City. In the event, some 9,500 turned up and paid just £2,500 – nowhere near enough to cover Dickson's costs. And his promotion of the infamous Jack Doyle v Jack Peterson British heavyweight title fight – ironically, the only title fight he promoted where the NSC consented to let a Lonsdale Belt be on offer – led to repercussions and controversy for years to come.

Doyle was the 'glamour boy' of British boxing in the early Thirties, although his serious boxing career would be a short one. His KO of heavyweight contender Jack Pettifer in only his seventh pro-fight in 1933 catapulted him into contender status and led to his contract with Dan Sullivan being bought by the Greyhound Association president, General Critchley, for £5,000.

Critchley immediately turned to Dickson and the latter promoted Doyle's next fight – a KO victory over a rated German. Suddenly the talk was of Doyle meeting champion Petersen, a match Dickson opposed, being convinced that Petersen's undoubted experience would be too much for Doyle, who was still very much a novice.

Critchley, anxious to reap some benefit from his outlay, persuaded Dickson to proceed, but it would turn out to be an expensive venture. First, 'Pa' Petersen, Jack's astute father/manager, demanded a £5,000 purse for the champion, a demand repeated by Dan Sullivan acting for Doyle. Dickson had no option but to agree, so much already having been invested in arranging the fight at White City.

In the event, due to delays and postponements, the vast auditorium was barely a third full – 25,000 turned up when 70,000 had been expected. The total 'take' was a mere £13,000, a figure dwarfed by expenses, purse money, etc.

The fight itself also proved a farce. The raw Doyle, achieving some success in the first round, rocking the champion with a wild right swing, came out for the second, arms flailing, landing blows to all parts of Petersen's anatomy. Unfortunately, a series of low blows led to referee 'Pickles' Douglas disqualifying Doyle before the round had ended.

Board secretary Donmall immediately asked Dickson for Doyle's purse-money to be handed over, pending an investigation. Dickson claimed in later articles that he handed over £3,000, deducting £2,000 for 'expenses'. The subsequent suspension of Doyle and the court cases that followed resulted in the Board eventually pocketing the £3,000 almost entirely, ignoring Dickson's justifiable pleas for compensation for the substantial losses Doyle's behaviour had inflicted upon him.

However, despite such disasters, not to mention the palpable lack of truly world-class fighters in Britain during the 1930s, Dickson, along with matchmaker Broadribb, gradually worked his way to becoming the most influential promoter in the country.

He was helped in no small way by the decline of the NSC as a top-line promotional organization. The continuing on-off saga of the proposed new Club venue (the financing of which had been fatally undermined by the 1929 financial crash and the slump that followed), plus a series of poorly judged promotional ventures in late 1933, led to the Club's principal financial backer, Commander Leake, announcing in September 1934 that he was forming a completely new organization.

In a *Sunday Dispatch* article headed: 'New Boxing Dictator for Britain', Leake outlined his intention to control top-flight boxing in Britain:

> So far as I can see, boxing has outgrown the NSC as at present constituted. Like all sports nowadays, boxing has become a gigantic public spectacle and an intricate commercial undertaking. Dickson has control over most of the boxers. Naturally he could always put on more attractive shows than the NSC.
>
> As I have spent £40,000 so far on boxing you will understand that I could not allow this to go on indefinitely.
>
> Now I have taken over the greater share of his responsibilities.

Although the NSC was 'moribund', according to Leake, he retained the services of Lionel Bettinson and also mentioned Ted Broadribb in his plans:

Lionel Bettinson

My dream is that eventually a new NSC will arise from the ashes of the old. I do not mean a club in the narrow sense of the word. I have consulted Lord Lonsdale about my plan and he is sympathetically interested. Obviously we cannot go on living in the past.

By 1934, therefore, the role of the NSC in respect of British championships was all but ended. With no London premises in the capital it could only mount one Belt match that year – Nel Tarleton v Dave Crowley at the Empire Pool where the principal promoter was Arthur Elvin.

During the whole of 1935 only four championship contests took place – three in Manchester and one in Wales. The last Belt match under NSC auspices would be the Jock McAvoy v Al Burke middleweight clash at Belle Vue in January 1935. By the time the next belt was fought for – in September 1936 – it would be under the auspices of the rebuilt, redesigned BBBC.

By then the NSC was on the verge of dissolution and although a 'new' NSC was launched in 1937, by the end of the year the Club's permanent seat on the BBBC had been abolished.

Ironically, the Club's demise probably ensured the survival of the BBBC, which had been engulfed in bitter arguments and controversy in late 1933. Trouble had begun at the start of the 1933–4 season when, with little promotional activity evident in London, Jeff Dickson had attempted to set up a featherweight title fight between Seaman Tommy Watson and Tommy Rogers, the winner apparently being in line for a lucrative fight with the legendary Kid Chocolate.

However, the BBBC stepped in and refused to sanction the

title fight, claiming that Dickson had not followed 'correct procedures' and that he was ignoring an eliminating series designed to
produce a challenger. An angry Dickson decided to take the fight
to Paris, claiming that the withdrawal of official sanction had
killed public interest in it.

Unfortunately Kid Chocolate then decamped to the USA and
Dickson was left with a promotional 'turkey' on his hands. The
blame for this was placed squarely on Board, whose actions highlighted the growing gulf between the demands of professional
sport in hard times and an amateur administration: all of which
was exacerbated by the extremely undiplomatic, high-handed
behaviour of Charles Donmall – now referred to by some as the
'Mussolini' of boxing.

Dickson's plight ignited a sudden flurry of activity – principally
a demand by the pros to be allowed to exercise more control over
the actions and procedures of the Board.

At a Board meeting in October, discussion centred on motions
put forward by northern boxing manager Fleming aimed at giving
professionals powers to hire and fire Board officials, and so heated
did the discussion become that Board chairman Lord Tweed-
mouth left in disgust. Col. Middleton of the Board hinted that
the end of the BBBC was nigh. Indeed, if the stewards had
resigned *en bloc*, as they were now threatening to do, it might well
have been the end of boxing's principal administrative organization.

However, Lord Lonsdale rallied them at an emergency meeting
on 17 October, the 'revolution' was repulsed and the demands
for powers to repeal and rescind decisions and laws made by the
stewards rejected out of hand. In particular, the powers
demanded by licence-holders to appoint (and sack) Board officers
(i.e. Donmall) were turned down flat.

Instead, some increase in the numbers of stewards was proposed along with some promised discussion regarding eliminating
contests (the ostensible cause of the present discontent). In
response, the southern branch of the Board resigned *en bloc*
(including Jeff Dickson, Victor Berliner, Charlie Rose and Harry
Levene).

The eventual crisis meeting held in Australia House in
December 1933 was confusing and chaotic, with interminable

WILL THEY REVIVE?

*Boxing, 1933*

arguments concerning the use (or misuse) of proxy votes. The result of a vote of confidence in the existing Board appeared to be a narrow victory for the latter which thus staggered into 1934 to be saved eventually, not so much by its own efforts, but by a combination of events and decisions.

Particularly important was the victorious outcome of a court case involving Jack Doyle – who lost his appeal for the repayment of his £3,000 purse. Then there was a second court victory against American manager Dave Lumiansky who had been appealing against suspension for alleged breaches of rules at the weigh-in for a contest between Jackie Brown and Dick Corbett in 1932. Indeed, by the end of 1934 it was Charles Donmall who was taking *Boxing* and journalist Gilbert Elliot to court for alleged libel – not the last time he would have to take such action.

Most significantly, however, Jeff Dickson had finally seen off the NSC. Its demise, and its departure from the ruling body of the BBBC, broke a link that had been at the root of so much acrimony and bitterness ever since 1919.

# 10

# The Rise of the Regions

During the troubled years 1926–36, when boxing politics seemed to take up more column inches than the fights themselves, the two divisions to suffer most in terms of Belt contests would be the light and welterweight. In the latter division, in nine championships between 1926 and 1936, only three were for a Lonsdale Belt – all involving Jack Hood.

As for the lightweights, the position was even worse: in twelve championship contests during the same decade, just three involved a belt, two of these featuring Al Foreman, the only fighter to promote his own championship.

Foreman was born in Whitechapel and had his first few bouts (under the ring name of Bert Harris) at Manor Hall. Making little impact, he went to Canada to join his brothers who were running a successful physical culture establishment. There his career blossomed – he became US Navy featherweight champion in 1926, then Canadian lightweight champion.

His chief asset was a terrific right-hand punch and an eagerness to use it – indeed, he held the world record for some years for the fastest KO (11½ secs, including the count). His ambition to take a World title was thwarted, however, by the presence in the USA during the early Thirties of Britain's Jack Kid Berg. Foreman thus returned to the UK in 1929 in order to secure the British lightweight title: it would be a campaign dogged with controversy.

The champion, Fred Webster, had not defended for a year, while the BBBC, struggling for survival anyway, was having difficulty in setting up a defence, challengers Izzard and Harry Corbett both having won eliminators. Despite Foreman's successful campaign, however, he was unpopular with the Board – first because he was backed by John Murray, then editor of *Boxing*, that ever-vociferous critic of the Board; second, because Foreman arrived in the UK tied to a sponsorship deal with boxing glove manufacturers Everlast. Thus each of Foreman's opponents had to be persuaded to wear these same gloves, a less than enticing prospect since the gloves (being thinner, less padded around the knuckles) appeared designed to increase the impact of his already formidable punch.

When the Board decided, however, that the lightweight title bout should be between Fred Webster and George Rose, Foreman and his brothers moved quickly. They secured an agreement with Webster to sidestep Rose: they paid him all he demanded and even waived the use of the controversial gloves; and because no promoter felt able to put the contest on within the restricted timetable laid down by the Board (who had reluctantly agreed to ratify the contest, though it would not involve a belt) the Foremans decided to hire Premierland themselves.

Webster received his money on the afternoon of the contest and a large crowd turned up despite the fact that the fight was taking place on a Wednesday night. It was a gamble, but it all paid off for Foreman, the contest lasting little more than two minutes.

The opening few seconds saw Webster jabbing Foreman back but, when Webster momentarily stepped away, Foreman sprang, both feet off the canvas, and caught the champion with a terrific right-hand punch to the temple – a high-up punch, but enough to put Webster down.

He rose at six but was bundled to the ropes where a succession of rights and lefts saw him down again – and counted out by referee Jack Smith. Foreman was mobbed and carried shoulder high to the changing room. It had cost him £800 of his own money, but he had the championship.

His two defences would both be Belt matches: five months after the Premierland contest he fought George Rose at Belle Vue – a more difficult encounter for the new champion who nevertheless ended it by KO in the sixth. Foreman, however, had been outboxed and outscored by Rose – as well as giving away 5 lb.

Against Johnny Cuthbert in December, however, Foreman's

# BELLE VUE, MANCHESTER

### Under the Joint Promotion of the

# NATIONAL SPORTING CLUB

#### (LONDON) and

# BELLE VUE (MANCHESTER) Ltd.

---

## On MONDAY, OCTOBER 20th, 1930, at 7.45 p.m.

---

*15 Round Contest for the LIGHT-WEIGHT CHAMPIONSHIP OF GREAT BRITAIN and the LONSDALE CHAMPIONSHIP CHALLENGE BELT*

# AL FOREMAN *v* GEORGE ROSE

#### LONDON.

#### (LIGHTWEIGHT CHAMPION OF GT. BRITAIN).

#### BRISTOL.

### *AND OTHER BOXING, PARTICULARS OF WHICH WILL BE ANNOUNCED LATER*

PRICES: Reserved Seats. Ringside **£1 11s. 6d.** (strictly limited). 1st Stalls **£1 5s. 0d.** 2nd Stalls **£1 0s. 0d.** 3rd Stalls **15s.** Unreserved Seats **8s. 6d.: 5s. 9d.: 2s. 4d.**

##### (All prices include Entertainment Tax).

**Seats can be booked at the National Sporting Club, 21, Soho Square W.1.**

Arrangements have been made with the L.M.S. Railway to run a Special Train or Trains from London on the day of the contest, leaving Euston at or about 2 : m.

### RETURN FARE: £1 3s. 0d.

heavier punch failed to prove decisive: though flooring Cuthbert five times, he ended up level on points, according to referee Douglas – a controversial verdict, but evidence that, despite a terrific career total of 133 victories from 164 contests, he lacked that extra quality to make him a great fighter.

Foreman did not defend the belt; nor, indeed, did he return it to the Club. For some mysterious reason, he pawned it before decamping to Canada to become a photographer. The belt was later acquired by Jeff Dickson who used it as a promotional gimmick to boost ticket sales for a lightweight title fight he was staging at the Albert Hall.

Foreman's successor, Johnny Cuthbert, beat Jim Hunter from Scotland in ten rounds at White City, Glasgow, but Cuthbert was principally a featherweight. The next champion of significance at the weight was Harry Mizler, who outpointed Cuthbert in January 1934 at the Albert Hall.

Mizler was a copy-book fighter with a straight left, who disproved the old adage that a great amateur champion rarely makes a champion professional. Mizler won ABA titles at bantam, feather and lightweight as well as taking the Empire Games gold medal in 1930.

Born in the Jewish East End, in Whitechapel, his elder brother Moe was also a boxer (indeed, a flyweight contender in 1929) and both were popular at Premierland. When Mizler burst upon the professional scene, he was at first hailed as a KO fighter, his first contest lasting under two minutes. His first fourteen contests (all victories) included ten KOs while the last was the points victory over Cuthbert for the title – a remarkably low number of fights for a champion in those days.

But Mizler was not really a heavy puncher – indeed, his suspect hands were to dog and mar his career. He defended the title some months later, beating Billy Quinlan, a talented Welshman in Wales, before taking on Jack Kid Berg – a Dickson favourite – at the Albert Hall.

It was for this contest that Dickson offered the 'unofficial' Lonsdale Belt that he had acquired, indirectly, from Al Foreman. Berg, a relentless, two-handed battler, dominated Mizler physically and psychologically before stopping 'Hymie' in ten rounds and, though Mizler's career continued until 1943, it would con-

MOSS DEYONG

1930s referees and managers

C. H. DOUGLAS

JOHNNY SHARPE

JACK SMITH

SAM RUSSELL

JACK HART

tain only one more championship fight: in October 1936 he was defeated by Jimmy Walsh, Berg's surprise conqueror, on points at the Empress Hall.

The errant belt, however, was never handed over by Dickson, neither to Berg nor Walsh. In fact, legend has it that Ted Broadribb received it as a gift from Dickson. Where it went after that is unknown.

London was now to suffer a relative decline in importance as a championship centre, while in the provinces boxing was never healthier, never more popular and producing excellent, exciting fighters.

In Manchester, for instance, Harry Fleming's growing influence rested principally on his control of three of Britain's most illustrious champions of the 1930s: Jackie Brown, Johnny King and Jock McAvoy; Jack Madden, meanwhile, was matchmaker for Belle Vue, a venue which, under the astute direction of John Henry Iles, was, in championship terms during the mid-Thirties, the capital of British boxing.

The first of Fleming's trio of champions was Jackie Brown. Born in Collyhurst, where Fleming's famous gymnasium was situated, of Irish extraction and temperament, he was skilful, speedy and exciting. His first major fight in 1927, however, at Jack Smith's Free Trade Hall, resulted in defeat. Smith rather foolishly refused Brown a return engagement and so Fleming took his eighteen-year-old prodigy off to Wales where he rapidly established a reputation defeating local contenders Phineas John, Boyo Rees, etc.

After a string of impressive wins Brown earned an eliminating contest in 1929 for the right to meet champion Johnny Hill, who was then preparing to meet Frankie Genaro on Jeff Dickson's 'outlaw' promotion at the Albert Hall.

Sadly, Hill died of pneumonia while in training – the upshot being that the eliminator became a championship, the only one to have been held on a Sunday. Brown KO'd opponent Bert Kirby in three rounds and was flyweight champion, though not beltholder.

Five months later a return was staged by the NSC at the Stadium Club in Holborn. This time Kirby reversed the decision exactly, in a three-round KO. Brown's excuse for the surprise result was that he was suffering from an outbreak of boils, something that had affected him previously when preparing for a big fight.

A year later, in February 1931, Jack Madden succeeded in bringing the two men together again, with some persuasion from the BBBC, at Belle Vue in front of a sell-out 7,000 crowd for what was considered one of the classic flyweight contests in British boxing history.

Brown regained his title and in the process completely outboxed and outpunched Kirby until, at the end of the fifteenth round, the Birmingham boy was a dazed and baffled fighter.

Brown was an attractive, charismatic little man. Brian Fleming, in *The Manchester Boxers*, described him as 'dark and distinguished-looking. . . . He was witty with a fund of stories and a repertoire of Irish songs which he was always ready to voice. . . . In a word, he had glamour and many of the Manchester folk in those drab days were happy to bask in the glamour with Jackie.'

He was also of genuine international class. In October 1932 he won the NBA/IBU version of the World flyweight title by defeating Young Perez in thirteen rounds at Belle Vue – this the title Jeff Dickson had monopolized with Genaro and Pladner in 1929. Brown defended it successfully four times in London and Manchester, and so successful was he that when Fleming's option on him expired, he turned first to Dave Lumiansky, the American manager so influential in Europe during the Thirties, and later still, to Harry Levene.

By 1935, however, with the rise of Benny Lynch, Brown's glory days were coming to an end. Lynch drew with Brown in a non-title fight in early 1935 but in September of the same year Lynch succeeded in forcing the Mancunian to retire in the second round. Brown had attempted to take the fight to Lynch – never the way to tackle such a hard counter-puncher. In the first round Lynch began catching the champion with debilitating rights to the heart and then, switching his attack to the chin, stopped Brown in the second, just as discarded trainer Fleming had warned might happen.

Brown, however, was not finished. Now with Harry Levene, he decided that the difficulty he had experienced in reducing himself to flyweight for the Lynch contest suggested he would fare better as a bantamweight. This meant challenging his Collyhurst stablemate, Johnny King, then bantamweight champion.

Thus in May 1937 at Belle Vue, the two local men faced one another while the whole of Manchester looked on in fascination. Johnny King, born in Collyhurst, also discovered and guided by Fleming, was of a completely different temperament to Brown. King was the perfect trainer, always in excellent condition and, despite a reputation for possessing a devastating right hand, was also a fine defensive boxer, as testified by the fact that he never suffered from cuts or from broken hands.

Interestingly, the two men did share one thing – a championship opponent whom they found difficult to subdue. Brown's *bête noire* was Bert Kirby; King's would be Dick Corbett. In fact, in four title fights with Londoner Corbett, King only won one, losing two and drawing the last.

King's first chance at the British title came in December 1931. Teddy Baldock had relinquished the title and King met Corbett at Belle Vue. Corbett, a cagy, difficult fighter, won an unpopular, close decision. Ten months later King refused to let himself be outmanoeuvred by Corbett's crablike, negative style and earned a hard-fought victory.

King was an extremely busy fighter (222 fights in all); he fought on average twice a month, usually for purses ranging between £50 and £100. He was a crowd-puller and popular wherever he went. He was also loyal: despite lucrative offers from Lumiansky, King stayed with Fleming all his career and the two followed a regular, workmanlike routine, King driving himself and his manager to contests, their sole extravagances being 'pub' lunches, games of darts and the occasional visit to the cinema.

His attempt to take a World title from Panama Al Brown was considered by many to be his greatest fight. King almost KO'd him, catching him in the seventh with his celebrated right hand, but was unable to finish the experienced American off, the latter clinging on to earn a points decision that was hotly disputed.

In 1934 King returned to domestic title fights, failing in two fights with Dick Corbett. The two fought an open-air classic on a British Sporting Promotions bill at Clapton but King could only manage a draw. Corbett then found he could no longer make the bantamweight limit and forfeited the title.

Thus, in May 1935, King beat Len Hampston at Belle Vue to take the title for the second time in five attempts. Two years later (following an unsuccessful attempt to take Nel Tarleton's featherweight title) and King was fighting Jackie Brown for the Lonsdale Belt outright.

In fact, the two had met once before, in 1935, in a twelve-round non-title fight when Brown had been badly beaten in six rounds. Now, under Levene's managership, Brown was confident he could succeed: King, with Harry Fleming in his corner, was certain he would not. In Brian Fleming's words:

> Brown on this occasion boxed a much more clever fight but, to the initiated, it was obvious that the amazing speed of the old days was no longer there. Johnny King, boxing well within himself, was always in command of the situation as he invariably was against positive fighters such as Brown. Punishing left hooks, under and over, plus a plentiful supply of right hand 'Mary Annes' from King finally began to sap Jackie's strength. The fight continued with Brown's persistence and pride keeping him going but he was floored in the eleventh and twelfth rounds before being knocked out in the thirteenth.

If the struggle for supremacy in the bantam and flyweight divisions resulted in the emergence of Manchester as one of Britain's major promotional and fistic centres, then the featherweight saga, as it unfolded in the late Twenties and Thirties, involved yet another provincial success story – that of Manchester's great rival, Liverpool.

The featherweight division was also noteworthy for the fact that, despite the trouble and strife surrounding the role of the NSC, almost every championship bout at the weight carried a Lonsdale Belt with it. Indeed, during the twenty-three years after Jim Driscoll's outright win of the very first featherweight belt on offer in 1913, only one of the twenty-three bouts that followed did not involve a belt.

Only the fierce competition between a handful of talented men ensured that no more than three belts were won outright: Mike

JAKE KILRAIN

1930s champions and challengers

HARRY MIZLER

ARTHUR DANAHAR

EDDIE PHILLIPS

JACK (KID) BERG

FRANK HOUGH

Honeyman, George McKenzie, Johnny Curley and Harry Corbett all secured two notches, only to fall at the third crucial hurdle. And it was a division noted for very experienced, very active men: Curley eventually notched up 180 bouts, Corbett 219, Cuthbert 154 and Tarleton 144. All were skilful, tough, durable battlers who plugged away behind well-organized defences, jabbing with straight lefts, adept at footwork and possessing bags of courage. No surprise, then, that they could all be guaranteed to put on a show, and audiences loved them.

In March 1925, Johnny Curley from Lambeth took the title from George McKenzie of Leith, the first of three championship wins for the man whose shock of ginger hair belied his equable if rugged temperament.

Curley was really from another era entirely. Born in 1897, he had begun his career in 1912, only to see it interrupted, almost permanently ended, by active service in France. He was gassed and almost blinded, yet was back in the ring by early 1919, battling away at Manor Hall, the Ring and Premierland. He was a tricky, wily fighter, possessing all the wrinkles of his demanding trade.

A product of the famous 'Lambeth School of Arms' where the Corbetts also trained, he was a continuation of that great South London tradition that included Sid Smith and Jim Sullivan and would continue producing fighters right up to the present day. Moreover, he almost always seemed able to win the contests that mattered.

He beat Harry Corbett and Billy Hindley in 1926 but with permanent possession of the belt at stake, he finally succumbed to Sheffield's Johnny Cuthbert in January 1927, Cuthbert already having scored three non-title wins over the little veteran.

Cuthbert, though born in Sheffield and trained there by his father in the latter's public house (where locals could sip their pints at the bar and watch their lad sweating and agonizing to make the far-from-natural featherweight limit), was a great favourite in London – in particular at Premierland. A professional since 1921, his correct style and great tactical awareness allied to a teetotal, almost monastic regime, might suggest that he lacked charisma, or fan-appeal. His popularity, particularly in Europe, belied that. Quite simply, he was a joy to watch as he dismantled men of supposedly greater talent and possessing more powerful punches: Gustave Humery, André Routis – even Al Brown, with whom he drew in Paris in 1928 – all were expected to destroy him, yet none did.

But Cuthbert found the British title a hard one to retain, principally because of one man – Harry Corbett. From Bethnal Green, Corbett was Cuthbert's boxing contemporary: both made their pro debuts in 1921, although by 1925, when Corbett contested the British bantamweight title, losing to Johnny Brown, the little Londoner had fought some eighty-three contests to Cuthbert's modest thirty.

Once he had made his name (though not his real name, that being Henry William Coleman) Corbett came under the managerial wing of Ted Broadribb. Broadribb had great ambitions for Harry; indeed, in March 1927 he placed a £500 bet that Harry would win a Lonsdale Belt within a year. He made it, almost to the day, when he took Cuthbert's featherweight crown in March 1928.

Corbett was a stylish little boxer, a gatherer of points and a wearer-down of opponents. He was also a great friend of Johnny Curley with whom he trained at Fred Duffett's South London gymnasium.

Corbett was keen, too, on the corner-man skills of manager Broadribb. He described the Cuthbert fight in *Topical Times*:

I entered the ring full of confidence. I was raring to go, too, for Ted Broadribb had rubbed some sort of embrocation on me in the dressing room which seemed to put new life in me. Broadribb seemed to have picked up innumerable ointments, potions, and embrocations during his life in the game which were very helpful to me.

Broadribb also produced good advice: 'Try and judge two minutes of each round,' he said. 'During that time, go hell for leather. Don't give him any peace. For the last minute of the round, take a rest.'

This was because Broadribb thought Cuthbert was hesitant when placed under continuous pressure. And the technique worked. Cuthbert was thrown out of his stride and lost – against the odds, it must be said, because although contests between the two were usually close, Cuthbert generally came out on top.

The return, a year later, was also drawn – and two months after that they were back in the ring together, though much against Broadribb's better judgement. The BBBC had insisted that Corbett face Cuthbert rather than Johnny McMillan, the preferred opponent of Broadribb. Jack Smith, the Board's appointed referee, adjudged Cuthbert a narrow points winner – a verdict few argued with.

Cuthbert thus took the belt, presented to him inside the ring by Lord Lonsdale – more than happy to play his part in the 'new' spectacular NSC.

A year later, Cuthbert defeated Dom Volante, a mouth-organ-playing Liverpudlian who had busked his fare to Manchester to begin his pro-career as a teenager and who had scored victories over Johnny Curley, Harry Corbett as well as Cuthbert himself before earning his title shot.

Volante's was a sad career: his proud boast was that, at its height, he had bought his mother a house in Liverpool: 'with all modern fixtures and a wireless and a gramophone to provide music....'

But Volante was a prolific gambler; and by 1932, chasing a

# ARCHIE SEXTON

OF

BETHNAL GREEN

Contender for the Middle-weight Title makes history

With Lauri Raiteri he engaged in an Exhibition Bout which was televised from Broadcasting House at 11 p.m. last night

shot at the lightweight title (he was eventually to lose an eliminator to none other than Johnny Cuthbert) he badly damaged his left eye and was warned not to fight again. He ignored the warning, as he later explained to readers of *Topical Times*: 'Why? Because I had no money. Mother needed money. Then there was my sister Lucy. For years she had been an invalid. She had to have good food. Then there is my little brother Vincent who is tubercular. I had to see he got every attention and comfort.'

But Volante's eye got worse and he was forced to give up the game, blindness a real possibility. The house had to be sold and he faced an uncertain future: 'I have no trade beside fighting. I can play musical instruments but who would find me work as a musician? I was good when I was the boxing musician, but now I am just the musician; there is a difference.'

Volante's great friend and stablemate – also a proud Liverpudlian – was Nel Tarleton, whose career might well have provided Volante with some solace. Tarleton, like Volante and thousands of other fighters, turned to the pro-game because of poverty. The eldest of eight children, 'Nella', as he became affectionately known to the crowds at Liverpool Stadium, turned professional officially at twenty when it was revealed in a local paper that he had been boxing for money under an assumed name (Nat Nelson) while still claiming amateur status.

He made his name in the old Pudsey Stadium (rebuilt by promoter Johnny Best in 1930). He was a lanky (6 ft plus) fighter with a long reach, fine footwork and a great defence. What is more, he could 'bang a bit' – forty stoppages to his credit in over 140 contests.

A spell in the USA, courtesy of Broadribb, along with Dom Volante was credited with adding a more aggressive approach to his repertoire. In the States, Tarleton and Volante sparred with Jack Kid Berg who was preparing for his epic battle with Kid Chocolate.

Back in England in November 1930 at Liverpool, Tarleton fought a draw with Cuthbert six months after Volante's unsuccessful bid for the title. A year later, in October 1931, taking advantage of Cuthbert's difficulty in getting down to featherweight (Cuthbert would soon become a fully fledged lightweight and would actually take that title too) Tarleton completely outboxed and outfought Cuthbert in front of 25,000 spectators at Anfield Stadium, the first time a Liverpool-born fighter had taken a Lonsdale Belt.

A local journalist described the scene:

> One of the most sporting crowds I have ever seen were massed, tier upon tier, in the darkness around the ground, only the ring being illuminated and throwing fitful beams upon the green of the turf and the wet waterproof sheets over which the boxers were carried at the ringside. Spion Kop glowed with hundreds of lights as smokers lit their pipes and cigarettes. It was surely one of the strangest but most successful settings for a fight that has ever been devised. . . .

At the finish, after Smith had lifted Tarleton's hand, Tarleton was cheered and chaired by the crowd, kissed by his sisters and presented with the belt (a new one, as Cuthbert had made the previous one his own) by the mayor of Liverpool – the first mayor to give official recognition to a professional fight.

Cuthbert's response was typically, refreshingly honest: 'Ah well, I've had a good run for my money . . . Nel was too good for me.'

A year later, Tarleton defended his title at promoter Best's new stadium, built, after much local protest, it must be said, on the site of a church and burial ground. Opened in October 1932, the new stadium was the first in the country to be built especially for boxing and the Tarleton–Watson fight was the first British title fight to be held there.

Ironically, given the stadium's later nickname of the 'Graveyard of Champions', it would be Liverpool's favourite son who would be the first to suffer a shock defeat. It was a controversial decision, understandably booed by the massed local fans, but Seaman Watson was a solid, unflappable fighter who had steadily kept the pressure on Tarleton, not allowing the champion's elusive skills to flummox or dishearten him. The final round was a classic, the whole stadium in pandemonium as the two men fought ferociously, Tarleton, with his left eye badly gashed and blood streaming down his cheek, meeting the furious assaults of Watson punch for punch.

No wonder that, with emotions so roused, the eventual

announcement that Tarleton had lost was greeted with such a prolonged storm of booing, an uproar that eclipsed the novelty of Lord Lonsdale presenting the belt in person, centre-ring, another 'first' in that the great man had never before carried out the ceremony in a provincial city.

Though Watson offered a swift return, Tarleton set off for the USA and Australia, a learning experience that toughened him physically and mentally, battling away with experienced scrappers in New York and Sydney.

July 1934 saw him make a glorious return to Scouseland, retrieving the title from Watson, whom he hammered to defeat at Anfield Stadium. Later that year he took the belt outright at Wembley Stadium, defeating Dave Crowley on points – the only time, incidentally, in some twelve title fights that Tarleton would appear in a London arena.

Tarleton would continue his successful career in the 1940s and become the first boxer to win both an NSC original belt and a BBBC Lonsdale Belt. Victories over Johnny Cusick (to regain the title Tarleton had lost to Johnny McGrory), Tom Smith and Tiger Al Phillips (the latter contest in 1945 when Tarleton was thirty-nine years old) saw him end an enormous career (144 contests between 1926 and 1945) in triumph. He then switched to managing his brother-in-law, Ernie Roderick, who himself almost won two belts outright.

# 11

## The End of the NSC

Between 1929 and 1939 there were thirty title fights in the middle, light-heavy and heavyweight divisions, twenty-seven of them involving at least one of three men: Len Harvey, Jock McAvoy and Jack Peterson.

The 'big three' took twenty-five titles between them, Harvey a record eleven titles, Peterson eight and McAvoy six. At times it must have seemed there were no other contenders as Harvey and McAvoy clashed four times, Harvey and Peterson three times. Only Eddie Phillips at light-heavy and Ben Foord at heavy made any sort of impact before 1937 when Tommy Farr became heavyweight champion.

Thus for promoters at the time, available talent able to fill a reasonable-sized stadium was limited and the fact that Peterson and Harvey were extremely shrewd negotiators only made life harder.

Yet these top British fighters were really only big fish in a tiny pool. World title fights were rare: the 'big three', despite their years of domination, managed only four: Harvey losing to Marcel Thil at middleweight in 1932 and to John Henry Lewis at light-heavyweight in 1936; McAvoy also losing to Lewis in 1936; while Harvey and McAvoy met one another in 1939 for a British 'World' title. Peterson never fought for a World title nor did he meet anyone even approaching world quality. Thus it is a difficult task to assess precisely these 'giants' of the British game.

The closest British promoters came to staging 'international' spectacles were when they imported giant German heavyweights (Neusel, Guhring, Muller, Schonrath – though not Schmeling and Baer) or Empire champions like the excellent Larry Gains or South African Don McCorkindale.

As a consequence, at middleweight and above, the Lonsdale Belts assumed an importance they had not enjoyed in previous decades. Jack Petersen would make a belt his own – the first heavyweight to manage the feat since Bombardier Billy Wells – while Len Harvey would clinch a middleweight belt bearing the illustrious names of Ted Kid Lewis, Tommy Gummer and Tommy Milligan. Indeed, in the middleweight division the change in fortune for the NSC's symbol of excellence was dramatic: between 1920 and 1929, of fifteen title fights at the weight, only four had involved a belt; of the next ten, only one would not.

Len Harvey was arguably the best boxer of the 'big three': attractive and popular, he embodied all those qualities so dear to British boxing fans – he fought cleanly and skilfully yet was modest and almost devoid of 'ego'. Unfortunately, his lack of ruthlessness accounted for his two defeats at the hands of US champion Vince Dundee, which led one commentator to describe Harvey as 'too lackadaisical . . . a terribly disappointing fellow . . . who has let his opportunity slip by him.'

By the time that uncharacteristic verdict was delivered in 1935, Harvey had been boxing for fifteen years and had fought thirteen British title fights at welter, middle and light-heavy and heavy-weight. He began fighting in Plymouth, his birthplace, at twelve-and-a-half years old, as a 'paperweight'. His father – his long-time guide and mentor – brought him and the whole family to London when Len was sixteen in 1923 and Dan Sullivan, general manager at the Ring, soon adopted him as the venue's star performer. By the time he was twenty he was a fully fledged middleweight with sixty-three pro-fights under his belt, including a draw with Harry Mason for the latter's welterweight title.

His strengths were his powerful left hand – as jab or hook – his uppercut and an extremely powerful right cross. Unfortunately, as he moved up the divisions, his natural weight did not, thus rendering his punching less effective. However, it was a KO in the sixth round of ex-champ Frank Moody that saw him gain his opportunity at middleweight against champion Alex Ireland.

This was on the NSC's showpiece tournament at Olympia in 1929. Harvey and Ireland came on at 10.30 in the evening following the featherweight title fight between Cuthbert and Corbett and the bantamweight title fight between Baldock and Pattenden – the latter a rousing affair that had been followed by great cheers and sustained applause.

The Harvey v Ireland bout thus started in an atmosphere of anticlimax, not too many people paying attention for the early rounds. However, it eventually produced, according to C. B. Cochrane, 'better boxing than we naturally expect from the "big men" of the evening'.

Throughout the fight, Ireland found himself chasing Harvey, whose straight left and right counters succeeded in rendering the Scottish champion groggy by the third. Rounds four and five saw Ireland struggling to seize the initiative from a supremely fit and confident younger man. Put down by a powerful uppercut for a long count in the sixth, he came out at the start of the seventh still groggy and was floored again by a powerful right followed by a left 'to the liver' for a decisive and conclusive ending.

Five months later Harvey took on Jack Hood, the reigning welterweight king, in one of the 'dream' fights promoters scramble for. Hood was five years older than Harvey, had been beaten only once in fifty-five pro-fights, was winner outright of the welterweight belt and had impressed on a tour of the USA. At the age of twenty-six he was in his prime, though prone to damaged hands – the cause of at least one of the three postponements that had held up the meeting of Britain's two most glamorous boxers.

Though giving away half a stone to Harvey, Hood was regarded by dint of his experience and ringcraft the marginal favourite for the fight. For much of the first five rounds, Hood treated Harvey as his fistic junior, jabbing and hooking, picking up points while Harvey contented himself with counter-attacks.

But in the fifth, a Harvey uppercut sent Hood back for the first time and Harvey now took up the running so that by the end, Hood was clearly tiring. A close fight was thus awarded to Harvey by the narrowest of margins.

Two months later, at Olympia, the NSC staged a lucrative return and this time Harvey appeared much more confident, more aggressive from the start, and succeeded in cutting Hood over the right eye with a left hook. Hood battled on and eventually returned the compliment by cutting Harvey over the right eye –

but it was another evenly balanced contest, so much so that at the end the referee could not separate them and awarded a draw.

In May 1930, the club matched Harvey with Steve McCall, the Scottish champion, beaten just twice in forty-two fights, on another big Olympia bill featuring a second Belt contest between Johnny Cuthbert and Dom Volante. Harvey had little trouble in securing a third notch on his belt: he had McCall in trouble from the first, a heavy left hook sending the Scot staggering. Nine rounds of relentless, heavy punishment followed and a left hook floored McCall for a count of eight. Up he got, was floored again, rose a second time, went down a third time – after which his corner threw in the towel. Harvey had won the belt outright, just as Cuthbert had done earlier in the evening – yet another 'first'.

Len Harvey was now Britain's premier fighter, prosperous enough to convert himself into a limited company with £1,000 one-pound shares. His trip to the USA, however, in search of a World title was a disaster. Three defeats inflicted by Vince Dundee and Ben Jeby – both future World champs – saw his ratings slump badly.

Thus, in 1931, a return with Jack Hood, staged by Jeff Dickson who could now boast a unique contest between two men who had both won an Lonsdale Belt outright, looked financially promising.

It was a fight to settle all arguments, and proved that Hood was too light to match Harvey's power and strength. Hood spent much of the fight attempting to nullify Harvey's left hook/jab – a potent weapon – either by holding or diverting Harvey's blows to his midriff where the welterweight champ took a lot of punishment. Hood's own normally sharp, accurate left was neglected and rarely used, while his right – a punishing, potential KO weapon – was too often employed in clinging onto Harvey. Harvey, aggressive and strong, had Hood down in the tenth and at the end was well ahead on points.

Hood then returned to the welterweight ranks to defend his title while Harvey turned, in March 1932, to consider the threat from an up-and-coming Mancunian, Jock McAvoy.

McAvoy, whose real name was Joe Bamford, was born in Burnley in 1908 and started boxing aged twenty when living in Rochdale

– hence his soubriquet 'The Rochdale Thunderbolt'. His first three years as a pro saw him compile an impressive record but not until he approached manager Harry Fleming at Collyhurst did his career really take off. Fleming helped to tighten up the big man's defence and to straighten out his punch, devising a system of bandaging damaged knuckles that allowed McAvoy to exploit its full power. By 1932 McAvoy had gained a title shot against Len Harvey for the latter's middleweight title.

Harvey won this one – a close fight – on points, his extra experience and solid defence proving too much for McAvoy. In fact, Harvey caught McAvoy with a left hook in the thirteenth that would have floored anyone else. McAvoy survived but would clearly be back.

Sure enough, in April 1933 at Manchester's Belle Vue, he took Harvey's title by dint of non-stop aggression, though once again it was close.

Harvey then moved up a division to light-heavy and into the all-time record books. In June 1933, he took Eddie Phillips's title on points. Five months later, on 30 November, he beat Jack Peterson for the latter's heavyweight title. Thus, in one year, Harvey held middle, light-heavy and heavyweight titles – a feat unlikely to be equalled or surpassed. Although Harvey would not contend another middleweight title bout, his and Jack McAvoy's paths would cross again.

Seven months on, McAvoy met Archie Sexton, the 'classy cockney' – a crisp-punching box-fighter with a stiff left jab – over whom he eventually swarmed, absorbing Sexton's counters and finally felling the Londoner with a right uppercut.

McAvoy, anxious for more lucrative bouts, promptly followed Harvey and stepped up a division. Between January 1935 and April 1936 he met and lost decisions to European (later World) champion Marcel Thil, World light-heavyweight champion John Henry Lewis and British heavyweight champion Jack Peterson. During a strenuous US tour, he also took on various heavy and light-heavyweight contenders.

It was a punishing, ultimately disastrous programme devised for him not by Harry Fleming but by Dave Lumiansky, the American manager then operating in Europe, who had taken over his contract in early 1935. With too many bouts and too little rest in between, McAvoy's suspect knuckles sustained heavy damage that refused to heal. His constitution – never the strongest – also suffered and his reserves were stretched to breaking point.

Fleming had tended to McAvoy's hypochondria (bronchial colds, boils, constipation, back pains, etc.) and had coped with his suspect, unstable temperament. Once under Lumiansky's control, such considerations took a back seat in the race for cash and glory. In the middle of this chaotic period, however, McAvoy managed to secure for himself a Lonsdale Belt outright (one of the last of the 'original' NSC belts), clinching a third notch by defeating Al Burke at Belle Vue in June 1935.

His defeat by Jack Peterson for the latter's heavyweight title in April 1936 was the last occasion on which Peterson – the third of the dynamic trio of British boxing – would taste success in a title fight.

Peterson, three years younger than McAvoy, had dominated the heavyweight division for four years, winning eight of nine title clashes, not to mention the light-heavyweight title in May 1932. Peterson had, in domestic terms at least, restored to the premier division some kind of respectability. Prior to his accession, men like Reggie Meen and further back Phil Scott had made little impression on a public eager for someone to don the mantle of Bombardier Billy Wells – still a popular and successful figurehead for the sport, if hardly a world beater.

Lonsdale Belt contests in the heavyweight division were still few and far between. Since Wells's last belt victory in 1916 there had been twelve heavyweight title bouts, only two of which had involved a belt. In 1919 Frank Goddard had beaten Jack Curphey, a bout somewhat devalued by the fact that most of the boxing world considered Joe Beckett to be the true champion. Beckett himself had fought for the belt once in 1923 at Holland Park before retiring.

Four title fights in the succeeding seven years with champions Goddard, Phil Scott and Reggie Meen testify to the dearth of talent at the very top. The advent of Peterson, therefore, was both a commercial coup for his backers as well as a shot in the arm for a glamour-starved boxing public.

Peterson was to be hailed, over-optimistically, as Britain's Carpentier, principally because he was good-looking and skilful and packed a KO punch; but perhaps more tellingly because he was, like Carpentier, not a true heavyweight at all, more of a blown-up middleweight – a factor that would eventually tell against him.

Backed by a wealthy syndicate and managed by his astute father, 'Pa' Peterson, his rise was swift. ABA light-heavyweight champion in 1931, by February 1932 he was Welsh light-heavyweight champion, and by May of the same year he was entering the ring at the Holborn Stadium (also a part of the Peterson syndicate's operation) to contest the British light-heavyweight title with holder Harry Crossley.

After a competent points victory, some two months later he was matched with heavyweight champion Reggie Meen at Wimbledon on a super-promotion of the NSC and Thomas Hatton. The Lonsdale Belt played a prominent part in the promotion and fight – a new experience for the heavyweight division.

Meen, at 6 ft 1 in and 15 st, was winner of fifty-five bouts, twenty-three by KO; and he towered over Peterson who had had only nineteen pro-bouts up to that point. Yet Meen would be KO'd in two dazzling rounds.

Events were to continue at this breakneck speed as, five months on, Peterson faced Jack Pettifer – 6 ft 7 in and 17 st 4 lb. The fight had a sensational start – Peterson raced across to Pettifer at the bell and floored him for a count of three with the first punch of the fight! Pettifer rose, staggered Peterson with a stiff left and battle commenced.

A punishing twelve rounds later and Peterson put together a left, right, left combination to floor Pettifer for the full count.

It has been said that, well-managed as he was financially, Peterson and his connections were in too much of a hurry, that he took on top men, particularly top heavyweights, too soon. Thus Peterson had to cope with too much punishment at the start of his career while he never had time to develop an adequate defence to match his devastating right. As it was, eye trouble would prematurely end his career after eight action-packed years.

Seven months after the Pettifer fight, Peterson was matched with the newest glamour-boy, Jack Doyle, in a contest that, as has been demonstrated, would have repercussions for Britain's boxing administrators. What is often overlooked in discussions

# *WIMBLEDON STADIUM*

The Lonsdale Belt Awarded to the Heavy-weight Champion of Great Britain

## REGGIE MEEN AND JACK PETERSEN

are due to Fight for the Belt and the Title on July 5.

*MR. THOMAS HATTON*
*has pleasure in announcing that by arrangement with Mr. Lionel Bettinson and the Committee of the National Sporting Club, the Lonsdale Belt will be at stake in the contest for the Heavy-weight Championship of Great Britain between Reggie Meen (the holder) and Jack Petersen (the challenger) at Wimbledon Stadium on July 5.*

*It was in the year 1909 that the Lonsdale Belts were offered for competition at fixed weights. The first winner in the heavy-weight division was Bombardier Billy Wells in 1911, and the last time the trophy was fought for was in 1923, when Joe Beckett beat Dick Smith. Book your seat for Wimbledon Stadium on July 5 to see who will be the next holder of the trophy.*

*There has already been a tremendous, even overwhelming, demand for seats, and it is advisable that YOU book your reservations NOW.*

Mr. Thomas Hatton's Offices in London are at 19, PANTON STREET, LONDON, S.W.1. Telephone: Whitehall 1100. On Page 3 you will find a complete list of Offices where you can book your seats. There is a great—an unprecedented—demand for seats, so 'Phone or Call—AT ONCE.

concerning the fight is that it offered Peterson the chance to make the Lonsdale Belt his own just a year after first claiming the title.

Two postponements due to Doyle's illness were poor preparation for either fighter: indeed, there was some suspicion as to Doyle's true fitness when he at last entered the White City ring on 12 July 1933, for his behaviour during the fight was certainly odd. As Jeff Dickson put it: 'Doyle went stark fighting mad in the second round. He dashed in, his eyes blazing and threw punches from outside the arena. Where they landed, he didn't seem to care.' Doyle was warned but continued to throw punches considered illegal and, within a minute of the restart, he was disqualified and escorted to the dressing-room amid a blaze of booing and howling.

It was certainly one of the most sensational Belt fights at heavyweight – indeed, at any weight – especially as it meant that Peterson was awarded the Lonsdale Belt for keeps after just twenty-four fights.

Perhaps the strain was beginning to tell, however, because four months later he lost his title to Len Harvey at the Albert Hall. From then until 1937, when Tommy Farr became champion, heavyweight title fights were non-Belt affairs.

From 1935 until the outbreak the Second World War, the BBBC gradually, painfully established itself as the governing body of British professional boxing, although its acceptance as such by managers, promoters and boxers was always grudging.

With the decline of the BBA and the inability of its critics to establish an alternative organization, the role of official opposition devolved upon the Boxer's Union, founded in 1934 by boxers and journalists including such luminaries as Jimmy Wilde, Len Harvey, Jack Hood, Jack Peterson and John Murray, who had been a prominent member of the old Boxer's Union formed before the First World War. The Union, later renamed the National Boxing Association, lasted no longer than five years and failed to gain official recognition from the BBBC.

The NBA's struggles, however, were not in vain, and in the course of time the BBBC adopted many of the Union's proposals and recommendations, particularly concerning safety and the financial payment of young and journeymen boxers. Its demands

JACK PETERSEN

Heavyweight stars of the 1930s

TOMMY FARR

JOCK McAVOY

JACK DOYLE

LEN HARVEY

BEN FOORD

in the late Thirties that the BBBC take up considerably more responsibility than the governing body appeared inclined to do were somewhat unrealistic, however, principally because for much of the time the Board was in dire financial straits and virtually paralyzed.

In 1935 its overdraft, after taking in some £2,372 in licence fees, was £1,665 – which led to some harsh words (and libellous allegations) directed mainly at Charles Donmall who continued to run the Board's day-to-day affairs from the offices of his engineering supplies company. The Board's expenses and phone-bills were pored over by its critics and imputations were made that Donmall was using the Board's expenses sheet as a means of embezzling money for his own company. He took a journalist (and *Boxing*) to court and won damages.

In July 1936, however, the Board decided to introduce a levy of 5 per cent on tournaments at which gross takings were £2,500 or more, to be paid as follows: 5 per cent of the money received by each boxer contesting the major contest after deducting £50 training expenses, and balance from the promoter. In return the Board would supply referees (paid on one per cent of the gate) timekeepers, inspectors, gloves, bandages – and championship belts.

The proposal – which had been rejected at an open meeting a year earlier – was now generally accepted and even welcomed.

The levy was official confirmation that the Board was now in complete control of professional boxing and its decision to take over the issuing of the belts was more than symbolic. Henceforth nobody was permitted to stage a championship or issue a belt without the Board's permission. And just to emphasize the break with past practice, the Board decided to alter the design of the Lonsdale Belts, replacing the central panel, depicting two boxers shaping up to fight, with a portrait of Lord Lonsdale himself.

The reversal of roles was complete when, in October 1936, the 'new' NSC – now run by manager/promoter John Harding for a wealthy syndicate – staged a British lightweight title fight (between Jimmy Walsh and Harry Mizler) at the Club's new boxing venue, the Empress Hall, Earls Court. Some months later, champion Walsh was presented with his BBBC belt (the third to be awarded) at an Earls Court promotion and, though the Marquis of

# THE BOXERS' BULLETIN

### UNITY IS STRENGTH

| Vol. I. No. 7. | JANUARY, 1937 | PRICE 2d. |
| --- | --- | --- |

## THE VICE-PRESIDENT'S NEW YEAR'S MESSAGE

❖

" *The Boxers' Union is the best thing that has happened in British Boxing since the War. I ask all of you to help us in 1937.*"

### LEN HARVEY

---

### PRINCIPAL CONTENTS

Queensberry handed it over and C. D. Douglas made a speech in honour of the occasion, it was clearly a *Board* honour.

In fact, the new NSC was only distantly related to the old Covent Garden Club. It was now a middle-order promotional organization with a restaurant headquarters at the Hotel Splendide in Piccadilly and a lease on the Empress Hall, where it held regular boxing shows.

In March 1938, it staged an inaugural luncheon to open the Piccadilly premises and invited along as many original champions as were still alive. The list was impressive, and included Pedlar Palmer, Joe Bowker, Matt Wells and Young Joseph, as well as outright belt winners Tancy Lee, Jimmy Wilde, Dick Smith, Pat O'Keefe, Johnny Basham, Billy Wells, Joe Fox and Jack Peterson.

Their presence begged a question: what had happened to the famous pension awarded to those men who won the belt outright? Unfortunately, the original Club was now defunct and the new one was really just a commercial organization dressing itself up in fancy clothes. Two years previously, in November 1936, faced with enquiries from Dick Smith, Pat O'Keefe and Tancy Lee regarding the pension, the Club had approached the Board of Control and asked the latter to take the matter up as *it* now had responsibility for issuing the belts. Donmall replied for the Board that it could do nothing and that the *new* belts did *not* carry the promise of a pension.

The Club then offered to go 'halves' with the Board in the setting up of a fund to pay the pensions but, once again, the Board refused to get involved – wisely, as it turned out, as in 1939 the 'new' NSC went into voluntary liquidation, saddled with debts and unable to pay creditors more than 3d in the pound. Meanwhile, of the original belt-winners, three – Bombardier Wells, Pat O'Keefe and Jimmy Wilde – lived well into their seventies and each lost out to the tune of some £1,400, while men like Dick Smith, Johnny Basham and Tancy Lee also lost reasonable sums of money.

Just before the bankruptcy, the Club had managed to pay Tancy Lee – then in straitened circumstances, various business ventures having failed – for half a dozen weeks but it clearly had no real intention of honouring its commitments. Considering the vast amounts of money said to have been involved in the various grand

MAIN ENTRANCE TO LIVERPOOL STADIUM.

schemes to rebuild and relaunch the NSC during the Thirties, the payment of £1 a week to half a dozen ex-fighters (a sum insufficient to keep many NSC men in cigars for a week – certainly not Lord Lonsdale whose cigar bill for a year was £3,000) looks positively insulting.

Sadly, a systematic form of support for boxers was not really part of the Club's philosophy; nor did anyone else in the industry see it as a priority until the Boxer's Union put its mind to the problem of insurance. The 'Champion' policy was the result, backed by Lloyd's Insurance brokers, a scheme that ultimately led to the National Boxers' Insurance Association.

It was fortunate that the outright belt winners of the inter-war years were, by and large, in little need of the Club's much-vaunted 'pension'. Johnny King, Jack Peterson, Len Harvey, Jack Hood and Johnny Cuthbert all bought and managed various public houses. Joe Fox had a sweet shop in Birmingham for many years (his belt on display in the window), Johnny Brown invested wisely in various business interests in South Africa and enjoyed a comfortable retirement, while Nel Tarleton would continue to box until 1945, his ring earnings also sensibly invested. Jackie Brown – although he spent money as fast as he earned it (a reputed £30,000 in the mid-Thirties) – was always able to maintain a respectable standard of living. Only Jim Higgins fell on hard times, reduced to selling tips in his home town of Hamilton, while Jock McAvoy's fate – crippled by polio in 1947 and ultimately to die from an overdose of sleeping pills in 1971 – was a tragedy that neither a pension nor an insurance policy could have affected.

These champions were not untypical of many other top boxers of the pre-Second World War era, as is demonstrated by an analysis – albeit largely anecdotal – of some seventy-eight former champs and contenders still alive by the end of the inter-war period.

At least thirty-four were either proprietors, managers or tenants of public houses, hotels or small businesses (ranging from Jack Bloomfield's ritzy Leicester Square watering-hole to Ted Moore's general store in the Thames tidal basin.) Ten more were exclusively involved in training or gymnasium work either on their own account or for someone else. Seventeen were either unemployed or holding down manual jobs in factories (Bill Benyon was a miner, and died in a pit accident in 1932; Alf Kid Pattenden worked in a boot and shoe factory in Edmonton, North London). Five had established themselves in different professions such as journalism (Elky Clark and Jimmy Wilde) or the armed forces (both Harry Mason and Mike Honeyman were in the RAF). Three were retired, including Joe Beckett, living comfortably off his investment in local government stock – a recommendation from financier Jimmy White – although poor Frank Goddard's investments all failed in 1929, reducing him to unskilled labouring on a farm, in which employment he eventually died in penury.

# 12

## The Board Takes Over

In view of the NSC's doomed attempt to launch a series of 'World' Lonsdale Belts in the late 1930s, it is ironic that the first BBBC Belt match just happened to carry a World title tag, too. In retrospect, however, it might seem unfortunate that the Board's first belt should have been won by the man in possession of that World flyweight title – Benny Lynch.

It is now almost impossible to rescue the memory of Lynch's career from the clutches of myth and legend. Being the archetypal fistic story so beloved of fiction writers and romantics, his rags-to-riches-to-rags progress would seem to encapsulate, for many, certain essential, unpalatable truths about the sport.

Yet almost everything about him was untypical: both his excellence as an athlete and his shockingly sudden decline were rare occurrences in professional boxing. In that respect, the 'legend' does neither the fight game nor Lynch many favours.

His meteorlike rise and fall in championship terms came at the end of a long, hard apprenticeship. Born in 1913 in Clydesdale (the Gorbals), by turns a cabinet-maker's tea-boy, butcher's boy, messenger and newspaper-delivery boy, he had a short amateur career before he turned professional in 1931 with Sammy Wilson, a local trainer, who would guide him to the very top.

Lynch then fought in and around Glasgow at small halls and booths for almost two-and-a-half years, sometimes appearing as often as once a week, and amassing a total of sixty fights with just seven losses. Between times he travelled with Len Johnson's boxing booth which operated principally in Lancashire and the North, an experience credited with building his physique and strengthening his mental approach. When added to his huge

171

PETER KANE

**1930s belt-winners at lighter weights**

DAVE CROWLEY

BENNY LYNCH

JIMMY, WALSH

JOHNNY KING

ERIC BOON

lung capacity (which gave him immense reserves of energy) plus powerful neck muscles (which enabled him to absorb more than average punishment), he was clearly a formidable and ferocious opponent.

In addition, Len Johnson contributed to Lynch's already extensive boxing skills by teaching him a variety of ring strategies and a repertoire of punches which Lynch absorbed with a swiftness that would continue to amaze his various handlers – one of his principal characteristics being the ability to employ the unorthodox to stunning effect.

In March 1935 his trainer Wilson helped him bluff his way into a World title bout. In a non-title fight with reigning British and NBA World champion Jackie Brown, he told Lynch to hold back and allow the then fading Brown to imagine there was little to fear from the young Scot. Brown then agreed to a triple title match (but involving no Lonsdale Belt) for the following September, and was KO'd in just two rounds.

It did the BBBC no harm, therefore, to have its first officially sanctioned Belt fight, Benny Lynch v Pat Palmer on 16 September 1936, simultaneously described as a World title fight.

Lynch's opponent was a Battersea boy who had been a fine amateur, having won the British, European and Empire flyweight titles. He pinned his hopes on outboxing Lynch but, from the very start, in front of 40,000 Scots crammed into Shawfield Park, Glasgow, Lynch's power of punch was clearly going to prove too much. A left-hook combination to body and jaw, followed by a right cross, almost put Palmer down in the first round. His eyes glazed, his legs buckled, but he clung on to make a fight of it. At the end of the seventh, however, he was put down by a left hook and saved by the bell. The same punch, preceded by a left to the body, ended the fight at the beginning of the eighth.

Three months later, at the Stadium Club, Holborn, Lynch was presented with his BBBC Belt by Lord Lonsdale himself, along with a plaque and a cup commemorating his World and European titles.

Within four months, Lynch had beaten Small Montana at Wembley Stadium, on an Arthur Elvin promotion, to assume undisputed world status. Thus his second Belt fight, against Peter

ARTHUR J. ELVIN     JOHN E. HARDING     SYDNEY HULLS

Top pre-war promoters

Kane, would also be a World title fight – indeed, would prove to be one of the most dramatic flyweight title fights of all time.

Peter Kane could, like so many men in this talented class, also be said literally to have burst upon the scene. Born in Golborne, Lancashire in 1918, he had his first pro-fight when sixteen and three years later his hard-hitting style had earned him numerous accolades.

Kane was a colourful performer, always up on his toes, speedy and enterprising; and he would go hell-for-leather into his opponent in a non-stop effort to land a punch that might bring the contest to an abrupt end. Of his forty-one victories to date, over thirty had ended that way.

Thus the fight, indisputably between the world's top two fly-weights, assumed national significance, the English feeling sure they had discovered someone who might match Lynch in strength and skill. The 43,000 packing Shawfield Park, Glasgow, domain of promoter (and now Lynch's manager) George Dingley, thought otherwise.

The very start of the contest caused uproar. Kane, dashing

across to deliver what he hoped would be an opening KO blow, was caught instead by a left to the stomach and right to the jaw and found *himself* down! Although he scrambled up at the count of two, he was so concussed that he recalled nothing of the succeeding thirteen rounds.

Lynch slowly, inexorably wore Kane down over the next eight rounds. In the ninth, Kane took a painful battering to the accompaniment of a fearful din, yet he staged a rally towards the end of the round and actually staggered Lynch with a right. In the tenth and eleventh he chased Lynch, attempting to press home what he felt was his advantage, but in the twelfth, Lynch put the Englishman down with a perfectly timed left hook as Kane came charging in. Saved by the bell, in the thirteenth, by now open-mouthed and defenceless, he was floored almost immediately. Up at seven, he was battered down a second time and, having only managed to crawl up onto one knee, was counted out.

Incredibly, Lynch would have only six more professional contests – none of them championship affairs – the last coming almost exactly a year after the tremendous Kane fight. Alcohol, and his consequent inability to make the weight, reduced these last performances first to sadness, finally to farce. Ten years after winning the first-ever BBBC Belt, he died of pneumonia and malnutrition, destitute and alone.

The phenomenon of Benny Lynch was like a dazzling shooting star across the generally more prosaic night sky of British boxing – yet excellence continued to push its way to the top of this enchanted flyweight division: Tancy Lee, Jimmy Wilde, Elky Clark, Johnny Hill, Jackie Brown, Benny Lynch – these great names would now be followed by yet another – Jacky Paterson, who would also bring that characteristic mixture of brilliance and tragedy associated with the flyweights.

Born in Ayrshire in 1921, he emigrated to Scranton, USA in 1928 but returned as a teenager to work, among other things, as a steelworker at John Brown shipyards. Like Lynch, he fought briefly as an amateur and turned pro at seventeen-and-a-half, but his progress was swifter than that of his illustrious predecessor.

Paterson's qualities were his southpaw right lead that he would use as both jab and KO weapon, his left being confined to defensive duties. As recounted by Brian Donald in *The Fight Game in Scotland*, Joe Aitcheson, Scotland's premier trainer, considered the little Scot 'the hardest hitter, pound for pound, that Scotland has ever produced. As a young man, he had worked as a butcher, developing the digital tendons, most vital part of a boxer's body when he throws a left hook – and how Paterson could hook!'

His opponent for the vacant title was to be Paddy Ryan, northern area champion. Ryan, whippet-fast and built, as one writer put it, 'like a miniature oak', belonged to the same Collyhurst stable in Manchester as Johnny King and Jackie Brown. Manager Fleming had gradually nursed him along because of his diminutive size.

He went through 1937–8 undefeated in eighteen fights, including a draw with Jackie Jurich, World champion. Thus he was a super-confident challenger, but in a tough toe-to-toe contest Paterson's superior power gradually prevailed.

Ryan sustained a bad cut midway through the fight which grew progressively worse until he could hardly see his opponent. Put down in the thirteenth and with the cut beginning to slit across the eyelid, the referee called a halt.

Paterson, twenty-five days short of his nineteenth birthday, was overjoyed but no better off financially than when the fight started. The bout had occurred just days after the wartime restrictions had come into force: thus it had been fought in the open-air beneath barrage balloons, a situation that reduced the gate considerably. Added to all this, George Dingley, ex-manager of Benny Lynch and the fight promoter, admitted that the compulsory bond he had lodged with the BBBC would in no way cover the boxer's promised purses. Some years later, both men would receive a few pounds each.

A successful defence against Ryan a year later set up a second England v Scotland World title clash. Peter Kane, despite losing to Lynch in that famous encounter in October 1937, had taken advantage of Lynch's inability to make the weight in defence of his World crown and had slipped in to defeat World champion Jackie Jurich over fifteen rounds at Liverpool. Kane was the undisputed World title holder and a match with Paterson was the logical next step.

Thus, in January 1941 at Hampden Park, the boxing public were given their wish – a Lonsdale Belt holder putting up his belt against a World title holder – an event unique in Belt history.

Kane was now serving in the RAF and consequently extremely fit and very confident; and just as he had done against Lynch, he came charging across the ring the moment the bell sounded, intent on landing a decisive blow as soon as possible.

The pair swapped punches unceasingly for a minute or two but Paterson, like Lynch, was the truer hitter and suddenly he picked a short right that carried his full power, catching Kane flush to the jaw.

Down he went in a heap and, although up at four, his mind was clearly elsewhere; Paterson then put him down again for the full count with two more short rights. Thus it had taken Paterson a mere sixty-one seconds to win the first BBBC Belt outright.

Jackie Paterson's career, however, was only at the mid-point. In 1947 he would add the British bantamweight title to his collection but not before putting his flyweight titles (British, World and Empire) at stake in July 1946 against veteran Joe Curran.

Curran had been a pro since 1930 and official challenger since 1944. One of the game's natural flyweights at only 5 ft 2 in, his career was already over 150 fights old when he got his big chance – a long and winding road that had seen him beat and be beaten by men such as Jackie Paterson, Rinty Monaghan, Peter Kane, Bunty Doran, Paddy Ryan, Gus Foran and Norman Lewis.

A merchant seaman during the war, he'd been divebombed and torpedoed – but there would be little such drama to the Paterson contest, staged before an incredible 50,000 at Hampden Park: a dull and disappointing fight which ended with a points victory for Paterson who would wait another two years before putting his title at stake again.

The bantamweight title, meanwhile, remained uncontested for the duration of the war. Champion Johnny King, who had taken the first BBBC Belt in 1938 by beating old rival Len Hampston, joined the navy and the Board allowed the title to remain with him. In fact, King was given the belt at the end of the war and thus became only the second man to win both a new and an old championship belt.

Official Boxing
Programme
MONDAY, MARCH 28th 1938
At 8 p.m.
*Price   Sixpence*

NATIONAL SPORTING
CLUB
EMPRESS  STADIUM · EARL'S  COURT · S·W·6

The first man to achieve that feat had been the incredible Nel Tarleton – but he had earned his belts the hard way. He had fought for the featherweight title for the first time in 1930; fifteen years later, at Belle Vue, he would defeat 'Tiger' Al Phillips to complete his second hat-trick of wins.

Tarleton had, in fact, contested the first BBBC Belt put up in 1936 at Anfield, but had lost on this occasion to Scotsman Johnny McGrory. McGrory then failed to make the weight for a projected defence against East Ender Benny Caplan and had forfeited.

In November 1938 Jim 'Spider' Kelly beat Caplan in Belfast to become the first Irish boxer to hold both British and Empire titles. What is more, it was the first time a Lonsdale Belt had been won on Irish soil. Kelly's little son Billy, then just six, was hoisted over the ropes on that memorable night and ran into the outstretched arms of his father. Sixteen years on and he, too, would have a Lonsdale Belt buckled around his waist – in the same ring, at the same weight. . . .

'Spider's' reign, however, was short. In June 1939 Manchester's Johnny Cusick travelled to Belfast and took the title by stopping Kelly in twelve rounds. Cusick's promising career would then be ruined by the war. Following the loss of his title to Nel Tarleton in February 1940, he joined the forces and between 1941 and 1947 was on active service.

On his return, he found quality contests hard to come by, especially as the once vibrant Manchester boxing scene had dramatically declined.

For Nel Tarleton, however, home-town support was always forthcoming, his wins in 1940 against Cusick and Tom Smith being before ecstatic Scousers at Anfield. Yet, ironically, it would be in Manchester, at Belle Vue's King's Hall, that he would secure his second belt outright, by defeating Londoner 'Tiger' Al Phillips before a crowd of 7,000.

Phillips, tough, strong and relentless, had been expected to sweep the thirty-nine-year-old Tarleton away but it was Tarleton who ultimately triumphed, although not before suffering considerable facial damage.

Nel Tarleton and Jackie Paterson thus took the first BBBC Belts very early on. However, the fastest of the Board's new belts to be claimed permanently would be the one put up for the lightweight division. As mentioned, following Al Foreman's decision to pawn the last original belt, Walsh beat Mizler at the Empress Hall to be the first man to hold the new trophy. He held the title for almost two years but in his first defence, against the experienced Dave Crowley from Clerkenwell, he fell foul of the Liverpool Stadium 'jinx'.

The fight, though a box-office flop, was an absorbing contest, turned around in round six when Walsh sustained a cut over his left eye. After this Crowley gained in confidence and coasted to a points win. He was destined, however, to be swept aside within six months by a veritable whirlwind of the ring – Eric 'Boy' Boon, a fighter whose all-action style and hard punch would put him at the top of his profession before he was twenty years old.

In a way, the story of Boon's race to the title is also the story of Jack Solomons's entry into the big time – though as a manager rather than a promoter.

Boon, from Chatteris in Cambridgeshire, began fighting, as his nickname suggests, as a boy; like so many fighters before him he was a smith by trade – the reason, he later wrote, for his fearsome punching power. According to *Boxing*:

> When I was swinging the big hammer, my father always taught me to pull the hammer back immediately on the point of impact. That gave me greater force and greater accuracy. When I started boxing I did the same thing. My nasty nature helped too!

He entered the London scene in March 1935 fighting a draw at Solomons's Devonshire Club – a successor to the East End's Manor Hall as a testing ground for young, predominantly London talent. In fact, at fifteen years old, Boon should not have been in the ring at all, the BBBC's stipulated legal age limit being sixteen.

Nevertheless, Boon soon became a favourite at the Club; and Solomons, detecting a fighter who appeared ever eager to perform, found it convenient to use him almost relentlessly. Within four years of his Devonshire Club debut he had fought over seventy times, a statistic that rather undermines Solomons's later admission: 'I was a little scared of rushing him on too quickly.'

Soon Solomons, in his capacity as matchmaker for Sydney Hulls, then the principal promoter in Britain, was using Boon on both Harringay and the Royal Albert Hall promotions, his crash-bang style a great hit with fight fans. His break-through contest came in a non-title points win over lightweight champion Jimmy Walsh, staged out-of-doors in Boon's home-town.

In June 1938 Walsh lost his title to Dave Crowley; thus Boon v Crowley seemed a 'natural' contest for Harringay, Crowley able to draw upon his East London support, Boon certain to bring along a vociferous body of followers from the Fen country.

Boon ultimately triumphed, but not before suffering considerable damage himself. In fact, his left eye was almost closed when, in the tenth, he put Crowley down with a tremendous right uppercut – the shot that turned the fight.

Crowley survived, but in the thirteenth a series of left hooks, followed by a right cross put Crowley down for a count of nine. Upon rising, Crowley was caught by a left and a right which dropped him again, his head resting on the bottom rope – in which position he was counted out.

Two months and much managerial wrangling later, Boon was back in the Harringay ring to face Arthur Danahar, an NSC-backed boxer managed by the Club's matchmaker, John Harding, in what was considered by many to be a classic, principally because, as against Crowley, Boon was facing a consummate boxer, expert and skilful, able to give the raw youngster a boxing lesson for eight rounds, and close that damaged left eye again in the process. The impact of the fight was also increased by the fact that it would be the first-ever 'close-circuit' sports contest, transmitted by the BBC to a series of cinemas around the capital which were packed to capacity.

In the eighth round, however, came a crucial turning point, according to Harold Lewis of the *Daily Telegraph*. Boon was in a bad way – mouth and nose bleeding, his left eye practically closed, one side of his face swollen. However, following a tremendous uppercut similar to the one that settled the Crowley fight, Boon's seconds encouraged their man with cries of 'You've got him going!' At that point, according to Lewis, 'Danahar turned towards these seconds and laughed down at them. He felt so secure. He had so outboxed Boon that he had won every round – some by a wide margin. . . .'

Unfortunately, 'Some twenty seconds after Danahar had laughed, he was on the floor, for Boon again came darting in, feinted with the right, landed the left and in the same action brought his right hand like a flash in a short half-circle to the point of Danahar's exposed jaw. . . .'

Though battling back, Danahar was badly dazed; the tide had turned. Both men were now fighting toe-to-toe but Boon's superior weight of punch was destined to prevail: in the fourteenth another right put Danahar down – for the seventh time in the fight – and though he tried yet again to rise, referee Barrington-Dalby stepped between them and ended it.

'It was,' Lewis wrote, 'one of the most exhausting and punishing fights between men of this weight I can remember since the days of Kid Lewis. . . .'

Ten months on and Boon was back facing Crowley again in his third title fight in under a year. By now wartime restrictions meant that Harringay was limited to a crowd of 5,000 on a Saturday afternoon. In what turned out to be Sydney Hulls's last promotion, Boon again overcame Crowley – this time in the seventh round after a right hand had put Crowley down, and a sprained tendon forced his corner to retire him. Thus Boon had won a Lonsdale Belt outright before turning nineteen years of age!

At that moment, however, the 'pantomime' began. Solomons proceeded to make a meal out of the fact that, owing to wartime restrictions, the Board had not brought the championship belt along for Boon to take home. 'Jolly' Jack claimed that Boon had burst into tears in disappointment in the dressing-room, prompting Solomons to go back out to ringside and set up a chant of 'Where's Boon's belt?'

This and some subsequent critical press comment annoyed BBBC officials and Solomons was summoned to the Board's offices to explain his behaviour.

Because the Board would not allow press representatives to be present, Solomons ultimately refused to give an account of his behaviour and was duly suspended.

After a year or two in the 'wilderness', however, Solomons

quietly returned to the fold. Boon, too, returned to Solomons, though his career – interrupted by his enlistment in the RAF – would never quite touch the heights of those pre-war days. Boon's weight was the principal problem: he was now a welterweight but was far less effective, losing as many contests as he won.

In 1944, however, he was matched with Ronnie James in a lightweight title defence promoted by Nossie Sherman in Cardiff. Solomons later wrote that he had to be persuaded to help Boon (and no doubt take his cut), claiming that Boon was better advised to give up the game, particularly as he had suffered serious injuries early in the war as the result of a motorcycle crash.

Boon certainly struggled to get inside the lightweight limit and was subsequently KO'd by James in ten rounds. Though he battled on (in fact he only retired in 1952) and earned himself a tilt at Ernie Roderick's welterweight title in 1947, 'Boy' Boon's glory days were definitely over.

He had at least the satisfaction of possessing a belt, and when he stepped into the ring with Roderick he was facing another man who had taken a belt outright, although the two men's careers could hardly have been more of a contrast.

Roderick had also started out on his boxing career as a teenager, turning pro at seventeen in January 1931. An extremely clever boxer, he would exploit a stiff left lead with a superb right cross that ended many of his early contests inside the distance. Smooth in action with a sound defence – to many, including promoter Johnny Best, who staged many of Roderick's contests at Anfield, he seemed from the very start destined for success. Yet, unlike Boon, Roderick would serve a long apprenticeship: in fact, it would be some eight years before he got a title chance.

The welterweight competition at the time was not particularly daunting. By the time the first BBBC Belt was put up for competition, the title had passed from Londoner Dave McCleave to hard-hitting Jake Kilrain. Kilrain, whose real name was Harry Owen, was from Bellshill, close to Glasgow.

An all-action fighter, something of a rough-diamond, he specialized in body-punching – indeed, had broken the breast-bone of Dave McCleave, a superb box-fighter with a tremendous amateur record, but whose left jab had been insufficient to keep

Kilrain at bay. Kilrain had then been matched with Jack Lord at Belle Vue for the first BBBC Belt contest at welterweight.

Lord was yet another boxer who had served a long apprenticeship before getting his opportunity – indeed, it had taken him eleven long years before achieving his big chance. And in a rough, tough contest Kilrain won on points. A year later, almost to the day, Lord was being rescued from the beaches of Dunkirk.

Roderick had no such distractions when facing Kilrain in March 1939. In front of 10,000 local fans at Liverpool's Anfield stadium, he KO'd Kilrain in seven rounds to become the first Lancastrian to win the British welterweight title. Though subsequently outclassed by Henry Armstrong in a challenge for the World welterweight title, in the UK Roderick was supreme: and though he, too, joined the RAF at the outbreak of war, he was allowed sufficient time off to train and to defend his title. In July 1940 he beat Norman Snow on points at Northampton, and in September 1941 it was Arthur Danahar's turn to taste defeat on a Jack Cappall bill at the Albert Hall.

Thus Roderick's permanent belt had been won with relatively little drama; indeed, he almost won a second when Jack Solomons took him up and used him to establish the Harringay Stadium after the war as the increasingly influential promoter's power-base.

# 13

# Freddie Mills and the Rise of Solomons

During the first decade of the BBBC Belts, the heavier divisions – middle, light-heavy and heavy – provided relatively little action, principally because of a dearth of new talent and the continued dominance of veterans such as McAvoy and Harvey.

Among the middleweights, Jock McAvoy's reign extended from 1933 when he first wrested the title from old adversary Len Harvey until 1940 when, after defeating Ginger Sadd in 1939 at Belle Vue, he forfeited the crown after refusing to defend at the purse offered. This decision was prompted by the fact that his manager was now Harry Levene, who specialized in picking up the contracts of apparently 'spent' fighters and squeezing large amounts of cash from their fading careers. McAvoy thus rejected £200 out of hand, so spurning the chance of becoming the first outright winner of the middleweight BBBC Belt. Not that it mattered – he already possessed an original one.

It would be 1945 when Ernie Roderick stepped up to defeat Vince Hawkins at the Albert Hall before the title would be 'operational' again.

McAvoy had also taken the first light-heavyweight title in 1937, defeating Eddie Phillips at the Empire Pool; but an accident to his spine, incurred while riding, made training difficult and, although remaining successful at middleweight, he lost his light-heavyweight crown in April 1938 at Harringay to – inevitably – Len Harvey, who repeated the feat a year later in July 1939 at White City.

However, both men's careers were about to be halted – indeed, ended – in dramatic fashion by the same man: Freddie Mills.

In the late Thirties, Mills had been battling away on the south coast, thrilling audiences at such venues as Bournemouth Winter Gardens and Ice Rink until, spotted by Ted Broadribb in early 1940 while KO'ing Jack Powell at Reading Racetrack, his career took off. Broadribb bought Mills's contract for £200 and by 1941 he was appearing at the Albert Hall on prestigious bills – significantly, however, fighting heavyweights.

Mills was very much a two-fisted battler, lacking a clean punch, but whose non-stop aggression could overwhelm weaker opponents. He was also extremely courageous, necessarily so since most of his top-line contests were to be against men considerably heavier than himself who would often hand out unmerciful beatings. Not surprisingly, his boxing skills – and he had them – were given little opportunity to flourish in what were often battles for survival.

Broadribb's first sight of Mills – and the latter's terrific left hook – had convinced him that Mills could succeed at heavier weights. As Broadribb put it in *Fighting Is My Life*:

> I had always dreamed of handling a World champion. I had come so close to it with Farr and then missed, that I was really beginning to think with my advancing years this might well be my last chance.

Their single-minded odyssey, combined with Jack Solomons's fair-ground showmanship, would carry British boxing into a new era after the Second World War.

Broadribb's 'missed opportunity' with Farr had come in 1937 when the canny, skilful Welshman had been beaten on points by Joe Louis in the latter's second defence of his World title. Farr could have dominated the British heavyweight scene for many years but chose to exploit his US prominence – unsuccessfully as it happened – and by 1940 had virtually retired.

Farr's one notch on a Lonsdale Belt (BBBC) had come in March 1937 when, at Harringay, he had defeated the reigning British heavyweight champion Ben Foord, Foord having earlier beaten Jack Peterson, the principal British heavyweight of the Thirties.

Foord was notable mainly for his gameness, his ability to absorb punishment and his optimistic wild swinging punches that could either demolish the opposition or miss by a mile. At 6 ft 3 in and 210 lb, the South African-born Foord was popular with promoters Dickson and Hulls, both of whom had a commercial penchant for heavier men. In August 1936 he was matched with Peterson, who made him look clumsy and lumbering in the first two rounds, but in the third Foord launched a giant right hand that Peterson failed to avoid and that sent him crashing to the canvas. After two more deckings, Peterson was counted out. Foord thus became the first Commonwealth fighter to take both British and Empire titles.

It was the high point of his career; in March 1937 he was matched with Tommy Farr for the British title. It was a bout he was expected to win, being by far the bigger, more powerful man but, in a dreary contest – the very first heavyweight BBBC Belt fight – Farr won on points.

Farr was not a powerful hitter, but his crouching, weaving style made him hard to hit and, against a heavy, slow-moving man like Foord, he was able to dodge and duck, accumulating points while the champion's stamina ebbed away in wild, wasted effort.

With the chance to meet Louis, Farr then relinquished his British title (breaking in the process various contracts he had signed with Sydney Hulls, the man who had given him his big chance) and set off for the USA with Broadribb. However, the Broadribb/Farr partnership, never an easy one and bedevilled with argument and acrimony, foundered after the Louis defeat.

Farr went his own way; Broadribb, financially secure, in his own words, 'just drifted along . . . so thoroughly unhappy about boxing that for a time I felt that I didn't want to know about it all. . . .' A car accident put him completely out of action for some months and when he attempted to rebuild his managerial career he found himself cold-shouldered: 'Phone-calls were a waste of time. I felt as if I was someone who might well have been set aside labelled, "to be contacted when needed".'

Thus, what boxers suffered week in week out, Broadribb was now enduring for the first time in his long and colourful career. Fortunately, when he lighted upon Mills, the desire and the opportunity returned.

Mills proceeded to take the fight scene by storm, fighting as often as once a fortnight until, in December 1941, at the Albert Hall, he gave veteran Jack London three stone and beat him on points.

In February 1942, again at the Albert Hall, he was matched with Jock McAvoy in an eliminator for the British light-heavy-weight title – this only Mills's eighth fight for Broadribb. The much-touted and eagerly awaited showdown, in front of 4,500 spectators, was hardly thirty seconds old, however, when McAvoy, following a left hook from Mills, gripped his back and gasped: 'My spine. Hold it Freddie, I can't go on. I've hurt my back.'

The referee helped McAvoy back to his corner, and signalled that Mills was the winner – amid boos and catcalls. It tran-spired that McAvoy had pulled a lumbar muscle, perhaps a reac-tion to his earlier horse-riding injury.

If that fight had been something of a sensation, Mills's next, against Len Harvey for the light-heavyweight title, was even more dramatic.

The fight, on 20 June 1942, was staged by part-time promoter John Muldoon at White Hart Lane, Tottenham Hotspur FC's ground, before an audience of at least 30,000. Almost all the principal actors in the drama were then in the RAF: Harvey was a pilot officer, Mills was a sergeant, Muldoon was an AC and referee Eugene Henderson was a corporal.

Harvey was the clear favourite among the boxing cognoscenti; although thirty-five years old, he was considered sufficiently experienced and skilful to be able to outwit his younger, more impulsive challenger, and the first round went according to those predictions, with Harvey scoring cleanly and regularly with his left, Mills hustling to no obvious effect.

The second round began, however, with Harvey's surprising decision to take the fight to Mills. They stood toe-to-toe in the centre of the ring, trading blows and, as Harvey stepped back momentarily, Mills launched a looping left hook that put Harvey down for a count of eight.

The entire stadium, it seemed, was suddenly on its feet in a frenzy of excitement as Harvey, white-faced and shaken, was backed up by Mills throwing rights and lefts, all of them direct hits to the jaw, the final blow sweeping Harvey off his feet and through the ropes. As Jack Birtley described it in his *Freddie Mills*:

'There was utter pandemonium as the stricken champ slithered onto the ringside press benches scattering typewriters and papers among the scrambling reporters.' He was counted out, still clambering onto the ring apron.

It was a dramatic end to Harvey's long and distinguished career as Britain's premier fighter. For Mills it was the start of an action-packed few years that would see him lose more title fights than he would win, though that elusive World title would ultimately arrive.

His last big fight before the end of the war, however, was a tilt at Jack London's British heavyweight title which Len Harvey had relinquished. The fight, at Belle Vue before 7,000 spectators paying over £10,000, was a tremendous scrap considered by many as the best heavyweight title bout for a decade.

It was a fight in which both men took a great deal of punishment, London in the early stages, Mills after round ten. London used a straight left and clubbing right hands in a vain attempt to pound Mills into submission; Mills simply absorbed whatever was thrown at him and came ploughing on with his own two-fisted assaults. Ultimately, in such an unscientific encounter, weight and strength told: London switched to battering Mills's body in the later stages and Mills gradually became less and less effective, though earning cheers for his courage.

Although Mills would concentrate on the light-heavyweight division in terms of World titles, at home he would press on, after the war, in a vain attempt to win the heavyweight title. Whether he ought to have been fighting at anything above middleweight remains a matter for debate.

The career of Freddie Mills was a significant factor in the rise and rise of Jack Solomons who would, within the space of a few short post-war years, become British boxing's supremo – as powerful and influential as anyone since 'Peggy' Bettinson and the NSC glory days.

A promoter needs star turns, of course, and in Mills and later Bruce Woodcock – who became British heavyweight champion in 1945 – Solomons had the use of two of British boxing's most charismatic fighters, at weights that had always proved popular in the UK, no matter what the quality.

It was Woodcock, the young man from Doncaster, who helped provide Solomons with his first big breakthrough when he took on and beat title holder Jack London at White Hart Lane in the first big post-war boxing promotion.

In the late Thirties, Solomons was no more than a small-time operator in a scene dominated, following the promotional demise of Jeff Dickson, by men such as Wembley Arena founder and promoter Arthur Elvin, John Harding, NSC matchmaker and manager operating out of the Empress Hall, Earls Court, and Sydney Hulls who, following a period when he ran shows from Crystal Palace and acted as matchmaker for Elvin, opened Harringay Stadium to big-time boxing in 1937.

In 1939, however, Hulls resigned from the BBBC following disagreements over policy and played little further part in boxing. Illness restricted his operations from the 1940s on and he died, aged just fifty-three, in 1952. A popular and imaginative promoter, his shows were always meticulously run and his reputation for honesty and fairness made his premature death a sad event in the hard-bitten world of pro-boxing. His earlier withdrawal from big-time promotions, however, meant that a vacuum had opened up during the war-years – a vacuum that Solomons had rapidly moved to fill.

Solomons's only big promotional foray in the 1930s had come in 1934 when he had joined a syndicate (which included Joe Morris and Ted Broadribb) that had put on the British bantamweight title bout between Johnny King and Dick Corbett at Clapton Greyhound Track.

As a financial gamble, it was a failure and Solomons turned back to developing his interest in the small Devonshire Club – just a sideline while he built up his retail fish business and later the bookmaking enterprises that would cushion him in later years as he launched out in flamboyant style, wheeling and dealing for World title fights.

The Devonshire Hall was a small place that never put on anything more important than a Southern Area title but it was crucial in helping to establish the web of grass-roots contacts that would later prove essential in maintaining Solomons at the top.

His role as manager of Eric Boon led him into close association with Hulls at Harringay – plus friendship with Frank Gentle,

Greyhound Racing Association supremo and 'landlord' at Harringay, not to mention White City. It was through his association with Hulls that Solomons also established a friendship and partnership with Sam Burns, a crucial player in his rise to prominence.

Burns had been in boxing since childhood, being the son of boxer Syd Burns. Burns junior was first a journalist, then publicity manager for Jeff Dickson and later John Harding. He was also a boxing manager (Arthur Danahar had been one of his protégés) and when the war began he became general manager at the Albert Hall for John Muldoon and later bookmaker Jack Cappall. Both Muldoon and Cappall, on Burns's recommendation, used Solomons as a matchmaker; Solomons was keen, however, to buy into the promotional scene. Muldoon had always rebuffed him, but Cappall agreed to join forces with Solomons, only for Solomons to set up the Bruce the Woodcock v Jack London heavyweight title fight – a match so expensive that Cappall, with his own considerable debts to settle, was forced to hand the whole enterprise over to Solomons. Although the Woodcock v London promotion was no great financial success, the fact was that he was 'in' ('and I meant to stay,' he later wrote).

The war over, Solomons moved fast to exploit his foothold. He knew, as everyone else did, that a 'boom' in sports of all kinds would occur: the problem was to obtain sufficient quality 'product' and secure venues in which to display and 'sell' that product.

In late 1945 Solomons made uncomfortable, sometimes dangerous, trips to war-ravaged Europe, wangling his way to and fro via military aircraft, chartered planes, dislocated railways, buses, jeeps – anything that moved; and by dint of shrewd and often bold wheeler-dealing he established outposts in Sweden and France, at first finding work abroad for boxers such as Ernie Roderick, Nel Tarleton, Jackie Paterson, etc. as well as employing Europeans like Marcel Cerdan and Theo Medina.

Within a year or so he was using those same boxers on attractive boxing bills at a variety of venues in the UK. In December 1945 he even managed to get to New York and engaged in the tough business of trying to establish his credentials in the face of fierce competition from the likes of Mike Jacobs.

Solomons was thus prepared to go to places no one else considered going – cajoling, pleading, shouting, bribing, whatever it took – and his ultimate success was a triumph for hard-nosed market-trader methods plus an instinctive flair for publicity, good or bad.

There was also, inevitably, a streak of ruthlessness running through his work. In 1946 Freddie Mills and Bruce Woodcock were orchestrated to provide a series of quick-fire sensational contests involving top-line American fighters Gus Lesnevitch and Joe Baksi which had the fans flocking to Harringay, now Solomons's principal venue.

Mills was badly beaten by Lesnevitch, an experience that left him ill and dazed for weeks afterwards. He later claimed he recalled nothing of the fight after being knocked down in the second round (the referee stopped it in the tenth); he suffered blinding headaches and slurred speech and each morning had to be woken from a sleep that was, he said, more like a deep coma.

Woodcock, meanwhile, was in New York, also being badly beaten and cut by one Tami Mauriello. Yet less than a month later both men were in the Harringay ring to face each other in a punishing twelve-round points defeat for Mills.

Within six months, Mills was once more at Harringay, facing an even heavier man – Joe Baksi, number five heavyweight contender in the world – who pounded and battered him to a six-round stoppage. This was the fight when Mills pulled himself out after arguing with his manager Broadribb, who had wanted him to continue.

The press was scathing. Frank Butler in the *Daily Express* wrote: 'The fight was a massacre and must not happen again,' while the paper's editorial asked: 'Who staged last night's big fight? It contributed nothing to sport . . . Mills was nothing more than a chopping block.'

Solomons commented: 'I reflected that if the reporters never howled, I should never eat. . . .'

Solomons's real anger, however, would be aimed at the BBBC and *its* criticism of the Mills and Baksi contest, implying, incorrectly, that the Board had warned against the fight.

The Board, or rather Charles Donmall, had for years been a particular thorn in Solomons's flesh. The latter's control over the domestic scene would be crowned, therefore, in 1949 when he was instrumental, due to his chairmanship of the Southern Area Council of the Board, in having Donmall removed as secretary.

Solomons could not have achieved this without help, of course, and the groundswell of discontent and criticism aimed at Donmall and his methods had been gathering force ever since the end of the war.

The thrust of much of the criticism concerned democracy and accountability: the fact that there had been no AGM since 1939 and that no accounts had been published since 1940. But a more emotive issue in the early post-war period which would have a great impact on British championships – that of the 'colour-bar' – had revealed the Board to be insensitive and unnecessarily secretive, not to say wildly out of touch with conditions and assumptions in post-war Britain. It was this issue that probably did more than anything else to undermine Donmall's standing in the eyes of the press and public.

The question of coloured British citizens fighting for British titles had been raised with the Board as early as January 1946 by the Colonial Department of the incoming Labour Government. Pro-boxing was now the only sport with such a 'bar' enshrined in its regulations: even the amateurs made no such distinction and the success of Randolph Turpin in winning two successive ABA titles at welter and middle respectively in 1945 and 1946 raised the spectre of another Len Johnson situation.

In 1947 the issue virtually exploded in the Board's face. Colonial Secretary Creech Jones said in a written answer in the Commons: 'I regard the colour-bar as quite unjustified. I hope the Board may be persuaded to alter their practice and with that in view further representations will be made to them.'

Prior to this, the Board had always tended to hide behind vague allusions to Home Office approval of its stance – that black v white championship matches might lead to civil disorder in the Empire, etc. Donmall's last public pronouncement on the matter, however, had clearly been xenophobic: 'It is only right that a small country such as ours should have championships restricted to boxers of white parents – otherwise we might be faced with a situation where all our British titles are held by coloured Empire boxers.'

Such sentiments were clearly irrelevant in 1946 and swift action ought to have ensued. Instead, following a terse announcement by the Board in July 1947 that a colour-bar regulation 'modification' would be published 'in due course', Donmall appeared on BBC Radio to be interviewed by Peter Wilson and put up a poor showing, refusing to answer direct questions concerning the issue.

In September another announcement was made to the effect that the colour-bar would soon be removed, but too much damage had been done to the image of the Board. *Boxing News* in October 1947 published a front page editorial under a banner headline: 'Tell The Public', in which it pressed home criticism of the Board's 'dictatorial' powers which were 'ill-fitting to the democratic age that we are now living in'. The vast majority of boxers, managers, promoters, etc., the editorial continued, 'have no democratic voice in the rules

Advertisement in *Boxing*, 1948

or ruling of the controlling body', and the colour-bar question had been 'decided by the administrative stewards whose identity and credentials in the boxing world are not generally known'.

Once more, alternative administrative bodies were being mooted; the trouble and turmoil of the mid-Thirties threatened to bubble up and engulf the sport.

Although an AGM was at last held in mid-1948 which satisfied most people that the financial affairs of the Board were being conducted efficiently and although Jack Solomons closed the meeting by paying tribute to the president (J. Onslow Fane), the chairman and the secretary, relations between Board members, stewards and the professional rank and file were strained and destined to reach breaking point before too long.

The following year, in response to a proposal from the Southern Area Council that, in future, all area councils should be composed of people with a financial interest in the sport, the Board put forward a counter-proposal that all area councils be composed of non-financially interested parties. 'You must realize,' a Board official said, 'that the dismissal of non-financially interested persons from the game will result in boxing being controlled by persons whose main object is financial gain and who may subsequently be tempted to sacrifice the sport for their own financial ends. . . .'

With hindsight, these words could be seen as prophetic. Unfortunately, the discussion in 1948 was dominated more by personalities than broad principles. For instance, a proposal made by the Board at the 1948 AGM that a pension plan be set up for Board employees (i.e. Donmall and his secretaries) appeared to anger almost everyone. 'What about a pension for the boxers?' asked Peter Kane, the boxers' representative, with much vigorous nodding of heads from philanthropically minded promoters and managers. One senses that if the scheme had been intended for anyone else than Donmall it would have caused barely a ripple of protest.

A vigorous campaign was conducted against the Board's proposals, co-ordinated by the newly formed British Boxing Promoters' Association and the British Boxing Managers' Guild. (The latter had Sam Burns as chairman, Ted Broadribb as financial secretary and its offices just happened to be 41 Great Windmill Street, Jack Solomons's West End headquarters.)

The defeat of the Board's proposals spelled the end for Donmall. On 20 December 1949, the General Joint Committee of the BBBC announced that it had decided to terminate Donmall's appointment and, while explaining that it could not discuss the reason for the change, J. Onslow Fane, chairman of the Board, paid tribute to Donmall, describing him as a 'great personal friend'.

Donmall himself was reported to be 'shocked and hurt by the action of the stewards'. It had clearly been a battle of wills and the Board had decided to sacrifice Donmall in the interests of some kind of peace. Ray Clarke, then working in Donmall's office, recalled the sense of shock and unhappiness at the manner of Donmall's departure:

Promoter Jack Solomons and his supporters virtually told the

## A MESSAGE TO ALL LICENCE HOLDERS OF THE BRITISH BOXING BOARD OF CONTROL (1929)

IS YOUR LIVELIHOOD **PROFESSIONAL BOXING** ?

## IF SO, ARE YOU AWARE OF THE FOLLOWING FACTS?

1 That at the last Annual General Meeting of the Board of Control, the Stewards put forward a proposal to create a fund to pay PENSIONS to the administrative staff of the Board and their dependants (i.e., the secretary, clerks, typists, etc.). No mention was made in the proposal to cover BOXERS.

2 This proposal when put to the vote was HEAVILY DEFEATED by your ELECTED representatives.

3 During the discussion PETER KANE (boxers' representative) said : "*If anyone deserves a pension it is the boxer.*" With which statement we heartily agree.

4 The Stewards put forward another proposal to the effect that in future all AREA COUNCILS shall be composed of NON-FINANCIALLY interested persons, duly elected by licence holders.

5 MR. JOHNNY BEST stated that such a rule would deal a death-blow to boxing for all time.

6 This proposal, when put to the vote, was ALSO HEAVILY DEFEATED by YOUR representatives.

7 The Chairman of the Board has announced that the Stewards would take a ballot on all licence holders with the idea of getting this defeat reversed.

8 If the Stewards do not win—*they have threatened to resign* ! ! ! In other words—they say, in effect, that YOU, the licence holders, do not know what is best for you.

## OUR ANSWER

9 PENSIONS : We have no objection to a Pension Scheme being introduced PROVIDED such a scheme is for the BOXER.

10 AREA COUNCILS : For the past TWENTY years boxers, referees, managers, promoters, timekeepers, seconds, whips, in fact all categories, have elected their own representatives to sit on Area Councils.

11 This method has been the ONLY way by which licence holders have had a voice in conducting their own affairs.

12 If this rule has stood the test of time, if it has been good for five, ten, fifteen, twenty years, why has it suddenly become a bad rule in the twenty-first year ? Only the Stewards say so.

13 We say : KEEP TO THE EXISTING METHOD—let the professionals look after professional boxing in Area Councils—not amateurs who do not have the knowledge.

14 Remember it is the professionals who have taken the Board out of debt and also provided the present funds of over £30,000—IT IS YOUR MONEY.

## Don't be Misled!

### WHEN YOU RECEIVE YOUR POLL CARD

### VOTE

# "NO"

Issued by a Joint Committee of the BRITISH BOXING PROMOTERS' ASSOCIATION, BRITISH BOXING MANAGERS' GUILD, and a gathering of LICENSED REFEREES.

stewards that unless they got rid of Donmall they could expect a vote of no-confidence at the next AGM. And I'm sorry to say the Board chickened out. When the move came to oust him, he found he had no support. A lot of people who had been treated in a manner in which they thought they shouldn't have been treated all ganged up against him. He hated the press and they reacted accordingly. Relations were very bad. However, the way he went caused a mini-revolt at the Board offices. We weren't happy with the manner of his dismissal. It was a power struggle.

# 14

# Before the TV Age

In the decade that followed the ending of the Second World War, the pro-boxing scene would experience many changes, not least the swift replacement of pre-war men, many of whose careers had been extended unnaturally due to the dearth of young challengers eager and able enough to take their places. The Combined Services had monopolized the lives of most fit young men during the war and National Service would continue to dog the careers of pro-boxers until the early 1960s, but with the cessation of hostilities there would come a flood of raw young talent into 'civvy street' keen to make up for lost time.

However, as the 1950s progressed there were to be fewer full-time boxers on show, mainly because the opportunity to fight each week or even each fortnight would no longer be available. Small-hall boxing shows failed to return in their earlier profusion – indeed their numbers would steadily decline. Explanations varied – swingeing entertainment taxes, the gradual destruction of old working-class inner-city districts, or, probably more crucially, changing recreation habits of an increasingly affluent and more educated population.

Interestingly, fistic skills would continue to be inculcated in the traditional way by the scores of old-timers who still operated in small gyms up and down the country, some going back to pre-war days. One such was Professor W. Klein's Olympic Gymnasium situated in a Westminster basement in Fitzroy Street. Successor to, among others, the Ring Gym in Camberwell, it was presided over by eighty-seven-year-old Bill Klein, ex-trapeze artist, wrestler and weightlifter who had learned the trade from 'Bat' Mullins and had looked after scores of pre-First World War fighters such as Gunner Moir, Tom Causer and Bombardier Billy Wells. Jack Solomons had brought 'Boy' Boon to him just before the Second World War and now, in the early Fifties, he could still be found tucked away at the end of the gym by a crackling fire behind the little café counter, a cap pulled down over his head and a mug of tea warming his hands.

Klein and his ilk would disappear as the decade progressed, but these post-war fighters would be the last to have direct contact with a venerable past, of bare-knuckle men and old-time wrestlers and NSC habitués. They would also be the last generation of fighters to have had any extensive experience of the boxing booths – those garish and gory institutions that, although continuing until the late Seventies, were already vanishing, along with the social patterns that had produced and sustained them.

Jack Solomons, meanwhile, would rapidly become the most powerful man in British boxing since the heyday of 'Peggy' Bettinson and the old NSC. In many ways, Solomons was utterly appropriate for the 1950s, a period characterized by excessive red-tape – through which Solomons loved to slice – and petty bureaucracy – which he enjoyed bulldozing.

More importantly, in a period of shortages and austerity, Solomons provided glitter and glamour, his Harringay and White City shows being the equivalents of a series of West End first nights, with celebrities, fanfares, spotlights and a definite sense of spine-tingling occasion.

He was a kind of fistic Lew Grade, his promotions borrowing from two distinct traditions: New York's Madison Square Garden (cigars, wisecracks and glamorous women) and the East End's Wonderland (Cockney-Jewish wit, whelks and pantomime staging). With his tight authoritarian control over even the minutest of promotional details, his concern for the best of behaviour (ringside betting prohibited) and his strict observation of the necessary properties (evening dress was obligatory for a Solomons show) he managed to satisfy just about everyone.

Moreover, he put British boxing firmly back on the world boxing map, and though the home-grown material was probably not quite of US class, his imaginative matchmaking and unrivalled ability to persuade top American boxers to appear in British rings certainly helped the British game overcome its inferiority complex, born of the long barren inter-war period.

Those Harringay nights would represent the high-point of British boxing's pre-television days – a medium Solomons viewed with understandable suspicion, well aware of how it had all but destroyed traditional promoters like himself in the States. In that, at least, both he and the BBBC saw eye to eye. As J. Onslow Fane, chairman of the Board, put it in *Boxing* in 1952:

> There can be no doubt but that television has increased the boxing interest in America but it has also cut deeply into attendances. I have come to the conclusion that it is not advisable to open the field to television. It is definitely not advisable to televise major boxing contests. . . .

It was a position that would come under ever-increasing threat, particularly when commercial television entered the field in 1955.

As a consequence, however, the champions Solomons promoted in the late Forties and early Fifties remained virtually untouched by the glamour bestowed by television. In fact, the majority of top fighters remained reassuringly 'normal', holding down industrial jobs for the most part throughout their careers, their modest purse-money hardly altering their day-to-day lives to any great extent.

Take the middleweight champions of the period. Vince Hawkins, from Salisbury, received £750 for winning the British title from Ernie Roderick in October 1946, which became £500 after manager, seconds and trainers had been paid. Thus, throughout his career, as reported in *Boxing*, he continued working on the railway: 'Early shift was 4 am to midday, go home, wash, change, then train. Late shift was midday to eight so I trained in the mornings. . . .'

Albert Finch, the 'Croydon Woodpecker', who tussled with the famous Turpin brothers during 1949–50, trained for his fights by loading and unloading the lorries of his father's haulage firm, while Gordon Hazell and Johnny Sullivan, who clashed in September 1954, were heirs to fast-fading fistic traditions.

Hazell's father had been an old-time wrestler who had fought George Hackenschmidt, physical culturist and body-builder of

Programme cartoon by Roy Ullyett, 1950

the pre-First World War era, and Gordon followed in his father's footsteps in terms of muscle development: golden-haired, bronzed, he was a 'pocket Adonis' who might well have been a big hit on TV had the medium been as big an influence as it is today. Instead, for much of his early career, he worked in a cigarette factory.

Sullivan, meanwhile, from Preston, was the son of 'Battling Sullivan', a renowned booth fighter who by the 1950s ran his own booth in the North and Midlands. Sullivan recalled in *Boxing*: 'I was born on the fairgrounds. Right in the middle of a circus. The old man had a boxing booth attached to it – we were still babies when he had us giving exhibitions in the booth.'

Pat McAteer, who defeated Sullivan in June 1955, was a maintenance fitter at Wrexham Colliery. His daily diary was as follows: 'Rise at 5.30 with mother's help; roadwork until 6.30; return home for breakfast; 7.00 leave by car for Gresford Colliery, Wrexham, to clock-on for 8 o'clock. Clock-off at 4 o'clock; motor home, rest for half an hour, after tea leave for training, four nights a week . . . .'

Birkenhead-based McAteer was extremely popular up north and would win a Lonsdale Belt outright without once appearing inside a London ring.

As for the welterweights, Henry Hall – who took the title in November 1949 – was a carefree blacksmith's striker at a Sheffield steelworks and distantly related to Iron Hague. His title bought him a year in the modest spotlight. It gave him, according to *Boxing*, 'time to buy a modern home, and a motor-car which takes my young wife and two kiddies into the country'.

Hall's successor, Eddie Thomas, worked an open-cast mine with his family, while Cliff Curvis – title holder in 1952 – strengthened his arms by rowing up and down Swansea docks plumbing for sandbanks while working for the Great Western Railway. Wally Thom, whom Curvis had defeated, continued to work as an £8 a week docker throughout his boxing career.

He explained in *Boxing*:

One of the reasons I ever decided to turn professional was because I was out of work for six months with severe cartilage trouble. I had to claim public assistance which I did not like doing. I decided then to become a professional so I could put some money away for a rainy day.

Thom's identification with local shipyard workers in Liverpool and Birkenhead was total, and his ability to fill the Liverpool Stadium whenever he fought was tribute both to his fighting skills as well as his modesty and lack of overweening ego. He was not quite so enthusiastically thought of in the south – partly because, unlike his other welterweight colleagues, he rarely appeared in London, although two of his three Lonsdale Belt victories would take place at Harringay.

By the mid-Fifties, both middle and welterweight belts 'launched' after the war had therefore come to rest permanently in Liverpool with McAteer and Thom, miner and docker respectively, emphasizing the strength of the non-metropolitan post-war boxing scene. Thus, although Solomons's London venues promoted some thirty-three out of eighty British title fights between 1946 and 1958, traditional centres such as Liverpool (under Johnny Best), Glasgow (with Sam Docherty), Northern Ireland (Bob Gardner), Nottingham (Reg King) and Leicester (Joe Jacobs) all took a reasonable share of the spoils.

No surprise then that a superb British champion such as Ronnie Clayton could contest nine of his thirteen title fights outside the capital: indeed, during the early years of his career he rarely appeared south of Watford, even though he received the *Boxing News* silver award in 1949 for outstanding achievement to the sport.

He was, in many ways, the typical Fifties champion: a quiet family man with sensible investments (car-hire firm, gymnasium), his principal pleasure being a dance with his wife at the Tower Ballroom, Blackpool. With RAF regulation black curls falling over his forehead, he was the model sportsman: likeable, professional in all he did, his steady, upright style and stiff left lead taking him to two outright Lonsdale Belt wins.

Oddly, Clayton was sometimes criticized for a lack of 'colour' and for being a tepid performer. Lucien Sharp, however, wrote in *Boxing*: 'His appeal is to those who discern and delight in the shrewder, more shapely arts of the sport – the creation, detection and split-second seizure of openings, the timing, the balance, the intuition that turns tight defence into explosive attack.'

Born in Blackpool in 1923, a sheet-metal worker at a gasworks, he became a mechanic in the Fleet Air Arm during the war which interrupted a boxing career begun in 1941. From 1946, guided by his father, he rose steadily through the fly, bantam and feather-weight ranks, winning fifty-two, losing just seven before attaining contender status in 1947. Nel Tarleton then retired and Clayton found himself matched with Al Phillips, the Aldgate Tiger, for the vacant featherweight title.

Phillips was one of the last representatives of a long and honour-able tradition: a member of the Jewish Lads Brigade, from the beginning of his career he wore the Jewish Star of David on his trunks in the style of the Jewish East Enders of the 1930s.

A merchant seaman, he fought before the war for Jack Solo-mons at the Devonshire Club and travelled to the West Country in boxing booths, a rough, tough fighter, half of whose sixty-odd victories had come inside the distance. He had already fought Tarleton for the title, his challenge having ended when he sprained his ankle. He then KO'd Cliff Curvis to retain his contender status in 1946 and, while awaiting another championship shot, took on British Guyanan Cliff Anderson in a controversial Euro-pean featherweight championship fight at the Albert Hall.

Anderson lost but most spectators and the press thought he had won. In the return, Phillips went down from what was claimed to be a low blow and the luckless Anderson was disqualified.

Two months earlier Phillips had snatched the European crown from Ray Famechon, no less, also on a foul. Thus he took the ring against Clayton in possession of two titles. The thrilling fight was held at the Anfield Football Ground in a rainswept ring. In the early rounds Phillips was the better at inside work and in the third he suddenly cracked an overarm right which landed flush on Clayton's jaw to throw him back on the ropes, dazed and looking as if he might fall. Phillips, however, was unable to finish it.

In the seventh, Clayton suffered a split eyebrow and a severe cut underneath but he kept the pace, holding his own in punch-for-punch rallies until gradually Phillips grew weary. By means of long-range boxing, Clayton gradually drew away on points and eventually won a close but clear decision.

Clayton then dazzled Johnny Malloy to defeat at the Nottingham Ice Rink and a year later came to London's Albert Hall on a Jack Cappall bill to meet Jim Kenny for outright possession of the belt.

Twenty KOs out of thirty-nine career wins suggested terrific hitting power on Kenny's part: indeed, the twenty-one-year-old colliery worker from Armadale in Scotland was expected by many to carry too much fire-power for the older man. Yet it was Kenny who was put through the ropes in the fourth round and onto the timekeeper's table! Clayton went on to win handily on points.

His second belt came with less alarms: Phillips defeated again in February 1951 at Nottingham, Dai Davies in June 1952 at Abergavenny and lastly, at Harringay in May 1953, Londoner Freddie King – a full eight years Clayton's junior. King was clearly the crowd's favourite judging by the noise that greeted his entrance, yet Clayton needed no more than four rounds, catching King with a sharp right that sent the Wandsworth boy down for the full count.

Aged thirty, Clayton was presented with his second belt and London belatedly recognized him.

A year later, in June 1954, another Londoner with a great following – Sammy McCarthy – forced Clayton to concede that age was catching up with him. Gilbert Odd recalled the exchange between the two men as they met, centre-ring, before the fight that would see Clayton lose his title at last:

'Evening, Sam,' Clayton said. 'Let's have a nice fight.'

'Yes, of course, Mr Clayton,' McCarthy replied.

Clayton had been able to sustain a successful career without the help of Solomons or TV: the regular large audiences at his numerous contests (113 pro-fights in a thirteen-year career) ensured his independence – a feature of Fifties-boxing in the North, and certainly of the 'Celtic Fringe' north of the border. Men such as Peter Keenan and Charlie Hill won three belts between them, performing before sell-out crowds almost exclusively in Glasgow, while across the Irish Sea Rinty Monaghan, John Kelly and 'Spider' Kelly took part in six title fights at King's

MAY 21, 1954       BOXING NEWS     5

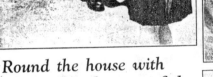

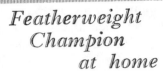

## Featherweight Champion at home

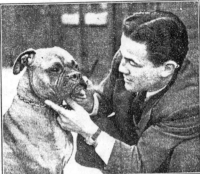

## Round the house with Ronnie, between fights

*Above:* A keen photographer, Ronnie Clayton takes a snapshot of his daughter Veronica in the courtyard of his Blackpool home. *Top right:* **One boxer to another, Ronnie with his dog Dinky.** *Below:* **The champion puts in some light work on his Austin.** *Bottom right:* Clayton is proud of the two Lonsdale Belts he has won outright and enjoys keeping them polished up.

Hall, Belfast where the fierce loyalty of supporters made travelling south an irrelevance.

Gilbert Odd once remarked how Keenan always looked 'fresh as a newly minted coin from top to toe with a matching demeanour that he maintained from first to last'.

The little Scot took the bantamweight title from Londoner Danny O'Sullivan, successfully defended against Bobby Boland and then defeated Birkenhead's Frankie Williams at Paisley in January 1953 to take his first Lonsdale Belt outright.

The Northern Ireland connection then began. John Kelly, with 10,000 Irishmen roaring him on, defeated Keenan and looked set to reign for many a year. Fight scribe Jim Davy wrote in *The Irish Press*:

> Kelly has all the attributes of a World champion. He is beautifully balanced on his feet, carries a KO punch in both hands and has a cunning defence. He feints, jabs, rides a punch as well as any fighter I have ever seen and, in addition has the most important attribute of all – a boxer's instinct to do the right thing at the right time. . . .

Sadly, French Algerian Robert Cohen shattered the image with a devastating three-round KO of Kelly, soon after which the Irishman lost his British title to Keenan. Kelly's career was all but over.

Keenan, meanwhile, with victories over George O'Neill in Belfast and John Smillie in Glasgow, earned himself a second belt and would later move into promotion on his own account. He would bring illustrious fighters such as Sugar Ray Robinson and Willie Pastrano to Glasgow as well as promote the title careers of Chic Calderwood and John 'Cowboy' McCormack – but he would be fighting a losing battle as Scottish boxing gradually declined in the late Fifties.

By contrast, John Kelly's meteoric rise and fall, Freddie Gilroy's triumphant capture of the bantamweight crown, not to mention yet another Kelly ('Spider') at featherweight – all were evidence of a resurgence of Northern Irish boxing when King's Hall, Belfast replaced King's Hall, Belle Vue as the home of diminutive champions.

Indeed, for a time it seemed that the fly, bantam and feather-weight titles were mere prizes in a private battle being waged between those two shipbuilding giants Glasgow and Belfast – a titanic clash epitomized by Cambuslang shipyard engineer Charlie Hill battling to defeat first Billy 'Spider' Kelly, then Jimmy Brown, both of Belfast, before defeating fellow Scot Chic Brogan at Cathkin Park, Glasgow to become the first Scottish feather-weight to take a belt outright since Tancy Lee back in 1919.

Not that Jack Solomons ignored the lighter weights entirely: the remarkable career of Londoner Terry Allen demonstrates the opposite. Allen, a Harringay favourite, turned pro in 1942 but only came to prominence after the war had ended, taking the Southern Area title in 1948.

He then met World champion Rinty Monaghan twice, beating him in a non-title fight, and then drawing when Monaghan's titles were at stake. In April 1950, however, Allen won both World and European titles at Harringay, and it was only after losing both that he finally took the British flyweight title, defeating Scotsman Vic Herman on points at Nottingham.

Oddly, despite his world pedigree, the annexation of a perma-nent belt would take three years and not a little controversy. In fact, he lost the title on his first defence to the veteran Geordie Teddy Gardner. Following Gardner's retirement, Allen was matched with Eric Marsden of St Helens at Harringay.

Marsden boxed well to build up a reasonable lead by the sixth round but then sustained a bad cut that forced him to retire. When next the two men met, in February 1954, again at Harring-gay, Marsden appeared to be winning the fight – indeed, he had Allen down in the third and fourth rounds and was consistently hurting him with well-timed rights to the jaw. In the fifth round, however, totally without intention, Marsden connected with Allen's nether regions, sending the champion squirming to the canvas. Referee Ike Powell directed Marsden to his corner and awarded the bout to Allen.

It was such a disappointing ending to the fight that the custom-ary awarding of the Lonsdale Belt was diplomatically waived.

# 15

## Jewels in Solomons's Crown

From the end of the war to the late Fifties Jack Solomons wielded power in the narrow world of British boxing primarily because he commanded the prominent London stages and, as a consequence, was able to operate on international terms. Once he had succeeded in tying up the availability of major London venues – Harringay, Earls Court, White City – suitable alternative space for mounting big shows was practically nil and it would be a decade or so before anyone remotely comparable in stature or influence would challenge him.

As we have seen, however, British championship boxing was not quite the monopoly that Nat Fleischer claimed it was in 1952 when he wrote in *The Ring*: 'Small promoters . . . cannot use big-time talent unless permission is granted for their use by the promoters holding an exclusive contract on the services of such talent.'

In London itself, the number of promoters who continued to make a living were few: indeed, smaller London promoters managed only five British title fights between 1946 and 1958 – the period of Solomons's greatest influence.

Clothing manufacturer Benny Schmidt did try, briefly and unsuccessfully, in the late Forties to compete with Solomons for top bouts, which he planned to mount at Olympia; but for the most part men like Stan Baker (Streatham Ice Rink), Jim Wicks (Wandsworth Stadium and elsewhere) and Jack Cappall (at the Albert Hall) were content to jog along, staging regular, modest programmes that attracted predominantly local audiences.

The only serious attempt to match Solomons for any sustained period came when two men – Ronnie Ezra and David Braitman

– who, having secured the NSC's old venue, the Empress Hall, launched themselves in 1949 with an ambitious programme featuring Marcel Cerdan (then World middleweight champion) versus Dick Turpin. Also on the bill were up-and-coming heavier men Don Cockell and Jack Gardner.

But the Braitman/Ezra partnership lasted little more than three years, squeezed out by Solomons and undermined by the Entertainment Tax. Their venue was passed on to Freddie Mills who would last until 1956 but who was clearly financed by Solomons. Braitman and Ezra managed just two title fights: a Commonwealth featherweight match involving Ronnie Clayton, and a European title bout with Billy Thompson. Mills, meanwhile, managed just one British title match – the lightweight clash between Joe Lucy and Tommy McGovern.

Not until 1956 when Harry Levene and Arthur Elvin reopened the Wembley Arena to the sport would competition become serious. Levene's first title bout would be another lightweight Lonsdale Belt match, this time between Lucy and Sammy McCarthy. In fact, there were good reasons why the lightweight division suited the capital's second rank of promoters.

With the fly, bantams and featherweights more or less monopolized by regional promoters, and with welters, middles and heavies snapped up either by Solomons or by northern promoters with venues such as Belle Vue, Manchester and the Stadium, Liverpool, only the lightweights remained viable in terms of local attraction and affordable price.

For some ten years the division and the belts were scrapped over by four men: two Londoners – Tommy McGovern and Joe Lucy; a Mancunian, based in London – Frank Johnson; and a Yorkshire-based Geordie from Hickleton Main with a London manager – Billy Thompson. Of this colourful, sometimes controversial, quartet, Thompson and Lucy would win a belt outright while Johnson would come desperately close.

An ex-miner, the stocky, curly haired Thompson was an honest, completely unspoiled character: a physical culturist and greyhound owner, he felt a great sense of responsibility towards his pit-worker supporters on whose behalf he often said he was fighting. In fact, he had turned pro in order to support his family, his

Programme illustration *c* 1951

## PROFESSIONAL BOXING at the EMPIRE POOL

### FIRST TIME FOR NEARLY TWENTY YEARS!

*presented by* HARRY LEVENE

**TUESDAY, JUNE 26th, at 7.45 p.m.**

| LIGHTWEIGHT CHAMPIONSHIP | HEAVYWEIGHT CHAMPIONSHIP |
|---|---|
| **OF GREAT BRITAIN** | **OF THE BRITISH EMPIRE** |
| 15 (3 MIN.) ROUNDS | (World Title Eliminator) |
|  | 15 (3 MIN.) ROUNDS |

### JOE LUCY
(Mile End)
(Holder)

### JOE BYGRAVES
(Birkenhead)

**V**

**V**

### SAMMY McCARTHY
(Stepney)

### KITIONE LAVE
(Tonga)

### INTERNATIONAL HEAVYWEIGHT CONTEST

### HENRY COOPER v GIANNINO LUISE
(Bellingham)     10 (3 Min.) Rounds     (Italy)

---

### *ALSO FULL SUPPORTING PROGRAMME*

**Plenty of Seats Available at £2 2s., £3 3s., £5 5s.**

(10s. 6d., 15s., £1 1s. Seats all Sold)

Bookable from Empire Pool (WEM 1234) or usual Ticket Agencies.

father having been forced to retire early from the mines suffering from silicosis.

Thompson gained his first title chance within two years of signing with manager Benny Huntman (having started out with Jarvis Astaire), being matched with Stan Hawthorne, a game and dangerous puncher who had already beaten him on points in an eliminator. Thompson overturned the form book, KO'ing Hawthorne in three rounds.

In May 1949 in Glasgow, he stopped Harry Hughes in five and his remaining championship victory was a points win in Hanley over Tommy McGovern to take the Lonsdale Belt outright.

It was a fight for which the BBBC had to give special permission, both boxers being managed by Huntman. Unfortunately, the Board censured and eventually suspended Huntman following the return. The Jim Wicks/Stan Cappall promotion at Wandsworth Stadium in August 1951 ended in chaos, McGovern KO'ing a clearly distressed Thompson inside sixty seconds, a single left hook being all that was required. Thompson had apparently drained his strength away the night before, losing weight in a Turkish Baths.

Tommy McGovern was then outboxed by Frank Johnson, and for the next five years the title was swapped between Johnson and Joe Lucy. Johnson was first scheduled to defend against Lucy on 9 January 1953 at White City but forfeited when he turned up an hour and a half late and ½ lb overweight.

Lucy, a Billingsgate porter, was then rematched with McGovern for the vacant title on a Freddie Mills promotion at the Empress Hall. Lucy ran out the clear winner on points but then lost the title to 'comeback man' Johnson, this in front of a live TV audience, pictures beamed from Solomons's Harringay stronghold.

The return, at Manchester's Belle Vue, saw Johnson striving to win the belt outright but after a quiet start Lucy suddenly exploded a tremendous right to Johnson's chin, an uppercut that almost lifted him off his feet. The result was a bad cut over Johnson's right eye that gradually worsened until the fight was stopped in the eighth in Lucy's favour.

In June 1956, therefore, on Harry Levene's first British title promotion at Wembley, Lucy outboxed ex-featherweight Sammy

McCarthy to become outright winner of the fourth lightweight belt launched by the BBBC in twenty years.

The arrival of Levene on the promotional map caused few ripples at the time. Only when Solomons lost his Harringay base in 1958 did Levene's foothold at Wembley appear ominous. The Fifties, however, had been all Solomons, his power underlined by the 'control' he exercised over the promotional destinies of charismatic fighters such as Randolph Turpin, Don Cockell and heavyweights Gardner, Williams and Erskine.

Turpin was clearly the jewel in his crown. Between the years 1950 and 1957 Randolph Turpin won and then relinquished a British title three times, returning at last to take the light-heavyweight belt outright when almost at the end of his incredible career. In the process, Don Cockell and Alex Buxton were to watch the cherished belt removed when almost theirs for keeps.

Turpin was acknowledged as being the best box-fighter Britain had produced since Kid Lewis – the greatest natural hitter since Jimmy Wilde. According to Frank Butler, Turpin's short left hook was the best of any middleweight in the world at the time; this, combined with his uncanny facility for launching murderous blows from all angles, made him far too good for any British fighter.

Yet his defeat by Sugar Ray Robinson set people wondering: how would he react, what had he learned technically from the experience, would he retire? His response was to move up to light-heavyweight and challenge British champion Don Cockell, at that point Britain's only other world-rated fighter.

In 1951, when Cockell took the European light-heavyweight title as well as defeating Albert Finch to confirm his status as British champion, he had been in line for a tilt at Joey Maxim's World title: indeed, March 1952 at Earls Court was already pencilled into Jack Solomons's diary.

Battersea-born Cockell was a powerful punching fighter with a great left hook, a veritable 'pocket-battleship', stocky and sturdy, cool and courageous. His problem was a genetic one concerning weight – he had a tendency to balloon up to heavyweight when he felt his best fighting weight, given his height and build, was light-heavy.

Thus there were questions as to his ability to perform at the very highest level. At Earls Court, as early as the third round, Cockell was bowled over by a powerful left hook, but after taking a count of eight he recovered well enough to hold Turpin off until the bell ended an exciting round.

For the next four rounds, Cockell managed to keep Turpin at bay and seemed likely to win on points. In the eleventh, Cockell was floored again (but up at six) by a sizzling left hook. From then on, it was all Turpin, who in the twelfth blazed in and put Cockell down again for a count of eight. One more time he rose, only to be sent staggering into the ropes by right and left swings – upon which the referee called a halt.

The belt presentation was an oddity: Turpin was given his own middleweight belt, the light-heavyweight belt having earlier been stolen from Cockell's home.

The trouble Cockell had experienced in getting down to the light-heavy limit persuaded him to move up to heavy, while Turpin decided to relinquish the light-heavyweight title and turn his attention to regaining his World middleweight title.

The British middleweight title was thus kept on 'hold' while the Board decided to match Dennis Powell and George Walker for the vacant light-heavyweight title, a somewhat surprising pairing.

Walker, managed by Sam Burns, was a hard-hitting American-style fighter whose game plan was to press forward throwing body punches in the hope of wearing his opponent down, when he would throw the pay-off punch – and he possessed quite a 'dig'. An ex-Billingsgate porter, he had turned pro after winning the ABA cruiserweight title in 1951. Thus he was little more than a novice with only twelve fights to his credit.

Powell, on the other hand, was approaching veteran stage: an ex-Second World War navy man, a builder by trade, he had graduated from unlicensed shows in North Wales to winning a Jack Solomons light-heavyweight contest at Harringay. Something of a protégé of Johnny Best, he had won the Welsh heavyweight title in 1948 (conceding over a stone) since when he had pursued a somewhat up-and-down career, dogged by cuts.

Both men could command vociferous support when the occasion demanded, but the fight was not considered attractive enough to stage in London (as every other light-heavyweight contest had been since the war). Instead, Johnny Best brought it to Liverpool where the locals were treated to a real blood-and-guts affair, thrilling, if gruelling, for both participants.

In the end, Walker's eye injuries proved the more debilitating, but Powell's greater experience and ringcraft would probably have prevailed had the referee not called a halt in the eleventh.

Seven months later and Powell was back in the ring making his first defence against Alex Buxton, who might well have felt aggrieved at taking his turn behind Walker. For Buxton was approaching veteran stage, having been boxing for some eleven years and now approaching twenty-nine years of age.

Alex's father was a West Indian, born in Antigua, who had settled in Watford to run a removals business and raise a family of four boys and a girl. All the boys boxed: Joe was a useful middleweight; Laurie a talented writer, student of law, Intelligence Service Corps man who also boxed as a middleweight after the war, winning two *Boxing News* merit awards; while the youngest, Allan, would win an ABA welterweight title in 1949.

Buxton was always one of life's battlers. As a child he had suffered with rickets and a hernia; as a boxer he broke both his jaw and his hand, added to which he had to overcome something of a temperamental nature: he could dazzle one week but fail completely the next.

Nevertheless, he was a skilful fighter, sympathetically managed by Jim Wicks who at that stage was putting together a quite successful 'stable' – including Joe Lucy, Jake Tuli and the promising Cooper twins.

Oddly enough, Powell had entered the ring as favourite: his display, however, was abject. Buxton dominated the encounter with his superior skills, completely outboxing his opponent for eight of the fight's ten rounds, the champion sustaining a nasty cut over his left eye that ultimately caused referee Tommy Little to call a halt.

For Buxton, presented with the belt in the ring by Lord Scarsdale, it was a moment of jubilation and celebration – for himself and for all his boxing brothers – the third time since the colour-bar had been lifted in 1948 that a coloured fighter had taken a title.

The following year, Alex took on 'evergreen' Albert Finch,

contesting his fifth British title, and KO'd him in eight. Then came the moment of truth.

Randolph Turpin was now back challenging at light-heavy and, somewhat surprisingly, considering his poor form, was nominated to meet Buxton. Solomons snapped the bout up and Buxton prepared to make his debut at Harringay. It would be a significant contest – the first all-coloured championship bout in British boxing history.

The two had already met in 1952 when Buxton had been stopped on cuts in the seventh. Their championship fight, however, would last just two rounds. Admonished by the referee for providing little by way of action, Turpin, visibly annoyed, pushed Buxton out of another clinch and then tossed a high right hand that caught Buxton on the temple. Alex stepped back, dazed, and Turpin charged. His left swept into Buxton's body and a mighty right crashed onto the champion's chin.

A roar went up as Alex buckled at the knees and fell flat on his back, blood spurting from his lacerated mouth. He managed to rise as 'Out!' was called and had to be helped back to his corner.

But the Buxton-Turpin saga had not ended. Turpin relinquished the title again following a defeat at the hands of Gordon Wallace, Empire light-heavyweight champion. Almost a year later, West Ham's Ron Barton was paired with Albert Finch for the vacant title, Barton triumphing with an eight-round stoppage. However, Barton's brief career would end prematurely because of eye-trouble.

In 1956 it was Buxton and Turpin once again, this time with both men fighting for the right to take the belt home permanently. By now, however, interest in the division was declining, and this second all-coloured title fight took place at Granby Halls, Leicester, drawing upon Turpin's still loyal Midlands following.

In a poor contest, Buxton seemed unable to launch more than tentative, one-shot attacks, while Turpin's once-shattering left hook was rarely seen. The end came in the fifth round, when Buxton threw a rare left hand – unfortunately just as Turpin was launching a right. It caught Buxton as he came in, lifted him off his feet and sent him crashing to the floor. Somehow he managed to get up at nine, only to be pounded down again. He struggled to beat the count another three times before the referee finally called a halt. Thus Turpin took the belt home for keeps and Buxton went home bitterly disappointed.

Turpin would defend the title just once more, in 1957, when he took on Arthur Howard and beat him on points in a battle that was fast, furious and exciting – if almost devoid of skilful boxing. Howard was said to have sailed in 'without method, without thought and without a clue', yet he had Turpin wobbling three times but could not finish him off. Turpin, tremendously fit and game, lasted the course and won well on points but it was his last title fight. He retired the following year – and in 1966 committed suicide.

Turpin, whether defending the titles or not, had dominated both middle and light-heavyweight divisions since 1950. In the heavyweight division, the same period would see a trio of fighters play musical chairs with the title, no one assuming complete control until 1956 when Joe Erskine recorded two successive victories – the first man to manage the feat since Jack Peterson in 1936.

It was a division, in fact, that had seen little sustained activity since the war: Bruce Woodcock, after defeating Jack London in 1945, waited four years before defending against Freddie Mills, but was denied a belt outright in 1950 by Jack Gardner – a result that opened a completely new era.

Don Cockell, Jack Gardner and later Johnny Williams would be the dominant forces in the division for some five years and, oddly enough, all three shared a similar passion: farming. In many respects, they fitted the traditional pattern of British heavyweights: quiet, reserved, almost retiring men, all possessing great courage but lacking that extra something to succeed at world level – be it a KO punch, confidence or possibly raw desire. Farming, perhaps, was too bucolic a pursuit to instil the necessary cutting edge needed at the very top.

Gardner and Williams first met in June 1950 at Leicester in an eliminator to decide who should take on champion Woodcock. Although both were the same age, Williams was by far the more experienced, having been a pro for two years longer and having had twice as many fights.

Gardner, meanwhile, had a record of twenty-two fights and just two losses, both to a Canadian called Vern Escoe and considered as mere blots on a promising landscape.

Big men both, they had different styles. Gardner, with great physical strength, was somewhat static in the ring and thus vulnerable to a succession of swift punches. Williams was much faster on his feet, moved easily about the ring and boxed with a great deal of skill. He also possessed a classic punishing left jab/lead which journalist Bill McGowran considered one of the most damaging he had ever known in such a heavy man.

This stylistic difference produced a classic fight, probably one of the most bruising, damaging and bloody encounters in British heavyweight history. At the end, Gardner took the decision and Williams was carried off to hospital with manager Ted Broadribb fearing that he might never fight again.

Gardner was considered the underdog when he took on Woodcock some six months later, yet he surprised everyone by doggedly, mechanically outpunching the veteran until Woodcock was forced to retire in the eleventh round. Although Woodcock threw every punch he possessed and connected with a good many of them, Gardner pressed relentlessly, ruggedly on, his performance suggesting that he might develop into a world-class prospect.

Four months later he took the European title from Austrian Joe Weidin and all seemed set for a clash with Lee Savold, Jack Solomons's 'World' champion. But Gardner's connections turned the fight down, considering that it had come too early for him. Within a year, Gardner had lost both British and European titles and was out of World contention entirely.

In March 1952 he took on Johnny Williams for the second time in defence of his British title. Since his earlier defeat, Williams had made a comeback guided carefully by the canny Broadribb. A keen student of the game, he showed more desire than Gardner, who seemed to remain locked in one particular style, unable or unwilling to adapt and learn. A second bloody encounter (Gardner suffered from bad cuts throughout his career) and a somewhat disputed decision saw Williams snatch the title – after which Gardner announced his retirement.

Don Cockell now entered the scene. Having given up the light-heavyweight challenge due to weight problems and the dominance of Randolph Turpin, Cockell took on and defeated the ageing

Tommy Farr (thirty-nine years old), then in the middle of a surprise comeback, before being matched with Williams at Harringay on 12 May 1953, the fourth heavyweight title in a row for Solomons.

Cockell was regarded by most experts as a no-hoper, being too slow and too small; yet he would prove the swifter mover at the outset, landing left and rights to Williams's body as well as beating Williams to the punch with his left. His first three punches – a left, followed by a left-right combo – had rendered Williams openmouthed and on the retreat. In the course of the fight both men suffered bad cuts and Cockell's left eye was almost closed at the end; but the smaller man bullied and bustled his way forward to take a decisive points decision.

Heavyweight activity at home then ended as Cockell progressed towards his momentous match with Rocky Marciano, a fight that put him briefly at number one in British fight fans' estimations, replacing the fading Randolph Turpin.

In 1956, however, while contenders Joe Erskine and Johnny Williams were sorting out who should challenge him, Cockell met defeat at the hands of one Kitione Lave and decided it was time to retire, leaving Erskine and Williams alone and centre-stage.

Cardiff-born Erskine certainly marked a radical change in style from the heavyweights preceding him. He was a skilful, clever boxer with a good defence and terrific ringcraft. He was, according to long-time adversary Henry Cooper, in *An Autobiography*, extremely difficult to hit because he was so flexible and adaptable: 'Whenever you thought you were out of distance, sure he couldn't sling a left hand, he did, the crafty so-and-so. When he was in the distance, you would think, "He can't see my right or left coming", but he could. He was unorthodox in that way.'

Erskine's record when he met Williams was impressive: twenty-six wins and a draw. But against Williams, he had to fight the battle of his career in a hard-fought, unrelenting grand-slam between two efficient tradesmen – a contest that ended in a torrential downpour that soaked spectators seated outdoors in Cardiff's Maindy Stadium.

Erskine generally controlled matters, scoring more frequently, although Williams inflicted more damage; as early as the fourth,

Erskine was cut under his left eye, which inspired him to attack Williams with vicious left-hooks, one of which almost had Williams down. Williams then tended to hold and spoil – he was much better at in-fighting – and after some close work in the ninth, Erskine emerged with a nasty gash over his right eye, his right eyebrow having split.

Williams made strenuous efforts to capitalize on this but Erskine (his corner having patched up the damage) used the ring well, countering with his left; and towards the end it was Williams who tired, his legs gone, and who, when the final bell rang, walked over to Erskine's corner and raised his hand. How times have changed.

Thus Joe Erskine donned the only solid gold belt then still in circulation and was mobbed by his supporters whom the *Boxing News* described as 'Calypso-singing "Tiger Bay" admirers! . . .' The reference to calypsos was a sidelong hint at Erskine's origins. Though little was made of it at the time, Erskine was of mixed-race parentage and his securing of the heavyweight title a symbolic moment in British boxing history. However, although British champion, he was already, in publicity terms at least, being over-shadowed by the future 'golden boy' of British boxing – Henry Cooper.

In February 1957, Erskine was matched with Nino Valdes – the prize, if he emerged victorious, being a chance to fight Lee Savold for the European version of the World heavyweight title. On the same bill, however, Cooper – though holding no British title – was challenging Joe Bygraves for the Empire title; an odd arrangement. As it was, neither British fighter won that night, but Cooper promptly set off for Stockholm to challenge, again unsuccessfully, for the European title (he was KO'd by Ingemar Johansson).

No wonder Joe Erskine was reported to be a little unhappy with his manager Benny Jacobs. Then there was the fiasco of Erskine's match with Peter Bates, a heavyweight challenger whom Midlands promoter Alex Griffiths felt merited a shot at the British title. The BBBC refused to ratify the match and so Griffiths was forced to stage it over fourteen rounds, thus ensuring that Erskine would not be stripped of his title if he lost. Had Erskine been part of the Wicks/Solomons empire, such indignities might not have befallen him.

Matters within the Erskine camp, however, were quickly patched up (as most disagreements were, Erskine being the most phlegmatic and amiable of characters) and Erskine then met Cooper in September 1957 at Harringay in a contest that unfortunately failed to thrill anyone.

When Erskine was declared the winner, fights broke out in the hall but Cooper, according to most experts present and on his own admission, had done nothing like enough to merit a victory. Cooper, however, would learn from the defeat.

# 16

# A Communications Revolution

By the late Fifties Jack Solomons's pre-eminent role as Britain's top promoter was being threatened by a combination of factors: the rise of a substantial rival in Harry Levene who would bring into play other younger matchmakers, managers and promoters, principally Jarvis Astaire, Mickey Duff and later Mike Barrett; the development of television, especially the introduction of commercial TV in 1955; the parallel, inexorable decline of boxing as a mass spectator sport and its contraction in terms of venues, promotions and active boxers.

Solomons's 'control' of top boxing in London had always been a matter of 'influence' although there was also a certain amount of bullying via the Southern Area Board of Control where he and his acolytes could comfortably 'regulate' the capital's affairs – blocking, reprimanding, niggling those whom Solomons felt might harbour ambitions beyond what he considered acceptable.

Braitman and Ezra were thus regularly given dressings-down, as was a certain energetic, ubiquitous ex-boxer turned matchmaker, Mickey Duff.

According to Jarvis Astaire, then a boxing manager but soon to become a major player through his close-circuit TV company Viewsport, Solomons never resorted to illegalities as such; nevertheless he was ruthless when the occasion demanded and was not, according to Astaire, above interfering (in unspecified ways) with a rival promoter's non-boxing business if necessary. (Most promoters had business concerns of some sort: Astaire had, among other things, a substantial interest in a chain of men's outfitters; Benny Schmidt was in the cloth business as was Ronnie

Ezra; Jack Cappall and Jim Wicks were bookmakers; Alex Lucas in Scotland had a furniture business and George Connell in Belfast was in the motor-trade.)

But Solomons in his heyday had fingers in numerous pies, contacts and friends in all the necessary places high and low. The opening chapter of his autobiography, published in 1951 when he was undoubtedly at his peak, is devoted to giving the reader an imaginary tour of his Windmill Street gym and offices – actually a semi-humorous demonstration of the forces at his command, the contacts he could call upon whether in show business or on the Boxing Board of Control, the Metropolitan Police or the press, boxing managers, agents – all are described, some even named, patiently waiting in the anterooms of the court of King Solomons.

In a sense, with his grip on prime London boxing venues, his retinue of managers, not to mention his regional contacts, Solomons could have been accused, if anyone had dared, of operating a monopoly of sorts. It is ironic, therefore (though typical of such a clever publicist) that in the years to come it should be Solomons who would make most of the warning noises about sinister 'syndicates', of monopolists poised to take over boxing and bleed it dry.

As early as 1954 (significantly just prior to the introduction of commercial TV) Solomons and Jim Wicks made a number of statements reported by Tom Phillips in the *Daily Herald* concerning the imminent danger to boxing of a 'syndicate' which, according to Wicks, was hoping that Solomons would leave the game (as he was regularly threatening to do because of the punitive Entertainment Tax) so that it (the syndicate) might take over.

Wicks declared that the syndicate's policy 'is not calculated to help boxing as a sport and as a public attraction. . . . Only Jack Solomons can save the sport from this menace.'

Gradually, however, Solomons found the ground beneath his feet shifting. In 1956 Arthur Elvin decided that big-time boxing could return to Wembley, and this allowed Levene, already promoting at the Albert Hall following Jack Cappall's death, to secure a venue big enough to mount 'Solomons-style' promotions in direct competition. Then, in 1958, came probably the hardest blow – the closure of Harringay by the Greyhound Association.

Solomons was thus thrust out into the marketplace with everyone else and, two years after losing Harringay, his other base power was removed. A *coup d'état* among licence-holders saw the 'financially-interested' Southern Area council replaced by a 'non-financially interested' council consisting of professional men: doctors, lawyers, etc., who owed no one any favours. It was a move supported by Jarvis Astaire and Mickey Duff but resisted by Solomons, who insisted that those with no direct interest in the sport had no real idea as to what was going on.

True to form, the 'monopoly'/'syndicate' accusations surfaced again. Indeed, for the next four to five years, bitter, sometimes libellous, accusations would rend the boxing scene, leading to enquiries and soul-searching, much of the bitterness stemming from Solomons as he fought a losing battle to sustain his pre-eminent position.

The BBBC responded quickly to the current accusations of the Southern Area council upheavals by setting up an enquiry under appeal steward Judge Eaglebach, and followed this with a Board investigation led by Alexander Elliott into 'the possibilities of drawing more boxers, more promoters and more spectators into the sport'.

In 1963, *Boxing News*, clearly unsatisfied with the Board's efforts, ran a series under the general heading 'The Hidden Menace', while influential journalist Peter Wilson ran a parallel piece entitled 'The Canker in Boxing'. Both suggested, in necessarily vague terms, the existence of nefarious practices (not to say individuals) then ruining the pro-game. This in turn led to yet another 'official' enquiry under David Karmel QC which concluded in 1964 that 'no real evidence to support the allegations that a monopoly, so-called syndicate, or any person controlling boxing, exists . . .'.

Eventually such accusations simply died away, to be replaced by a regular bemoaning of the 'rivalry' that disturbed what would otherwise have been a cosy cartel at the top.

The accusations – though not without some substance – actually heralded the death throes of Solomons, as the jolly Nabob of Sock's reign came to a bitter and undignified end. For even to the most casual observers of the sport, it was clear that Solomons was being edged out by a group of powerful and influential men.

Boxing News, July 28, 1967

'I'll Meet Ali Whenever He's Ready'—Joe Frazier. See Page 3

**BOXING NEWS**

*World's Premier Fight Weekly*

Vol. 23 No. 30 58th Year — PRICE ONE SHILLING — Registered at the G.P.O. as a newspaper — JULY 28, 1967

# BATTLE FOR POWER IN BRITISH BOXING

JARVIS ASTAIRE — MIKE BARRETT — MICKEY DUFF — HARRY LEVENE — JACK SOLOMONS

Harry Levene, along with matchmaker/manager Mickey Duff, in conjunction with boxing manager, businessman and television mogul Jarvis Astaire, had joined forces in a loose marriage of convenience to reap the benefits of the increasingly TV-dominated premier boxing scene.

Solomons would continue to do well during the Sixties and Seventies but he had no right-hand man of the calibre of Mickey Duff, particularly when Sam Burns moved with boxer Terry Downes to join Levene. Solomons also made the mistake of investing the affair with too much of his own personality. As Sam Burns put it, Solomons came to believe that *he* was the attraction and not the boxers.

The struggle, however, was being played out on a rapidly shrinking boxing stage. In sheer volume (number of boxers active, number of promotions mounted) British boxing was in gradual decline, and for reasons that had little to do with the way the sport was run.

No syndicate could be blamed for the fact that, whereas in 1947 there had been some 760 promotions in Great Britain, by

1967 this figure had shrunk to 164. Mr 'X' was not responsible for the fact that in 1947 paying customers might visit any one of 150 venues large and small in the UK to watch boxing, yet by 1967 ten private sporting clubs were responsible for almost half the promotions in the country.

Boxing was not the only sport to suffer a massive decline in paying customers. Football, too, found itself in a similar crisis during the Sixties and Seventies. The reason was a changing society: people with more money and more choice as to leisure opportunities, and altered social arrangements as slum clearance projects swept away established communities that had once fostered 'traditional' sports.

Few football clubs, though, went out of business. They could put in more seats, employ a commercial manager, sell players to one another, borrow money from the local bank-manager. For boxing, without a similar physical base, the decline was more serious. As small halls closed their doors to the sport, preferring bingo and even wrestling, there were fewer openings for aspiring boxers, thus fewer boxers. There were fewer gyms and fewer old-timers to pass on the secrets of the trade. Boxing was truly a contracting industry.

Those caught up in the decline found it hard to grasp exactly what was happening. During the early Fifties the blame for smaller promoters ceasing to operate was placed on the crippling Entertainment Tax. When the tax was lifted in 1957 and the decline continued, there was much bewilderment, which only helped to foster the increasingly hysterical claims that boxing was being slowly destroyed by sinister forces in the early Sixties.

However, the principal response by promoters to declining attendances during the Sixties was to turn away from commercial public tournaments and to open private membership clubs along the lines of the National Sporting Club at the Café Royal – during this decade operating extremely successfully. In 1964 the Anglo-American Club was opened at the Hilton Hotel, followed by the Clarendon at Hammersmith, the Wyvern in Manchester and the Midland in Birmingham, while in 1965 – a sure sign of the times – Jack Solomons opened the World Sporting Club at the Grosvenor Hotel, Park Lane. Meanwhile the NSC had sufficiently improved its status that in 1962 it successfully bid for a

British title fight. Thus in February of that year Chic Calderwood
fought John O'Brien for the light-heavyweight title.

Such high-profile venues, involving sponsorship and possible
links with slot and close-circuit television (not to mention live
relays) appeared to be the future of the sport, certainly the
immediate future. By 1967 private clubs were promoting 50 per
cent of all tournaments in the UK, the NSC more than anyone
else.

The principal worry concerning the clubs was that the average
working man might be excluded – clubs were not cheap. These
fears were assuaged by the inescapable fact that the average
working man was simply not turning up in sufficient numbers
when there *was* an opportunity to watch 'live' boxing – at any
level.

However, a trend had set in by the end of the 1960s whereby
a promising young boxer (Ken Buchanan is the most celebrated
example) could progress through the ranks and even win a title
without actually appearing before a traditional paying audience,
perhaps not even a television audience.

The decline also contributed to the increasing emphasis placed
on television – both as villain and possible saviour. When commercial TV opened up in 1955 much was hoped for the medium
and its relationship with boxing. In fact, on commercial TV's
very first night, fifty minutes of live boxing was transmitted from
Shoreditch Town Hall, Lew Lazar beating Terry Murphy on
points for the Southern Area middleweight title.

It was a Solomons promotion, of course, and apparently a great
success with everyone on their best 'TV' behaviour – the boxers
all had neatly ironed trunks and new white laces while some had
even cleaned their shoes.

The debate in boxing circles regarding television had already
been raging for some years, Jack Solomons famously declaring as
far back as 1950 that, unless properly handled, the new medium
would destroy small-hall, grass-roots boxing besides emptying the
bigger stadiums – just as it had done in the USA.

After the initial excitement, however, ITV gradually lost
interest. From the heady days of 1959 when a special deal was
announced between the BBBC and ITA to take fortnightly Satur-

day night fights for a trial six months, it petered down to 1965 when, of ten live transmissions, ITV took just three.

Television – whether BBC or ITV – only wanted the best. It wanted champions and championships. The BBBC, backed by promoters, consistently refused this throughout the Fifties and Sixties, trying instead to persuade programmers to show small-hall promotions, to take an interest (in fact to sponsor) the sport at the grass-roots. In this respect, the BBBC could be accused of misunderstanding the whole nature of the television medium. Unless given what it really wanted, TV would, and did, simply turn elsewhere. (For commercial TV, wrestling became its major 'live' sport for many years – thrills, spills and manufactured excitement galore.)

When confronted at various times during the late Sixties by angry licence-holders who accused the Board of not ensuring that provincial promoters received a fair share of TV's limited 'spoils', the Board seemed to have grasped that television could not be forced to take an unwanted product. But as the controlling body, it seemed unable or lacked the imagination to develop a strategy to *sell* boxing in a way that ensured everyone got something out of it.

In July 1969, amid such publicity, Midlands promoter Alex Griffiths threatened to give up commercial promoting and resigned from the Midlands Area Board of Control in protest at the fact that London, and Duff in particular, was receiving almost all the money emanating from television. Duff countered that he, in turn, was using such finance to get more and more young fighters opportunities to work. Who, if anyone, 'controlled' television would always be a barren, ultimately irrelevant argument. What is certain is that the new medium was soon affecting – perhaps even distorting – pro-boxers' careers. In this respect, the different fortunes of three British champions both reflected the changing TV times and mirrored the shifting power relationships at the very top.

On 18 April 1958, at Harringay Stadium, welterweight champion Peter Waterman fought his last fight, while lower down the same bill Terry Downes was celebrating his first year as a pro by knocking over a 'Mexican roadsweeper'; the following night in

Germany, Henry Cooper was suffering a home-town verdict, being disqualified after KO'ing his opponent.

Peter Waterman, ex-ABA welterweight champion, ex-grammar schoolboy, dashing and good-looking (he married a debutante), was an important member of the first Jarvis Astaire/Mickey Duff 'stable' which would include Terry Spinks, Bobby Neill and Sammy McCarthy.

Waterman turned pro in December 1952 and in three knock-about years shot to the top of the boxing world. Aged just twenty-one, he was a bright, articulate host of ITV's Cavalcade of Sport – an ambitious venture that ultimately foundered after a couple of years, but not before making Waterman a national celebrity. In fact, he celebrated his twenty-first birthday on the 'box' cutting a cake with Jack Solomons et al. in attendance. And in April 1956 he duly took the British welterweight title from Wally Thom.

Peter Jones, Waterman's friend and surrogate father, recalled, in *A London Life*, those heady, somewhat innocent days: the champagne celebrations at the Astor Club with Jones clutching the belt wrapped in a blood-stained towel, the taxi ride home with Waterman flaked out on the back seat:

> As I was paying off the taxi, I dangled the beautiful Lonsdale Belt in front of the taxi-driver. 'Good Gawd,' he said. 'Is that a Lonsdale Belt? Did you win it?' 'No,' I said, reaching into the back of the taxi and pulling out the new welterweight champion who by this time had lost all interest and was like a rag-doll. 'He did!'

Six months later Waterman defeated Frank Johnson – a fight that demonstrated Waterman's worrying tendency to absorb tremendous punishment before subduing his opponent. He had been counted out by all but the referee after Johnson had knocked him down in the fourth, but had dragged himself off the canvas and won. It had been a similar story in January 1958 when he had won the European crown – knocked down twice in the eleventh but still triumphing on points.

That was Waterman's forte – hit and be hit – and in boxing terms it was successful: in a career of forty-six fights he won forty-one – only seven of those on points. He would only be stopped once himself, significantly in his last fight against light-weight champion Dave Charnley on that April night at Harringay. In a catchweight 'super-fight', Charnley administered a five-round thrashing but by then Waterman had already shown signs of having, in boxing parlance, 'gone' – reflexes awry, his durability suddenly suspect.

In fact, he was suffering from severe neurological damage and soon after his retirement paralysis set in down his left side. Crude and painful surgery only made it worse and so Waterman – a kind, philosophical man – drifted into a long, sometimes distressing retirement, ending in 1988 with his premature death (aged fifty-four) by heart attack.

Meanwhile, that other shooting star of the late Fifties had roared into the limelight. Terry Downes, although (like Waterman) gutsy, fearless and possessing a raw natural talent, personified the rapidly changing times more accurately, being more obviously a 'rebel' in both appearance and behaviour. He was also luckier, his crash-bang style resulting in more superficial – though sometimes equally gory – damage.

Although born in Paddington, he lived in America for some years and boxed with great success in the US Marines. Back in the UK, after a brief period with Fisher AC, he was welcomed with open arms by Jack Solomons who passed him on to be managed by Jarvis Astaire (the big rift had not by then occurred). Downes would always have the right connections: later Sam Burns would take up the managerial reins while Mickey Duff would serve in his corner.

He was an instant hit: appearing on a Solomons Harringay show in April 1957, he KO'd Peter Longo inside a round. It was his extrovert behaviour that caught the public's eye although at first, this being England, his confidence and gusto were misunderstood. As he explained in his autobiography, *My Bleeding Business*:

I'd got some booing for bouncing in the ring, white boots and scarlet shorts with scarlet-and-gold Marine colours gown and doing my punch-up dance. I hit the air and bounced around the ring. I was just lettin' 'em know I meant business. In America it was all part and parcel of the scene, but the English fight fans got the needle to this show-off stuff and gave me the 'bird'. The more they jeered, the more I kept going. They couldn't win.

The 'war-dance' was almost as much a talking point as his boxing performance, but from then on Downes's love-affair with the press (who dubbed him 'The Whizz Kid') and subsequently the public – who flocked to cheer him on – would ensure his swift route to the top, just as long as he turned in the results.

In fact, it was to take him only nineteen fights, spread over less than eighteen months, before a title chance came – though his progress had not been unblemished: stopped by Dick Tiger in his third fight, losing to Les Allen on points and then on cuts to Bermondsey-based Welshman Freddie Cross – this last illustrates the cruel realities of boxing at the top.

Cross could well have thought his victory over Downes would lead to a title chance; the fight had been mooted as an 'unofficial' eliminator. Solomons promised there would be a return within a month, presumably for Downes to redress the balance, but, according to Downes: 'We never fought again. Cross went out of the picture.'

Some months later, Downes defeated the then champion Pat McAteer in an eight-round non-title fight and McAteer announced his retirement. Downes again:

> With the British title vacant, Solomons did a smart bit of matchmaking, pairing me with Phil Edwards of Cardiff and applying to the Board for it to be recognized for the title. They agreed. Freddie Cross put up a bit of a scream, but it didn't count.

What did count, of course, was political muscle and commercial clout. Downes took the title, stopping Edwards in the thirteenth round of a one-sided contest, displaying great skill, outjabbing a renowned jabber, cutting him and battering him about the body until referee Billy Williams stepped between them and raised Downes's arm.

His career now took something of a nosedive – literally, as damage to his famous 'hooter' plus cuts over both eyes would plague him and almost force his retirement from the ring. When he took a severe beating from US fighter 'Spider' Webb (losing on cuts) followed by another defeat at the hands of tough Senegalese Michel Diouf, his bright future looked to be in jeopardy, a prediction reinforced by his first title defence against Scotland's Cowboy John McCormack.

McCormack was a boxer whom many now consider could have been much greater than he was but for a suspect attitude. Years later McCormack confirmed this in *Boxing*: 'I never really liked boxing,' he admitted. 'To be truthful, boxing was just a job – a means to an end to me. It gave me lots of money to spend and a certain fame. I loathed the training – it was a grind.'

Forced to box for a living in order to supplement the family income (his father died when he was only thirteen), his awkward southpaw stance and powerful right hand and left hook took him to a Scottish middleweight title in just a year and he was considered more than ready for a crack at the British title.

Indeed, he entered the ring a slight favourite, odds that looked generous when Downes floored him in the fourth with a right cross. After this the fight grew more and more confusing as Downes's powerful body-shots (his penchant) were frequently made by McCormack's antics to look like low blows: 'As a fight it was a farce. He'd fold up with the first sign of a body punch and with the referee pulling me off and him squirming and face-pulling I still didn't know how I kept my temper. What kind of a championship was this? It stunk. . . .'

Clearly McCormack did not see it like that, nor the referee Ike Powell, although many at ringside felt that the final 'low blow' that convinced Powell to award the fight to McCormack was an unlucky accident.

McCormack, however, had little time to savour his triumph. The outcry was so intense that a return was fixed (without McCormack's knowledge, as he was on holiday at the time) for a mere seven weeks later. Downes made no mistake in the rematch. After boxing carefully through the first few rounds, in the fifth he sustained damage to his left eye, then was caught by a right that opened a cut above his nose, so bad that it seemed the fight might be stopped there and then.

With little time left, however, Downes proceeded to batter McCormack unmercifully. By the eighth, McCormack, having been down four times, was draped across the top rope unable to defend himself and the referee stopped it.

The victory marked the beginning of a new phase in Downes's career. After losing his title in the first McCormack fight, Downes had been incensed by the BBBC's decision to fine him: 'I still think the fight and the fine was a diabolical liberty. It knocked all the pride out of winning a championship. I couldn't care less – and my opinion still hasn't changed. They can keep their titles.'

He was also increasingly dissatisfied with the purses he had received fighting for Solomons. When the opportunity came, and it soon did, Downes accepted a fight on a Harry Levene bill – despite Sam Burns's warning that Solomons would never employ him again.

Downes, however, was adamant: 'It was a chance I had to take. I was too anxious to get cracking again to concern myself with politics.' He thus took a fight against a Belgian, Carlos Vanneste, at Wembley and following that he fought on a Mickey Duff promotion in Liverpool. From then on, he was firmly entrenched in the 'non-Solomons' camp.

A title defence against Phil Edwards was arranged for 5 July 1960 and once again Downes proved much too strong for a game challenger. Edwards was stopped in the twelfth, Peter Wilson in the *Daily Mirror* enthusing: 'Tearaway Terry! Edwards had gradually been unfleshed, hammered and beaten and tossed from one set of ropes to another. He was a slack-legged marionette, sagging and lurching helplessly. . . .'

Six months on and Downes, now the possessor of his very own belt, was in America tackling Paul Pender in the first of three exciting, bloody and extremely lucrative World title clashes that not only secured Downes's financial future but was instrumental in launching the close-circuit boxing operation of Jarvis Astaire, a factor of crucial importance for boxing politics and economics in the 1960s.

Downes never defended the British middleweight title. In November 1962 he and Burns refused the Board's ultimatum that he defend against Cowboy John McCormack, declaring that the £5,200 purse (his cut of a successful £8,600 bid by Jack Solomons) was not enough money, when he, Downes, was the principal 'draw'. He also resented the role of the BBBC in general, notably its 'dictatorial' powers which had the effect of making him feel that it was 'no privilege' to be a champion at all.

Downes also disputed the Board's assertion that it had taken his title away (prompting premature headlines that this was the first time in boxing history that a champion had been 'stripped' of a British title). He, Downes, had given the title up. The Stewards of Appeal later confirmed this was correct.

If Downes was British boxing's 'stormy petrel' during the 1960s, then Henry Cooper was the sport's still point in a rapidly turning world. Unlike Waterman or Downes, Cooper would establish himself as a champion without being boosted or packaged by TV. Television would ultimately serve Henry Cooper, not vice versa. He first fought for the heavyweight title in 1957, took the title at last in 1959 and held it through eight successive defences until 1967 when (shades of Downes) he relinquished it for 'political' reasons. He returned to beat his successor Jack Bodell in 1970, finally bowing out amid controversy and tears in early 1971.

Thus for fourteen years Henry Cooper was either champion or champion-elect – spanning the generations from Johnny Williams and Joe Erskine, through Brian London and Billy Walker all the way to Joe Bugner and Danny McAlinden.

If, as many believe, he was not the greatest of British heavyweight champions, it is admittedly hard to think of any former wearer of the troubled crown who might have beaten him with ease.

What is certain is that Cooper, unlike so many of his predecessors, gave British boxing credibility: he was durable, extremely likeable, a battler who overcame a series of setbacks and even humiliations on his road to triumph. Above all, he possessed a left hook ('Enery's 'Ammer') that always held out the promise of something exceptional, not a wild swing nor a clubbing thump, but a thing of beauty, his own touch of genius, perfectly, gloriously fulfilled when he dumped the incomparable Ali on the seat of his pants – one of the sublime moments of sporting history when expectations, hopes, dreams of the impossible are suddenly, miraculously realized in one bright flash of lightning.

In that respect, Cooper was to boxing what Bobby Charlton was to football – another English hero who, as he grew older, became an essential fixture and who, during a period of style and attitude 'revolution' remained reassuringly sane. Oddly, they both possessed a powerful 'dig' that could either take the breath away or leave one groaning with disappointment; and both set targets that will probably never be equalled – Charlton's goal-scoring record for England, Cooper's three Lonsdale Belts won outright.

In stark contrast to Terry Downes, Cooper was able to remain more or less above the fray, thanks mainly to his manager – the 'Bishop', Jim Wicks.

Wicks was astute and wise in the ways of boxing's seamier political side. He had been a manager and promoter for decades before taking on Cooper and had worked with both Solomons and Levene before either had risen to prominence (indeed, he had set up his first betting shop with Solomons).

By the mid-Sixties, Wicks was approaching seventy years old and concentrating all his energies on Cooper. As Cooper put it in *An Autobiography*: 'Fortunately for me, because Jim Wicks never tied me to one camp, we always played one against the other.'

In fact, Cooper's career serves as a barometer of the changing fortunes of Solomons and Levene. In 1963 it was Solomons who matched Cooper against the then Cassius Clay (the famous split glove fight); in 1966 when Cooper met Muhammad Ali for the latter's World title, it was Levene who promoted and Jarvis Astaire who controlled the close-circuit transmission of the fight that caused so much controversy at the time.

Cooper's quest for belts had an inauspicious start. In 1955 Joe Erskine defeated him in an eliminator to meet Johnny Williams, while in 1957 Erskine defeated him a second time at Harringay in Cooper's first bid for the title.

Cooper's career could be said almost to have ended before it had begun. However, he dug deep and two years on he beat Brian London at Earls Court to assume the title that he would make synonymous with his name.

London was the son of ex-heavyweight champion Jack London – a rather dour (and thus probably misunderstood) young man whose career seesawed alongside Cooper's (he fought Henry three times and Henry's brother Jim once) for almost as long: 1955 until 1970.

He won only one of his six championship fights, however, the first one against Erskine whom he stopped in eight rounds in 1958.

London was the sort of man only good fighters beat: he was rough and tough and, as Reg Gutteridge described him in a programme in the late Fifties, 'ruthless, rough, scared of no one. Scowls at would-be interviewers – hates publicity. "I'm boxing for money. I don't like publicity because I might not live up to it." '

He was certainly tough. At the end of their title fight, Cooper admitted to feeling 'worse, more exhausted and in more pain than after any other'. Swallowing blood from the first round, he also sustained cuts beneath both eyes. London suffered, too, however, so much so that at the end of the fourteenth round he raised Cooper's arm, thinking it was the end of the fight.

Such are the oddities of boxing that four months after losing to Cooper, London was in Indianapolis challenging Floyd Patterson for the latter's World title. It took Patterson eleven rounds to subdue him. Seven years later a much less effective Patterson came to London and KO'd Cooper in four rounds.

Cooper's next three defences of his British title were against Joe Erskine, a saga that, once Cooper had sorted out how to handle Erskine (that is, go for him early, pressure him and never let him settle), became predictable and somewhat undignified.

In fact, in their first contest with Cooper as champion, Erskine was floored by a series of combinations that left him draped grotesquely over the bottom rope for all the world as though his back had been broken. It was some anxious moments before he was revived.

Their next encounter was less dramatic: Erskine's eyes were damaged so badly by the fifth round that the referee stopped it. What made the occasion special was that Cooper had now won his first Lonsdale Belt outright – in fact, it was the last of the old gold belts in circulation, bearing the names of Cockell, Williams, Gardner, Woodcock, Jack and Brian London, Len Harvey and Tommy Farr – and, of course, Joe Erskine.

For it is often overlooked that, had Erskine managed to beat Cooper in any of their encounters in the early Sixties, then he, too, would have earned a belt outright. Instead, he holds the record for the most number of times a boxer failed to clinch a crucial third notch.

The final Cooper v Erskine fight, in April 1962, again ended when Erskine's eyes had closed – this time in the ninth. A chapter had ended. Although Erskine went on to beat Jack Bodell and Johnny Prescott, he dropped a decision to the new 'Golden Boy', Billy Walker, and called it a day.

In February that same year Cooper clinched his second belt outright by defeating Brian London again, having already, a year earlier, beaten Dick Richardson, a fighter Cooper classified as a 'bully boy', someone who 'if you let them get on top, they would bash the life out of you'.

Richardson, a Welshman from Newport (a next-door neighbour had been a brother of Johnny Basham) had turned professional in the same year as Cooper – indeed the two had first met when on National Service in Aldershot.

In their first meeting as pros in September 1958, Richardson, according to Cooper, came charging in, first round, 'fighting with his head down, bom, bom, bom! I was ready for him, yet still he did me!' Richardson cut Cooper's eyebrow, splitting it vertically to the middle of his forehead. In the fifth round Richardson rushed in, guard down – 'Then wallop! I caught him with a peach of a left hook.' Richardson did not get up.

Their title fight ended in a similar fashion, Richardson felled in the fifth round in what was to turn out to be his last fight, which was an oddity as his first had been a defeat at the hands of Henry's brother Jim.

Cooper's third belt came within the space of two and half years, fights slotted in around his epic challenge to Ali in 1966. Johnny Prescott – a game battler – succumbed in ten rounds on a rain-swept night in Birmingham; two years later Prescott's 'stablemate' Jack Bodell, an awkward southpaw, lasted just two rounds (but he would come again). And finally, in November 1967, 'Golden Boy' Billy Walker became Cooper's ninth victim on the trot – in many senses ironic because Walker, for all his courage and dura-bility, was almost exclusively a creature of the television age, rushed on too soon to have learned any valuable lessons about his chosen trade. Instead, his blonde good looks and tremendous physique excited television audiences who knew next to nothing about boxing and who only wanted thrills and spills.

Walker had been signed up by Harry Levene for a massive sum amid much hype, but his forte always appeared to be an ability to soak up punishment, his destruction by Brian London in 1965 being a classic example of how out of depth he really was.

Cooper more or less worked Walker over for six rounds before unleashing a fusillade of blows that Walker could neither avoid nor counter. The referee stepped in and ended it.

Two years later, Cooper was attempting to fix up a World title bout with Jimmy Ellis in the chaos that followed the deposition of Ali as World champion. The BBBC chose to back the WBC as against the WBA, who were sanctioning Cooper v Ellis – a decision that Cooper considered a betrayal, particularly as he reckoned the Board had done extremely well financially out of his career. He therefore relinquished his title in protest.

Jack Bodell was matched with Carl Gizzi at the Ice Rink, Nottingham – and won. Thus the decade that Cooper had so dominated closed without him. It was not, however, to be the end of the Cooper/Lonsdale Belt saga.

# 17

# Legends of the Sixties

During the years 1960–8, British fighters would challenge for World titles at every one of the traditional eight weights then recognized by the BBBC: in all, eleven men would take part in twenty-three World title fights, thirteen of them in the UK. This was an important factor in stimulating the communications 'revolution' taking place in pro-boxing, not to mention inflating purse expectations of men reaching championship (or near-championship) status. In turn, this played a major part in destabilizing traditional promotional arrangements in Great Britain.

The year 1966 was dominated by the Ali-Cooper World heavyweight title fight, promoted by Harry Levene and relayed to selected cinemas via Viewsport close-circuit TV. Arguments raged as to whether such a nationally significant sporting event should be available only to those who could pay. Even the incumbent Labour Government became involved through minister Tony Benn who invited all interested parties to a round-table conference, thus providing Jarvis Astaire, Harry Levene and Co. with some excellent free publicity. Benn ultimately refused to interfere with the workings of the free-market particularly when Astaire made it clear that without the revenue generated by close-circuit TV, the fight could never have been staged in the first place.

Solomons's attempts to compete with Viewsport by transmitting Walter McGowan's World title fight with Salvatori Burrani via his own network generated less controversy and, sadly, for Solomons, a great deal less money, while his 'coup' in securing the return of Ali to fight Brian London backfired as London appeared to concede in ignominious fashion, reducing what was a mismatch anyway into an undignified farce.

By the end of the year, Solomons, having been beaten to the wallet by Levene in bids to stage the Rudkin v McGowan British title fight (also transmitted via Viewsport), was threatening to pull out of big tournaments and concentrate on his World Sporting Club, opened with fanfares earlier in the year.

Solomons had more than played his part, however, in projecting British champions onto the world stage. The careers of Howard Winstone and Brian Curvis in particular had been largely shaped by his adroit matchmaking and promotional skills.

Winstone, for instance, won two Lonsdale Belts outright by the age of twenty-four, after which he concentrated almost entirely on European and World bouts, there being no one good enough to challenge him for the domestic title.

Winstone's superiority lay in the timing and precision of his left-hand work, probably the sharpest weapon of its kind in the whole game. His footwork and judgement of distance were equally superb – he could be within his own punching range and still sway away from an opponent's body shots. Moreover, he possessed an enormous fund of courage. Managed by Eddie Thomas – an outstanding welterweight champion in his day – the two made a strong, emotionally integrated partnership and Winstone became, thanks to television, probably one of the best-known fighters in British fistic history.

ABA champion in 1958 and Empire Games champion in 1959, he made his pro debut at Wembley Arena and after thirteen straight wins was leading contender for the British featherweight crown then held by another great ex-amateur, Terry Spinks.

In a sense, it would be one 'Golden Boy' replacing another because Spinks – an Olympic gold medallist in 1956 – had from the very start of his career been a box-office hit. His choirboy looks and frail appearance belied his toughness and courage and his two title wins over Bobby Neill during 1960 were dramatic, almost tragic, struggles.

The first fight saw Neill stopped in the ninth on a cut ('no bigger than a shaving nick', according to Neill – a classic understatement). The return – for a record purse for featherweights and part of Harry Levene's assault on the Solomons empire – saw Neill comprehensively outboxed for thirteen rounds before being KO'd.

Neill collapsed in his dressing-room and was rushed to hospital where a blood clot was removed – the closest a Lonsdale Belt match has ever come to producing a fatality.

Spinks himself, by the time of the Winstone bout, was probably on the decline, having taken so many hard knocks during his short career (not least having remained unconscious for a full four minutes after being KO'd by Neill back in 1959). His hopes of making the belt his own were to be rudely shattered: outboxed and outpunched in a thrilling contest, Spinks was so exhausted by the tenth round that he was unable to continue.

Spinks retired soon afterwards. What with Charlie Hill having taken so much punishment during his reign (battered to the floor ten times by Neill before retiring), Neill himself almost dying and Spinks quitting the sport when aged just twenty-four, it is evident that featherweight was a tough division during these years.

Winstone would also suffer pain and damage at the hands of opponents – but they would be World champions. At home, the competition was somewhat more benign. A year after the Spinks fight, wins over Derry Treanor and Harry Carroll saw Winstone take his first belt.

Securing the second belt took slightly less time – just over ten months, in fact. Johnny Morrissey was stopped in eleven in Glasgow, Billy Calvert was outpointed in Porthcawl and John O'Brien was competently dealt with in December 1963 at the National Sporting Club. After that it would be another three years before anyone from the British Isles was considered of sufficient quality to enter the ring with him. In December 1966 Lennie 'The Lion' Williams, the Welsh featherweight champion, was stopped inside eight rounds at the Wyvern Social Club, Aberavon.

After that, Winstone's career ascended to World level, his compelling battles with Vicente Saldivar, Mitsunori Seki and Jose Legra establishing the good-looking, thoroughly likeable Welshman as one of Britain's boxing immortals. Only when he finally hung up his gloves in July 1968 was the featherweight title released from his mesmeric grip.

That other supreme Welsh boxing artist, Brian Curvis, also found British titles, if not simply there for the taking, then often merely occasions to demonstrate that he had no equal in Britain or the Commonwealth. Curvis, a southpaw, not only knew how to box: he was an exceptional hitter for his weight. Not that he indulged in 'slugging'. What impressed the cognoscenti was the accomplished way he went about his work. He would pinpoint an opponent with an accurate straight right and swiftly follow with a left bang on target.

Curvis took the welterweight title from Wally Swift at Nottingham Ice Rink in December 1960, the start of an unprecedented seven-championship-win sequence. Swift was defeated a second time at the Ice Rink in May 1961, followed by Irishman Mick Leahy in October 1961 – a perfect left hook felling the Irishman as if he had been shot. Brian handed his first belt to his brother Cliff, by now his manager.

His second belt took over two years to secure but the three victories – over Tony Mancini, Tony Smith and Johnny Cooke – were more emphatic than the first three, each ending well inside the fifteen-round championship distance. He handed his second belt to his wife on their honeymoon.

Curvis was very much a 'Solomons' fighter; indeed, as early as 1960, when Brian was an untitled twenty-three-year-old, the promoter promised the young Welshman a Lonsdale Belt acquired 'some time ago' if he won a particularly crucial fight. With Ted Broadribb serving in Curvis's corner, the suspicion is that the belt was an original NSC one, discarded by Al Foreman and snapped up by Jeff Dickson.

Solomons also pulled off a typically dramatic piece of match-making when he paired Curvis with lightweight champion Dave Charnley in a lucrative catchweight fight in the summer of 1964, Curvis winning on points after being floored early on by the dynamic Charnley.

However, Curvis could not manage to overcome the legendary Emile Griffiths who thoroughly outboxed him over fifteen long and painful rounds in the same year. Two years later, in 1966, the unbeaten British champion retired – significantly, perhaps, the year when the Solomons star really did begin to wane.

The arguments and accusations concerning 'syndicates' and 'monopolies' during the 1960s had most relevance for the provinces. If proof were needed that 'independent' promoters were a

dying breed, then the situation in Manchester, Liverpool, Newcastle and South Wales – all once prolific boxing centres and now
virtual 'ghost towns' – appeared conclusive enough, particularly
where British championships were concerned.

Between 1962 and 1968, of forty-six British title fights, only
eleven were staged in London, yet throughout this period, Belle
Vue, Manchester mounted no more than six title fights – every
one of which was promoted by 'Londoner' Harry Levene, the
matches made by Mickey Duff, with occasional involvement of
Manchester bookmaker Gus Demmy.

Liverpool, once the famous 'Graveyard of Champions',
managed no more than two title fights – once again, Duff/Demmy/
Levene events. Meanwhile, that other 'monopolist', Jack Solomons, continued to be active up and down the country, putting on
title promotions in Birmingham, Belfast, Glasgow, Coney Beach,
Porthcawl and St James' Hall, Newcastle.

In a sense, it was often not so much a matter of provincial men
being squeezed out as a lack of new men taking over from earlier
provincial 'giants' such as Johnny Best of Liverpool. Best had
ruled his particular patch since before the war, but when he died
aged seventy in 1956, the Stadium was already in decline. In fact,
Best had already announced that, due to the Entertainment Tax,
the old Stadium would only be opening once every three weeks
instead of once a week. Understandably, in such a climate, no
one stepped into his shoes.

Title fights staged by promoters not associated with the two
big cartels were few and far between. Peter Keenan – boxer turned
entrepreneur – managed a couple in Glasgow; Alex Griffiths
in Wolverhampton, Stan Cottle in Cardiff and Lew Phillips in
Birmingham all put on single championship shows. But the man
who really kept the independent flag flying throughout this period
was Reg King, operating from that unlikely venue, the Ice Rink,
Nottingham.

King was a Nottingham bookmaker who began promoting just
after the war at the local Victoria Baths, a small hall that served
as his regular base, while the Ice Rink, which could hold between
5,000 and 6,000, was reserved for the gala occasions.

During the Fifties champions like Ronnie Clayton, Dick
Turpin, Alex Buxton and Pat McAteer had defended their titles

at the Rink, and throughout the Sixties King managed at least one title fight a year, specializing in welter and middleweights. In fact, from 1963 to 1969 Nottingham fans had a monopoly of the middleweight title as local lads Wally Swift and Johnny Pritchett regularly packed the place.

For a period in the late Fifties King also dabbled in Scottish featherweights – in particular, British title-holder Charlie Hill who defended his title twice at the Ice Rink, on the second occasion losing his crown to a man who would later play a large part in the career of Nottingham favourite Johnny Pritchett: Bobby Neill.

King also secured, in December 1961, a British lightweight title fight that neither champion nor challenger would look back upon with much pleasure.

For Dave Charnley, considered by many as one of Britain's best post-war champions, the fight was something of an irritation. It was certainly a rare occasion; since winning the title in 1957, defeating Joe Lucy on points at Harringay, the powerful little 'pocket Marciano' had been too busy chasing European, Empire and World titles to have time to defend his Lonsdale Belt.

Managed by Arthur Boggis, Charnley, the ex-blacksmith from Dartford, an elegant, fiery, two-fisted southpaw who liked to end his contests inside the scheduled time-limit, had powered his way to the title, losing just twice in twenty-four contests.

Charnley's only limitations, if they can be so termed, were his diminutive size and his tendency to cut. With short arms and legs, he liked opponents to come to him and he was at his best when he could hook, uppercut and jab without moving forward. A determined, relentless opponent who never contemplated defeat, his ringcraft enabled him to surmount his natural deficiencies, so much so that in two tremendous scraps for the World lightweight title he gave Joe Brown – a supreme boxing champion, mobile with tremendous reach – the fights of his life.

During the same period he KO'd Willie Toweel to take the Empire title and won and defended the European title three times. However, five years between British title defences was considered long enough by the Board who nominated one Dave 'Darkie' Hughes from Cardiff as challenger.

The fight would be remarkable for two reasons: the record

quick finish (the two men were in combat for less than thirty seconds) and the fact that Hughes was the only black boxer to feature in a British title fight throughout the 1960s.

Hughes was a veteran, having been fighting professionally for some seventeen years after starting out with the George Middleton/Randolph Turpin 'stable' in 1953. He was clearly overawed by the occasion, *Boxing News* reporting:

> Hughes, looking drawn at 9 st 6 lb, surprisingly stepped into the centre of the ring as though shaping up for a spar-session. Charnley unleashed his southpaw right-hook – and the punch knocked any semblance of fight out of his outclassed challenger. Darkie staggered and almost pitched face-first out of the ring. He glanced appealingly at his corner as though in search of a friendly face. Then another hook sent him on his haunches.

Hughes rose, Charnley crashed home another right and it was over – the quickest-ever finish to a British championship fight.

Charnley, in fact, was to taste little more championship success. The following year he lost his Empire title to Bunny Grant and in 1963 he secured his Lonsdale Belt with a points win over Maurice Cullen. A year after that, he retired.

Charnley, Hill, Neill, even Cooper and Erskine in 1962 – Nottingham fans could hardly complain about the quality of fighters being placed before them. Yet it would be local men Wally Swift and Johnny Pritchett who would provide the majority of the drama, one or other of them featuring in some nine title fights over the next ten years.

Managed by George Biddles, the Nottingham-born Swift secured a surprise shot at Tommy Malloy's British welterweight title in February 1960. Although the underdog and relatively inexperienced, he responded to the local crowd's enthusiasm by boxing Malloy's head off, his educated left hook-cum-jab jerking Malloy's head back with sickening regularity as the veteran champ attempted to fathom out what to do.

Swift then came up against Brian Curvis, who took his title and defeated him in a return some six months later. However, by December 1964 Swift was operating successfully at middleweight, earning the right in an eliminator at the Ice Rink in May 1964 to challenge for the title.

In December 1964 Swift's all-round boxing craft put paid to the middleweight champion, Irishman Mick Leahy. But within months he was faced with a challenger destined to split the local support he had hitherto exclusively enjoyed.

Johnny Pritchett, a native of local village Bingham, had turned pro in 1963, the year Swift won his first championship. A fine amateur – indeed, ABA welterweight champion – he was an intelligent, two-handed boxer, immensely strong and always superbly fit. As a boy he had admired Swift, and indeed, as an amateur had helped him in the gym.

Pritchett's route to fame had been a roundabout one: he had gone to Bobby Neill in London when turning pro and was now living there. With Neill's London contacts, Pritchett had been able to start his career in the most glamorous of circumstances – at Wembley Pool in 1963.

The Swift v Pritchett middleweight title fight in November 1965 was thus the perfect Nottingham promotion: the 'young pretender' (one of the first generation of boxers, incidentally, not to have gone through National Service) versus the much-loved 'old campaigner'. And in a close-fought battle there was little in it going into the twelfth round, when Harry Gibbs decided that a cut over Swift's swollen and closed left eye was too bad to let him continue.

It was a bitter blow to Swift and a result that was greeted with mixed emotions by the crowd. For manager Bobby Neill, however, it was confirmation that Nottingham Ice Rink was his lucky venue; following his own title win in 1959, he had brought Alan Rudkin to the Rink earlier in 1965 to see him take the bantamweight crown.

The good form would continue. Because it had been a voluntary defence, Swift was granted a return and fourteen months later the Nottingham fans were treated to an even better clash between the two committed rivals. Pritchett by this time had become a much more accomplished boxer: seven more wins had followed, including a second title win at Nottingham, against Nat Jacobs. Consequently, victory over Swift would secure the Lonsdale Belt outright, the sixth to be won since 1909.

Even to this day there are people in Nottingham who argue that Swift won the second title encounter. Wally himself certainly thought he had done enough but after fifteen of the most exciting rounds ever seen at the Ice Rink, referee Wally Thom scored it 74¾ pts–73¾ pts in favour of the reigning champion.

It was a tremendously emotional night and at the end the whole arena was in uproar as Swift fans whistled, booed and stamped their feet in disapproval. But it was not the end for Wally Swift. Pritchett defended once more, against Les McAteer, but following a defeat at the hands of Roberto Duran, he retired. Thus in July 1969, almost nine years after he had first challenged for a title at the Rink, Swift stepped out again, this time to contest the vacant middleweight title with McAteer.

Sadly, his final championship bout would end in disappointment. Les, whose uncle Pat had won the same title and an outright belt in the Fifties, was too strong for Wally, then in his thirty-third year. Swift was forced to retire in the eleventh round. Thus the middleweight title was at last prised from Nottingham after five eventful years.

Pritchett and Swift were fortunate in having a local promoter and a popular local venue that guaranteed them a healthy payday whenever they challenged or defended a title. Nottingham was almost the only provincial venue in England in a healthy state during the Sixties. For a champion from any other region or city not tied to an influential promoter nor gifted with a style likely to excite a London audience, the possession of a Lonsdale Belt meant little in terms of hard cash or exposure.

Maurice Cullen was one of Britain's most accomplished lightweights – essentially a boxer but with a brilliant left hand that was no 'tap-and-away' prop but a damaging punch that tended to sicken rather than KO opponents. Between 1959 and 1968 he lost just five contests out of fifty-two and in 1963 gave Carlos Ortiz, lightweight World champion, a fearful struggle before Ortiz scraped home.

Yet Cullen found that in metropolitan circles he was considered 'box-office poison', *Boxing News* commenting: 'Fans don't exactly break down doors to see him perform.' Why this was so remains a puzzle, as veteran boxing scribe George Whiting described Cullen thus: 'He pursues his trade with the elusiveness of an eel, the pace of a whippet, the guile of an escapologist and the agility of a cat-burglar.'

Whatever the truth about his skills and appeal, he would find it very hard to earn good money in British rings. He took the vacant title in Liverpool where he was matched with local boy Dave Coventry by local promoters Ray Peers and Jack Turner – the first lightweight title fight in the famous stadium since 1947.

Cullen scored a fine, emphatic victory over the tough, USA-style Coventry and while Lt Col. J. W. Graham placed the Lonsdale Belt around his waist, Cullen's Geordie supporters sang the 'Blaydon Races'. As British champion at a popular weight, however, he found the major promoters reluctant to employ him.

In 1965, when he was matched with Londoner Vic Andreetti in a first defence of his title, the BBBC put the fight out to tender, only to find no takers. Eventually, Alex Griffiths decided to stage it at Wolverhampton where it proved an exciting contest, with Andreetti wading through Cullen's regular accurate left jabs to launch a string of attacks that had his London followers cheering wildly.

At the end, however, Cullen, to loud jeers from Andreetti's supporters, was declared the winner. The following year, Cullen made the belt his own, defeating Terry Edwards in Newcastle – a home-town title fight at last; but his triumph went almost unnoticed in the rest of the country.

For a bona-fide champion of such quality, such lack of attention was galling, particularly as this was the period when non-title fights such as the Walker v London heavyweight clash were being snapped up for close-circuit transmission, when Howard Winstone never seemed to be off the TV screen, and when a succession of 'Golden Boys' such as Mark Rowe and Ralph Charles, Walker and Johnny Prescott appeared to be making vast sums of money for simply putting in an appearance.

It got to the point in 1967 when Cullen, offered a paltry £500 to defend his title, threatened to retire from the game and take a job as a physical training instructor. However, Jack Solomons stepped in and made a bid to stage the contest – yet another return with Andreetti – for a purse of £2,465 at King's Hall, Newcastle.

Cullen ran out a unanimous points victor, but no better off

financially, and it would only be in 1968, when Mickey Duff matched him with the then merely 'promising' Ken Buchanan, that he would be offered a London title date, and this at the private Anglo-American Sporting Club before an audience of no more than 1,000.

Sadly for Cullen, he was on the end of a shock defeat, being KO'd in the eleventh round after a painfully chastening fight. Down as early as the fourth round, down again twice in the sixth and once more in the ninth, it was a comprehensive defeat that more or less ended his career.

Cullen's fate – not popular enough in the capital, but lacking a powerful provincial promoter to back him – would not be shared by a famous quartet of champions from across the various borders of England. During the 1960s, the traditional Celtic dominance of the lightest weights, fly and bantam, continued apace as Irishmen Freddie Gilroy and Johnny Caldwell, Scotsman Walter McGowan and Welshman Alan Rudkin took titles and belts galore.

With fanatical audiences in Belfast and Glasgow, men like McGowan did not need to travel south to make a good living; Freddie Gilroy fought every one of his five British title fights in Belfast, only gracing the Wembley boards when a European or World title was at stake.

At the very start of the decade it was the Irishmen Caldwell and Gilroy who were at the top of their respective divisions, both having defeated and forced into retirement talented Scotsmen to get there.

Caldwell, the younger of the two, had taken the flyweight title from Freddie Jones who had been champion since 1957. Great things had been expected of Jones who had turned pro in 1955 under the management of Walter McGowan's father and who had taken the flyweight title after just seven pro fights. But after successfully defending against Alex Ambrose in Glasgow, he took his title to King's Hall, Belfast in October 1960 where he crashed to defeat inside three rounds – counted out lying face down after taking two precise rights to the jaw.

His conqueror, Caldwell, aptly dubbed the 'Cold-eyed Irish Killer', came from a hard background. Born in 1938 in Cyprus Street off the Falls Road, he had a long and successful career as an amateur – 240 fights and only six defeats. No wonder he was welcomed with open arms by Glasgow promoter Sam Docherty in 1958 when as an apprentice plumber he travelled to the city in search of work.

Caldwell's devastating punching and his all-round ability to combine jabs, hooks and uppercuts made him such a sure-fire hit in Glasgow at Docherty's Kelvin Hall shows that, by the time Belfast promoter George Connell lured Caldwell back to Ireland for an appearance before his native audience, expectations were high.

His fans were not disappointed. After just seventeen pro-fights and seventeen wins, Caldwell became flyweight champion, his swift, devastating three-round KO of Jones ending the latter's career.

Within months, however, finding it impossible to make the flyweight limit, Caldwell stepped up to bantamweight, thus putting himself on a direct collision course with that other Northern Irish phenomenon, Freddie Gilroy.

Gilroy was two years older than Caldwell, with an uncannily similar upbringing and amateur career (also gaining a bronze at the Melbourne Olympics and meeting with defeat a mere three times in over 100 amateur bouts).

He had a southpaw style and a powerful punch which, according to writer Patrick Myler, made him the hardest hitter in Irish boxing history. After a mere thirteen bouts, he gained a championship shot against veteran double belt winner, Peter Keenan.

Keenan was no stranger to the King's Hall, Belfast, having lost his title to Billy Kelly there in 1953. After regaining it in Glasgow he had returned to Belfast to defend it successfully against George O'Neill. Against Gilroy, however, he found himself unable, despite his superior experience and know-how, to contain the more powerful, much younger Irishman. Put down several times in the course of the contest, Keenan failed to survive a torrid eleventh round, being rescued by the referee after his fourth trip to the canvas.

Keenan, nevertheless, endeared himself to the 16,000 crowd by putting his arm around Gilroy and singing 'When Irish Eyes Are Smiling' before announcing his retirement.

Gilroy seemed destined for big things – a European, then a

Commonwealth title followed, but soon after, in the first successful defence of his Lonsdale Belt against Billy Rafferty, his career
began to go awry.

In 1960 he lost to Alphonse Halimi in a challenge for the EBU
World title; a year later, the European title went. Meanwhile,
Johnny Caldwell had taken Halimi's World crown. Thus, despite
KO'ing Billy Rafferty in twelve rounds to earn himself a Lonsdale
Belt outright – the first Irishman to achieve such a feat – Gilroy
could no longer claim undisputed sovereignty of the bantam-
weight division.

Johnny Caldwell subsequently lost the title in Brazil in January
1962, but defeat in foreign climes rarely dents a fighter's popularity at home and Caldwell was now considered the obvious
challenger for Gilroy's British title. It was, as Patrick Myler wrote,
'one of the most natural pairings in Irish boxing history', and
George Connell teamed up with Jack Solomons to mount the
Irish fight of the decade, if not the century:

> The fight began at a tremendous pace and never faltered. The
> punch-for-punch exchanges in the opening three minutes set
> the pattern for the rest of the bout and even though Caldwell
> was on the floor within seconds of the first bell, he stormed
> back to win the second round with lightning fast, strength-
> sapping hooks to the body.

And so it continued – first Gilroy, then Caldwell seemed to
have the upper hand as the crowd roared itself hoarse with
excitement. In the sixth, however, Caldwell suffered a cut eye –
an injury that gradually worsened as Gilroy tore in. At the end
of the ninth, Caldwell's cuts man, Danny Holland, decided it was
all over.

It had been an epic struggle, but though a return seemed
inevitable, Gilroy never fought again. Disputes over the contract
resulted in delays and a fine by the BBBC, non-payment of which
in turn led to Gilroy's licence being temporarily withdrawn.

Although he claimed that it was weight troubles that had been
the problem and that he would resume his career at featherweight,
it may well have been a lack of desire, and perhaps Gilroy had
the right idea after all. Caldwell, though continuing to fight, also

found that the lustre had faded. In 1964 he did create a little bit of Belt history by taking the bantamweight title by outboxing Englishman George Bowes in Belfast – forcing him to retire with a cut eye in the seventh – to become the first Irishman to win two British championships. Looming on the horizon, however, was a young man who would ultimately end Caldwell's career.

Alan Rudkin, though a Welshman born in Corwen, North Wales, lived and grew up in the Dingle district of Liverpool. As he rose to fame, his Scouse associations were a gift to hard-pressed sub-editors ('Mersey Man Rudkin Has The Beat In His Fists') while his baby-faced, sub-Beatle haircut fitted neatly into the 'Swinging Sixties' image.

Yet his career owed nothing to such superficialities. In the unchanging workaday world of pro-boxing, the qualities that guaranteed success had little to do with passing fads. Rudkin was a tiny powerhouse of a man, a two-fisted box-fighter with a good punch and seemingly bottomless reserves of stamina and strength.

Like Gilroy and Caldwell, Rudkin travelled widely as an amateur, boxing for England. When he turned pro in May 1962, he joined another amateur team-mate, Frankie Taylor, under the management of Bobby Neill, which meant moving to London and lodging in Islington where he had a job as a warehouse-packer at a sausage factory.

Rudkin's career certainly got off to a good start, his first pro-fight being at Liverpool Stadium where he was paid £1,000 – the highest purse a preliminary fighter was ever paid at the famous arena. But although his progress to a title fight was well-nigh spotless, when he was paired with Johnny Caldwell in March 1965 the betting slightly favoured the champion as the more experienced, perhaps more ruthless man.

Caldwell, nevertheless, looked a battle-weary veteran as he shaped up to the younger, fresher challenger whose relentless pressure inflicted a badly damaged nose as early as the third and a bad cut in the ninth. When Rudkin turned his attentions to Caldwell's body in the tenth, forcing him to collapse into the ropes, the referee intervened.

The final player in the magical quartet was Walter McGowan. Hugh McIlvanney said of him, in *On Boxing*, that he possessed the 'best hands I have ever seen on a boxer from these islands.

His extraordinary, fast, varied, damagingly selective punching made him the most precociously brilliant amateur in my experience.' His huge talent, however, would be compromised, like Caldwell, by a tendency to cut.

His progress through an admittedly thin flyweight division was swift. In his third pro fight in October 1961, he lost narrowly to the Scottish champion Jackie Brown, then a leading contender for the flyweight title. Brown was a fine classy boxer, a master craftsman who relied on poise and punch rather than power to beat an opponent. In February 1962 he travelled to Birmingham to defeat Brian Cartwright to take the title, hanging the Lonsdale Belt over the counter (suspended on black velvet with a spotlight trained on it) in his hostelry, the Station Bar, Abbeyhill in Edinburgh.

In May of the following year, however, Walter McGowan laid claim to the belt. Although in only his tenth fight, he proved to have too much skill and ultimately strength for Brown – a fighter who was even then struggling against nature to stay in the flyweight division.

McGowan would never have to hand back the belt. Brown stepped up a division and for the next three years no one of sufficient class in the eyes of the BBBC established a right to challenge McGowan. Then in May 1966 he was given the belt for keeps at a ceremony at Jack Solomons's World Sporting Club – the first man to make a BBBC belt his own after just one contest.

Although McGowan was to take the World flyweight title in 1966, it was clear that on the domestic front, bantamweight offered greater, more lucrative opportunities and the resulting McGowan v Rudkin British title fight in September 1966 would turn out to be the best big contest of the year. Yet, when the fight began, the stadium was barely two-thirds full.

The first eight rounds belonged to Rudkin. The little Liverpudlian was the aggressor, attempting to coax his Scottish adversary into a close-quarters punch-up, but McGowan was too shrewd to risk this while Rudkin was fresh and fit.

Rudkin concentrated his attack to the body, paying particular attention to McGowan's rib-cage – when he could hit it, because McGowan was boxing beautifully on the retreat at this stage.

Then McGowan, though suffering some ugly cuts, gradually piled on the pressure to take a points decision, a verdict that was greeted by a tremendous storm of booing. Many present had felt that a draw would have been a fair result.

It was two years before McGowan and Rudkin met again; and it cost Harry Levene £10,000 to win the right to stage the return, which he promoted at Manchester's Belle Vue stadium.

Once again, it was Rudkin who dictated matters at the start, preventing the champion from mounting his own offensive by forcing him back continuously: and though warned for use of the head and suffering a nasty cut, by half-way Rudkin was clearly in the lead.

In the ninth round, McGowan's left eye started to bleed once again, prompting him to fight back furiously. He had Rudkin troubled by a left-right combination to the head and this was the shape of things in rounds ten to thirteen with the Scots champion handing out punishment to his challenger in liberal doses.

The tactic failed, however, to pull the fight out of the fire and from the fourteenth round onwards Rudkin reasserted himself by boxing smartly on the retreat and amassing more points. At the end, Harry Gibbs went to Rudkin's corner to proclaim the new champion of Britain and the Commonwealth.

Rudkin would continue fighting for titles for another four years; McGowan had contested his last. In 1970, when Rudkin, who had already won a belt outright by defeating Evan Armstrong in June 1969, refused McGowan a return fight, preferring to take on Johnny Clark instead, McGowan decided to retire.

# 18

## Levene Supreme

In November 1979 the BBBC celebrated its Golden Jubilee with a grand 'bash' at the NSC's new home, the Café Royal. The glossy brochure produced for the occasion provided not only a potted history of British pro-boxing and the Board itself but also an accurate glimpse of the state of play where promotional power was concerned, the principal 'movers and shakers' such as Levene, Duff, Barrett and Lawless being pictured prominently or featured in large ads.

Two big names – Jack Solomons and Teddy Waltham – were nevertheless conspicuous by their absence from the vast and impressive guest-list that included over a hundred former champions.

Waltham had been Charles Donmall's successor as general secretary of the Board in 1950. An ex-fighter and referee of great repute – indeed, one of the top half-dozen referees in the world – he was steeped in the professional game, with fistic family connections stretching back into the nineteenth century. As such, he was a pro's pro – although the wisdom of having an active referee in such a prominent and sensitive position (as such, an employee of promoters) might have been questioned.

Even so, Waltham had raised the Board from its precarious post-war position to its current status as the firm, unquestioned authority in British professional boxing, and had enhanced its reputation abroad with his skilful and popular diplomacy. In 1972, after twenty-two years in the 'hot-seat', he had retired, replaced by his deputy Ray Clarke. In 1978, Waltham had died, aged seventy-two, much mourned and respected.

Jack Solomons was still alive, albeit extremely ill and close to death – indeed, he would die the following month. Yet reading the Jubilee brochure, which contained just one passing reference to him, one might have thought he had never existed. He repaid the compliment, of course, in his will, bequesting the Board just one penny and leaving nobody in any doubt as to his feelings towards the organization with which he had battled long and consistently.

His gradual eclipse during the 1970s had at least taken much pressure off the Board. The emotional turmoil, the uncomfortable (and inconvenient) accusations of 'monopoly' that had soured the early Sixties were gradually replaced by a long-running, bitter but containable 'dispute' between two distinct 'camps'.

Solomons, despite steadily losing ground, had never, of course, given up the struggle. His World Sporting Club at Grosvenor House mounted some nine championship bouts during the Seventies and his alliance with Nottingham's Reg King had helped keep the Ice Rink afloat in championship terms until the mid-Seventies, while the relaxation in rules concerning promoters' rights to manage fighters meant that he had been able to oversee men such as Charlie Nash and Danny McAlinden to championship challenges.

In the Seventies, however, championship shows increasingly came to mean the Albert Hall (under exclusive control of Mike Barrett) and Wembley Pool (Harry Levene's 'Home of Big Time Boxing'), with matchmaking for these two very much the domain of Mickey Duff, and management of many featured champions the preserve of Terry Lawless. And with TV and close-circuit transmissions always by courtesy of Jarvis Astaire, these men were boxing's Big Five – and the Seventies their triumphant decade.

They were sustained by close, almost incestuous, links with the BBC which, being a natural monopoly itself, probably preferred dealing with similar creatures in the wider world. (It was established as early as 1972 that Mike Barrett was receiving some £3,000 per promotion from BBC TV whereas provincial promoters, even with attractive bouts to sell, were regularly turned down.)

Television would be a key factor in the battle at the top during the Seventies, the 'live' promoter, even when protected by the Board's fourteen-day rule, generally coming off second best. For instance, on 27 June 1972 Jack Solomons and Alex Griffiths promoted the British heavyweight title fight between Jack Bodell and Danny McAlinden at Nottingham. It was a box-office flop – and it is not hard to understand why, considering that on the very same evening ITV beamed Ken Buchanan v Roberto Duran into people's homes for free, while in the early hours of the following morning Muhammad Ali's fight with Jerry Quarry had been piped into various cinemas up and down the country by Jarvis Astaire's Viewsport. ITV followed this up on the night of the 28th with a double bill of Ali v Quarry and Bob Foster defending his World title – very good for television viewers, but hopeless for Solomons and Griffiths.

Television, of course, was by now well out of the Board's control or even guidance; and even such influence as the Board might try to wield generally seemed to work against the smaller promoters – the very people who could have done with some TV cash.

In February 1970 the Board introduced a rule to the effect that in order to qualify for a TV 'date' a promoter had first to have mounted three small-hall shows. The idea, naturally, was to give promoters an incentive to put on more live shows, but it simply made things much harder for provincial promoters who calculated that it was too risky to try mounting three potentially loss-making shows in order to gain the chance (no more) of earning some TV cash.

For the big boys, such as Mickey Duff – who operated regularly at York Hall and Shoreditch Town Hall – it was relatively easy, of course: yet another case of the rich getting richer and the poor poorer. No wonder, therefore, that the exclusive dinner/boxing clubs continued to proliferate throughout the Seventies: by 1972 there were some twenty such sporting clubs in England and Wales, with two on the way in Scotland.

These clubs had mounted 66 of 101 shows thus far that year; and even championship fights were to be increasingly staged in members-only clubs. The Board – keen to keep boxing open to and within the means of the ordinary fan – had tried to make it difficult for them by insisting that clubs not be allowed to negotiate for title fights: only when a fight went out to purse offers could a club make a bid.

Nevertheless, Solomons's World Sporting Club, Duff's Anglo-

American Club at the Hilton, the Midland Sporting Club in Solihull, and later the Albany Hotel in Glasgow, continued to lead the way in staging championships. By the late Seventies, when the Board altered the rules to allow clubs to bid on equal terms (something Jack Solomons had regularly pressed for), clubs would be staging the vast majority of title fights.

It was the irresistible rise of Harry Levene that would nevertheless prove the key factor in a very special Seventies phenomenon – the emergence of British boxing 'superstars', tilting at World titles as regularly as they had once scrapped for Lonsdale Belts.

Levene, even when a simple boxing manager in the inter-war years, had specialized in obtaining title shots for his boxers even when they were not acknowledged as champs at home. Now, with a glamorous arena such as Wembley at his command, he came into his kingdom; and the Seventies would see Arthur Elvin's old stamping ground stage some thirteen World title fights, not to mention sixteen European titles as well as eighteen British titles. With Barrett's Albert Hall acting virtually as 'back-up', mounting another twenty-one British title fights and twelve European championships during the same period, it is not hard to see where 'power' lay during these years.

In all, some eleven British fighters between the years 1970 and 1980 fought for World titles – the same number as during the Sixties but, whereas the earlier champs compiled twenty-one title shots, the new men amassed thirty-six.

That was the principal difference between the two decades for men at the very top – title activity now almost ruled out run-of-the-mill contests. With so much money on offer for individual contests – at least, for those men 'in the frame' – there was no need (indeed, it was positively foolish) to contest bouts of lesser importance.

The consequences for domestic boxing, a gradual but inevitable erosion in significance, was noted as early as 1972 by *Boxing News* in an editorial under the headline: 'Sign of the Times': 'Clearly pride and prestige no longer matter if a British title does not carry enough for the fighter in money. . . .'

Now this had, to some extent, always been true. Champions such as Downes, McAvoy and Beckett, right the way back to

Freddie Welsh, had baulked at defending their crowns if the purses were too small. The Seventies, however, saw a new development: the wholesale relinquishing of titles once they had served their purpose of elevating the fighter to World or European contender status. As *Boxing News* commented:

> Is the surrender of titles a sign of the times we live in when ambition and chances in so many fields count for little unless accompanied by the right terms in cash? Considering what their forerunners had to fight for, even in this progressive age of inflated values, the swing-up of titles is not good for boxing or what we owe the greats of yesteryear.

What it meant, of course, was the virtual abandonment in certain divisions of the accepted practice whereby a British champion made regular defences against nominated challengers.

Indeed, during the Seventies some fifteen British title holders at almost all weights either relinquished or forfeited their British titles rather than defend them – some, such as Minter and Buchanan, doing it twice.

Compare this to the Sixties, when only three men gave up their British title for reasons other than retirement – one of whom, Henry Cooper, was merely protesting at the Board's refusal to back him in a World title bid, another, Calderwood, because he was in jail – and one can appreciate the 'sea-change'.

Cooper, in 1976, was himself moved to excuse fighters who handed their belts back with such alacrity thus: with fewer fighters involved in the sport and the more 'free' titles available, the more incentive there was for fighters to fight and promoters to promote. Moreover, a British champion holding a European or World title stood to lose a great deal of money if forced to defend his British title and in the process suffered a loss. Relinquishing the title and the belt was thus a simple precaution, as Henry Rhiney remarked in 1977: 'Lonsdale Belts do mean something. I mean, every fighter would like to have one, but they don't do much for you.'

Nevertheless, during the Seventies, British championships did produce some superb 'super-bouts' between men recognized either as World champions or contenders, fights that carried the increasingly rare tag – 'box office'. Unfortunately 'box-office' was not a term often associated with the first of the Seventies super-champions – Ken Buchanan. Indeed, Buchanan had more excuse than most for feeling that the British title was never going to earn him money commensurate with his status.

Buchanan's career is often cited as evidence of the destructive rise in importance of exclusive members-only clubs as against the commercial promotions in traditional 'public' arenas. Such 'exclusivity' was also used to explain the lack of support for him when he *did* fight in public – his apparent inability to fill a stadium of thousands, even in his own country.

Buchanan, while castigating his homeland and his home city for showing little enthusiasm for him, felt the blame lay elsewhere; his lack of exposure was due more to boxing politics than his own lack of appeal. Eventually he rounded on his manager/second Eddie Thomas who, in his role as manager of Howard Winstone, had fallen out with the Duff/Barrett camp, while Thomas's close links with Jack Solomons only exacerbated the situation: 'So my name failed to appear on the high-roller shows in London and, while I sat at home and occasionally earned peanuts for boxing journeymen professionals on the road to nowhere, others were piling up the readies and the glory in front of big crowds.'

Consequently, having gained the British lightweight title from Maurice Cullen in February 1968, Buchanan waited eighteen months in vain for the Board to provide him with an opponent before announcing in late 1969 that he was retiring. He claimed he could earn more as a joiner than as a fighter, but the wood chips on his shoulder must not be allowed to obscure the fact that, ever since Dave Charnley retired in 1963, the lightweight division had suffered in terms of viable, attractive contenders and thus audience-appeal. Charnley himself had been annoyed at having to defend for relative peanuts against 'Darkie' Hughes. A fine fighter like Maurice Cullen had been similarly aggrieved at the lack of interest shown in him by London promoters while Buchanan's successor, Willie Reilly, actually gave the title up in 1972 rather than defend for a purse of under £2,000.

With little credible opposition at home, matchmaking was a difficult business. Buchanan had, in that sense, 'classed' himself out of work. His World and European forays would be extensive enough, however, thanks initially to Solomons whose international clout made up for his inability to mount large-scale British title fights.

Having been persuaded to return to the game in 1970, Buchanan lost a disputed match with M. Velazquez in Madrid, defended his British title (the BBBC having conveniently refused to accept his earlier 'retirement') against Woodford's Brian Hudson, Southern Area Champion, and then four months later, in San Juan, took the WBA World title from Ismael Laguna.

When he finally decided to challenge for the Lonsdale Belt again, he had thus established himself as one of the world's greatest lightweight boxers, having developed from a boxer with elusive speed of foot and a style based on a 'classic' stand and prance behind a left jab' into a hard-hitting, dazzlingly two-fisted battler whose straight left, reinforced by sharp hooks with the same hand or swift right crosses, made him feared and respected.

Thus, when Buchanan was matched against Jim Watt in January 1973, the latter found himself facing a 'living legend'. Watt's apprehension – indeed, awe – has been cited as an explanation for his subdued performance. To quote Buchanan in his *High Life and Hard Times*: 'It was a crap fight. Jim Watt was not 100 per cent confident that night. Every time I hit him with a half-decent shot, he hung on.'

Although neither man was ever in any trouble, the referee's 10–3 score in Buchanan's favour, though perhaps a trifle harsh on Watt, reflected the superiority of the ex-champion, who had now earned himself a Lonsdale Belt for keeps.

The contest, staged at Glasgow's Albany Hotel, a club venue holding little more than 1,000, was Buchanan's fourth and last appearance in Scotland before retiring in 1975. In 1974, faced with a challenge from Watt again, he chose to concentrate on a European title challenge and, for the second time, relinquished the title.

The career of Watt, in many respects Buchanan's heir-apparent, would underline certain of Buchanan's complaints regarding the 'system' that he felt had operated to exclude him from domestic fame and fortune. Like Buchanan, Watt built his performances upon a firm base of a solid left jab which could double up as a hook. Never wildly exciting as a performer, he was tough, determined and much more dangerous than his benign appearance might suggest. Challenger Johnny Claydon from West Ham, who had a hustling aggressive style, good stamina and a solid punch in either hand, found his strength sapped by Watt's accurate and sickeningly regular short left jabs to the body, while Watt's southpaw jabs to the face, followed up with short-range upper-cuts, reduced Claydon's performance to ragged confusion. In round ten, referee Wally Thom halted the contest after Claydon's third trip to the canvas.

Watt was presented with a Lonsdale Belt to keep after the fight. His career, although almost ten years old at that stage, was taking a definite turn for the better, for in his corner that night was one of the most successful post-war fight manager/trainers ever: Terry Lawless.

After Lawless became his manager late in 1976, Watt started to get the opportunities that had eluded most British lightweight champions since the war. Yet to attribute Watt's success simply to Lawless's connections would be demeaning both to fighter and manager, for Lawless transformed him from a basically defensive fighter into a ruthlessly punching destroyer. Between 1977 and 1978 he had four European title bouts, all won, followed by a glorious sequence of World title matches beginning in April 1979 with a successful challenge to Alfredo Pitalua and continuing through until June 1981 when, in his fifth defence, he was out-pointed by Alexis Arguello.

Five of those matches were in Glasgow before enthusiastic audiences at Kelvin Hall and Ibrox – nights of passion and colour that must have had Buchanan grinding his teeth in frustration at what might have been.

Lawless was approaching the pinnacle of his success by the mid-Seventies, and would also be responsible for overseeing men like Maurice Hope, Kirkland Laing, John L. Gardner, Jimmy Batten and Ralph Charles, among others, guiding them to titles, fame and relative fortune.

In 1976, however, when Watt joined the 'stable', the jewel in Lawless's crown, the pride of the nation, was John H. Stracey, World welterweight champion in 1975 and 1976.

Stracey's contribution to British championship history would be limited to two fights with Bobby Arthur, the first, at the Albert Hall in October 1972 ending in controversy when Arthur, well behind after six rounds, collapsed in a heap following an innocuous-looking body-shot. Stracey was disqualified.

The return in June 1973 saw Arthur dispatched in four rounds. Stracey would never fight for a British title again but, intriguingly, he clashed in a non-title fight with another talented welter, Dave Boy Green.

In any preceding decade, these two men would have scrapped regularly for the welterweight title but the modern era saw them pursue largely separate careers dictated, of course, by economics.

Dave Boy Green was, like Stracey, an all-action crowd pleaser, uncomplicated, with vast reserves of energy and brimming with confidence and courage. He was a sort of modern-day Jack Kid Berg, although, because of Green's birthplace, Chatteris, he was regularly likened to another Fenland hero, 'Boy' Boon.

Green, like Stracey, would be a regular at the main London venues; indeed, in forty-one pro fights, nineteen would take place at the Albert Hall, thirteen at Wembley, and the crowds would flock to see him.

Because of his slighter build, Green took the light-welter route to a British title, beating two stylists, Billy Waith and champion Joey Singleton. He then took the European crown and, *à la* Stracey, relinquished the British title.

It was at this point that the two men's careers collided in spectacular fashion as Harry Levene brought them together to fight for the right to meet World welterweight champion, Carlos Palomino.

The fight created massive attention and lived up to all expectations. Green caused the early damage, closing Stracey's left eye and though Stracey was to come back, Green never stopped moving forward and throwing punches until a succession of big rights (known to Green's Fenland fans as 'muckspreaders') had Stracey looking unsteady in the early stages of the tenth. At that point Harry Gibbs waved the fight to an end and Wembley erupted.

Green's one other title fight was further evidence of the strange twilight world to which the British title was increasingly being relegated.

Throughout the Green-Stracey era, the British welterweight champion was Henry Rhiney, who had taken the title from Pat Thomas in November 1976. Rhiney could, at his best, be a marvellously fluid boxer. A good body puncher and nice jabber, with a beautifully timed short right hand and a hard uppercut, he was an attractive fighter, if possessing a suspect temperament. Nevertheless, Green took him on in January 1979 and stopped him in five rounds – but only for the European title. The latter was now set at twelve rounds while the British title was still fought over fifteen. Thus Rhiney, with special dispensation from the BBBC, remained British champion – an unsatisfactory situation.

As a demonstration of the crazy world boxing had become, however, the contrasting payments Rhiney would receive for different matches is hard to beat. When he defended (and lost) his title the following year against Kirkland Laing, Rhiney received a purse of £2,000. For his fight against Green, he was paid £20,000.

The welterweight division thus failed to produce the sort of rip-roaring Belt contests its two principals might well have staged. In the middle and light-heavyweight divisions, however, the mid-Seventies saw some titanic clashes, providing some of the best Lonsdale Belt action for many years.

At light-heavy, John Conteh, probably Britain's most talented fighter since Randolph Turpin, would – despite much behind-the-scenes acrimony and controversy – achieve great things on the world stage.

Strangely, however, Conteh's record at home, fighting for the domestic crown, was much less conclusive and satisfactory. His battles with Chris Finnegan were classics, raising the profile of a division that, since Chic Calderwood's untimely death, had produced some entertaining but hardly world-class entertainment. Cardiff's Eddie Avoth and Dublin's Young John McCormack (with a single intervention by Merthyr's Derek Richards) had dominated the division in the late Sixties to early Seventies, both men securing two notches on the belt until Finnegan, a hugely popular fighter from Iver, Bucks, broke the sequence in 1971, stopping Avoth in fifteen rounds.

Finnegan, who had sealed his fame by taking the gold medal at the 1968 Olympics, was a true 'character', hard-drinking, blunt-talking, with a rough and ready exterior, his rugged courageous approach to the game being based on a fine tactical brain. An effective southpaw with a punishing jab, he always gave of his best, though the lack of a KO punch and a tendency to cut was always likely to prove a stumbling block at the very top.

One thing Finnegan did *not* do was relinquish his title, perhaps because, although always an extremely active champion, his international sorties were not consistently successful.

Following the Avoth victory, Finnegan won and lost the European crown, and put up a gallant but unsuccessful fight for Bob Foster's World title. At twenty-eight, he might have appeared to be nearing the end of his career – but at this point John Conteh entered the picture.

In March 1973, at Wembley, twenty-two-year-old Conteh took on and defeated Rudi Schmidtke for the European title that Finnegan had lost. On the same bill, Finnegan successfully, albeit narrowly, defended his British title against Welshman Roy John. Two months on, and Conteh versus Finnegan was a 'natural' – a fight for three titles, bringing together the young pretender and the popular veteran.

Conteh was the complete box-fighter – gritty, full of self-belief, very ambitious. His victory over Schmidtke had been a sensational demolition job. With mean ruthless power, he had punched the German to a standstill after flooring him three times in the sixth. Conteh's punching power and Finnegan's know-how, combined with an ability to take a good shot, were sufficient ingredients to create uncertainty and excitement – enough to pack Wembley and fill numerous close-circuit venues, courtesy of Viewsport, around the country.

And the fight disappointed nobody. Finnegan was badly hampered by a cut nose in the tenth round but he never stopped coming forward, preventing Conteh from dictating the pace of the fight. The middle rounds were tough for Conteh with Finnegan punishing his every error, but Conteh's heavier hitting always gave him the edge, and from the tenth round on he took charge.

Finnegan rallied in a do-or-die last round but it proved too little, too late; and though the result was greeted with some booing, most ringside scribes agreed.

The return clash set up by Levene in May 1974, for the World title, ended in some controversy, halted after two mins twenty-five secs of the sixth by a bad cut to Finnegan's head. Until that point, Finnegan had been causing Conteh a great deal of trouble; and though many considered that Conteh's strength would eventually have prevailed, a gruelling contest seemed in prospect with Conteh already looking ruffled and missing badly. Indeed, it had been as a consequence of a wild swing that their heads had clashed – as Finnegan later wrote in *Self-Portrait of a Fighting Man* (dubbing Conteh 'pickle-head'): 'He came wading in with his loaf, like a good 'un.'

Conteh subsequently moved on to defeat Jorge Ahumada and win a series of World title defences that would place him at the centre of British boxing until the end of the decade. And for Chris Finnegan there would be one last campaign. A year later, with Conteh having relinquished the British crown, Finnegan was matched with an old friend, and an equally colourful character, 'Gypsy' John Frankham, for what looked to be his last chance to lift the Lonsdale Belt permanently.

Frankham, a bona-fide Romany, had, by the mid-Seventies, given up the travelling life to run a caravan site at Twyford, although his horse-dealing still took him round the country's fairs. He claimed ancient boxing lineage: Joe Beckett, he said, was related to his father and had, in fact, once been called Frankham. A fighter with lightning reflexes and baffling defensive moves, who delivered punches from all angles, Frankham liked to get the crowd laughing. But his victory over Finnegan – Harry Gibbs adjudging him a narrow points winner – caused anything but amusement in some quarters. Indeed, a potential riot was only avoided by Finnegan's good sportsmanship, a grin and a hand-shake reducing the protests to boos and a solitary bottle that crashed onto a reporter's typewriter.

Frankham was unconcerned: 'It was a real good week for me,' he told a *Boxing* reporter: 'I went to Epsom the day before the fight and a fortune-teller told me I was going to win. On the Tuesday I became the champion and on the Wednesday I went back to Epsom and won £2,000 playing pitch and toss. That's where all my money goes – every penny I ever made out of boxing I've gambled and drunk away.'

Frankham's good fortune would soon dissipate. A swift return (billed as 'The Fight To Settle All Arguments') was set up and this time, instead of resorting to strength and aggression in an attempt to knock Frankham out of his stride, Finnegan fought a more controlled fight, looking to hurt Frankham with well-placed shots. Although there were no knock-downs, several times Frankham had to hang on in order to survive.

At the end of a stirring fight, Finnegan's arm was raised – he had the belt for keeps, fitting reward for a career spent drawing in the crowds and providing them with compelling action.

The career of Finnegan's younger brother, Kevin, although at middleweight, was uncannily similar in many respects. In his case, the World title holder who found great difficulty in subduing him was Alan Minter.

Kevin was a more flamboyant, outspoken character than Chris. He cared little for boxing's establishment – nor did he sympathize with British middleweight champion Bunny Sterling's inability to earn good money. Sterling, in Finnegan's opinion, had only himself to blame for poor purses: 'Who wants to pay to watch him?' he demanded.

They certainly paid to watch Finnegan who, like his brother, was a fine technical boxer, blessed with great powers of endurance. In 1974 Finnegan took Sterling's title and almost immediately relinquished it in order to contest the European title which he won and then lost to Gratien Tonna.

In 1975 Finnegan was matched again by the BBBC with Sterling but when the latter relinquished the title to concentrate on European title ambitions, Alan Minter was drafted in. A former ABA middleweight champion and Olympic bronze medallist, he was a future 'golden-boy' crowd puller and a match with the more experienced 'veteran' looked promising.

Up to that point, Minter's progress had been erratic: he had a tendency to swing wildly when under pressure, but he possessed a useful jab and a solid left lead.

It turned out to be a great fight: Minter, who had never previously boxed more than ten rounds, showed unexpected staying power to outlast his opponent. Nevertheless, Finnegan had looked to be moving into a commanding position by the eleventh before unaccountably letting Minter get on top of him over the last few rounds. The half-point verdict satisfied nobody. Finnegan later admitted that he had not possessed the power and ruthlessness to finish it.

Following his win, Minter's manager Doug Bidwell declared that Alan would not be relinquishing his title as he wanted a Lonsdale Belt outright. Thus, five months on, he defeated Walworth's Billy Knight, KO'ing him in two rounds. He now felt confident enough to take on Finnegan again and in another controversial Wembley sell-out, the closest of decisions – once again to Minter – caused a great deal of ringside anger and protest. Finnegan had come back strongly in the middle stages and had spun Minter round with a short right hand, stopping him in his tracks. As Minter later recalled on television:

> He had me rocking and rolling, one round, I wasn't sure which. I went back to the corner and the cornerman said, 'Alan, this is the last round. If you don't go and win this round big, you've lost the title, and where are you going to go? Because the loser doesn't go anywhere. You've got to go out and give your all.' So I went out and I had a terrific round, I had a great round and as the bell ended, I walked over to the referee to have me hand put up and he said, 'There's still one round to go!' And I'd given me all in the fourteenth. And I couldn't come again in the last round. . . .

Indeed, as Finnegan stormed in, it looked all up for Minter, who was literally hanging on. And yet, as Minter put it, 'I nicked it.'

Minter now had the belt for keeps – and duly relinquished the title.

Kevin Finnegan meanwhile kept plodding and was matched with Frankie Lucas for the vacant title. Lucas was a tough, talented fighter but was only twenty-three, and having only his tenth professional contest. Finnegan was expected to have too much know-how for him but, before a small Albert Hall crowd, the two men contested a bloody, brutal battle which was only ended in the eleventh with Lucas so badly cut referee Harry Gibbs had no option but to stop it.

Thus, when Minter lost his European title to Gratien Tonna

some four months later, it seemed he needed the British title again in order to get his career back on track – and so, for a third time, it was Finnegan versus Minter.

Minter had by now sought the advice of Bobby Neill, and had sorted out one or two attitude problems:

> In my early career they used to say, hit Alan Minter and then wait for him and he'll come looking for you. In the first Finnegan fight he hurt me and in the second fight he hurt me and the reason was, he's caught me and I've lunged in, wide open, and I'm entitled to be hurt or picked off. . . . So this last fight, we thought to ourselves, look, there's no need to have a fight. What we'll do, we'll box properly, move and jab, sit behind the big jab and that's what won me the fight, just taking me time. . . .

A solid, uncontroversial points win for Minter ended this particular long-running argument. Like his brother Chris before him, Kevin was faced with a bleak prospect at this stage: thirty-one, with younger men now hustling into the limelight. Kevin plugged away, however, and in 1978 he travelled to the States where he took on no lesser men than Ayub Kalule (light-middleweight World champ the following year) and Marvin Hagler (who would take Minter's World crown in 1980).

Back in the UK, he watched as twenty-one-year-old Tony Sibson stopped Frankie Lucas for the vacant middleweight title. Sibson's defence against Finnegan, arranged for November that year, was thus regarded as a formality for the younger, stronger man – but Finnegan had a surprise in store. In a superb performance of guile and cunning he stole the title from the ten-years-younger champion.

Sibson seemed strangely subdued from the start, and Finnegan's clever feinting threw the younger man completely onto the defensive. Although Sibson succeeded in cutting him in the fifth, Finnegan continued to spear Sibson with his unerring left jab as the younger man came uncertainly forward.

Eventually, Sibson upped the pace and used his greater physical strength to force his way into the contest, smashing away to Finnegan's head with hooks and in the fourteenth setting up a sequence of punches that a tiring Finnegan later admitted to thinking would never end. Yet at the finish Finnegan came back and referee Harry Gibbs was persuaded to award him the fight by just half a point – though there were many at ringside who felt the margin should have been even greater.

Finnegan, like his brother before him, thus had a Lonsdale Belt of his own, and ended the decade, as so many other champions had done, relinquishing the title.

Minter, Conteh, Buchanan, the Finnegans, Jim Watt, John Stracey, Dave Boy Green – these were fighters worthy of entering any Boxing Hall of Fame. And yet, in broad historical terms, their achievements must take second place to another group of Seventies fighters who overcame more than simply fistic opposition to secure their place in the limelight. For the 1970s was the decade that saw, for the first time, black fighters making a significant impact on British boxing.

# 19

# Black Is Beautiful

The 'revolution' in British boxing began in 1970 with the crowning of Bunny Sterling as British middleweight champion – the first 'immigrant' boxer to hold a British title and the first step in a process that would see many more black boxers emerge at the top to claim the spoils so long denied them.

Although Dick Turpin opened the door to coloured fighters as early as 1948 when successfully contesting the middleweight title, only his brother Randolph, Alex Buxton and Joe Erskine had successfully followed suit, while 'Darkie' Hughes – KO'd by Dave Charnley inside a minute in 1961 – had been the only other black fighter to have been given a title chance.

Immigration in the 1950s and 1960s had of course dramatically increased the black population in the UK; but the BBBC ten-year residence rule effectively barred a generation of young men from competing for titles.

By the 1970s, however, a number of boys who had been born in the late Forties and early Fifties in the West Indies and who had come to Britain when they were of primary school age were now eligible to compete. Thus Jamaicans like Sterling, Henry Rhiney, Neville Meade, Des Morrison, Bunny Johnson and, later, Kirkland Laing, along with Antiguan Maurice Hope, St Vincent's Frankie Lucas and St Kitts's Pat Thomas would all win championships during the Seventies. At the same time, British-born coloured fighters such as John Conteh, Clinton McKenzie, Larry Paul and Vernon Sollas would also make major contributions.

It would not, however, be a painless revolution. As Bingo Crooks, Jamaican-born Wolverhampton-based featherweight contender put it to a *Boxing* reporter:

I'm not saying the rough times I've had are because I'm black; but the black man's got to fight harder, I don't care what no man says.

Maurice Hope, whilst conceding that some black fighters would be prone to lay undue emphasis on their colour if they failed or received a poor deal, also understood that being black in Great Britain was problematic. As quoted by Ernie Cashmore in *Black Sportsmen*:

I'm only human. Outside the ring you feel frustrated but you try to argue and get some facts . . . (but) it makes no sense arguing with them, so I had to walk away or get involved in fights. Most of the time I'd walk away. Now in the ring, its different: it's all legal there. . . .

For a time black fighters such as Hope would explain their desire to fight as being, at least in part, a reaction to being black in a predominantly white country. Frankie Lucas, who came to England when nine years old in 1963, explained:

I'm light-skinned because my mother was a white West Indian. Some of the English boys used to call me a wog but I'd run after them till I caught up with them and really give them a slap. . . .

As an amateur, Lucas's dual loyalties would work in his favour in a bitter-sweet way. He won bouts for England and was an ABA champion in 1972 and 1973 but was so annoyed at being overlooked by England selectors for the 1974 Commonwealth Games in New Zealand that he donned the colours of his native St Vincent, beating England first choice Carl Speare in the semis before going on to win the gold.

The suspicion that race made a difference to a boxer's chances was hard to banish. The fight game at all levels prides itself on its apparent colour-blindness. The emergence in the Seventies of so many coloured fighters eligible and talented enough to take titles placed that tolerance under a great strain. By 1980, although a great deal of progress had been made by black boxers in cham-

pionship terms, the resentments and the bitterness still simmered
as furiously as they had ten years previously when Bunny Sterling
made the crucial breakthrough.

Sterling certainly considered his progress up the boxing ladder
an unnecessarily difficult one, the majority of his early fights
being last-minute substitution affairs with promoters seemingly
uninterested in his 'awkward' style. Thus he would often have to
accept a third of what lesser fighters were being paid. His resentment was fuelled by the realization that his style was extremely
popular on the continent, where his great evasive qualities, his
ability to make the other man miss by a mere turn of his head,
plus his flashy, sharp flurries of punches, were much appreciated.

Basil Sylvester Sterling came to Britain aged six in 1954. While
boxing as an amateur with the St Pancras Club – where he
compiled a record of nineteen wins from twenty-two bouts –
he forged a relationship with trainer George Francis which would
be the key to his subsequent career. He once commented: 'If
George died tomorrow, I'd never box again. He has meant that
much to me.'

Together they turned pro and set off on the long road towards
the British middleweight title. In May 1970 Sterling beat Harry
Scott in a final eliminator to qualify to meet champion Mark
Rowe.

Two more contrasting fighters, both in style and background
could not be imagined. South Londoner Rowe was considered
the 'Golden Boy' of British middleweight boxing, a fighter whose
whole-hearted, two-fisted style guaranteed full-house signs outside the Albert Hall, where he was invariably a regular.

Rowe's connections had not been in favour of the Sterling
defence; in fact, the BBBC had found it necessary to insist on
the contest, even though Rowe, with a record of twenty-seven
wins and three losses to Sterling's sixteen wins and eight losses,
was the overwhelming favourite. Rowe had all the firepower, the
strength and the crowd; Sterling, as it transpired, had the skill.

For the first two rounds, Rowe chased and stalked while Sterling back-pedalled, jabbing on the retreat. Towards the end of
the second round, however, Rowe sustained a cut which led him
to step up the attack in the third, charging in, swinging his speciality body punches. Sterling responded by boxing better than at

any time in his career, employing a variety of clever punches that never allowed Rowe to pin him down and do damage.

Cut a second time in round four, Rowe launched a desperate attack that had Sterling reeling, though he lasted the round.

Then came the sensation. Referee Wally Thom walked across to Rowe's corner, looked at the cuts and shook his head. It was all over! Angry ringside scenes followed.

Rowe was particularly bitter:

The Board of Control forced me to put my title up against Sterling, and now he's got the British title. And he can keep it. He cut me with his head both times. I don't want to fight him again. . . .

For Sterling, however, the victory was particularly sweet:

You can't imagine what pleasure it was to find that I had come in out from the cold. I got a kick out of seeing the shocked faces around the ring when I won. So many thought I had no chance that night, but I knew I would beat Rowe.

The aftermath, however, was as ugly as some of the scenes at ringside that night. Sterling recalled: 'I kept getting threatening letters calling me a black bastard and the rest of it', while his manager George Francis was also abused: 'I kept getting letters saying, "You f. . . . g traitor, letting a black man win a British title" '.

Francis, however, who would also oversee John Conteh's rise to the top, always felt a strong bond of affection for Sterling:

With John it was easy – he had glamour and everybody was working to help him to the top. Bunny had to do it the hard way, just on his own ability. . . . The most emotional moment in my life in boxing was when Walter Bartleman rang me up to tell me that Bunny had won the Best Young Boxer award. I was so overcome that I sat down and cried. We were due to leave for Australia so I asked Larry Gains to collect it for him.

Larry was a great black fighter who had been denied the

breaks that Bunny was getting, so it seemed appropriate that he should represent Bunny.

In 1972 Sterling defended his British title against Phil Matthews at Belle Vue, practically toying with his supposedly hard-hitting opponent; in 1973, without moving out of second gear, he took the middleweight belt outright with a victory over Don McMillan at Solihull – this for a miserly purse of £1,500. Three months later he ended Mark Rowe's career with a fifteen-round points win and in February 1974 he took on Kevin Finnegan – his fifth title defence in three-and-a-half years.

Once again, the size of his purse – another £1,500 – brought complaints from Sterling and manager Francis who considered it 'degrading'. Neither the Albert Hall nor Wembley had bid for the fight, leaving the way open for the Solihull Sporting Club to pick it up for a song. Sterling was said to be depressed and upset; he was also bemused when Finnegan was adjudged a narrow points winner.

One more British title fight awaited him. Finnegan gave up the British title to pursue a European title challenge and Sterling was matched with fellow West Indian and already light-middleweight champion, Maurice Hope. Sterling proved too strong, stopping Hope in eight rounds to regain the title – which he promptly gave up for 'business' reasons.

Like Sterling, Hope would dominate a British division (the light-middle) and win a belt outright. However, in contrast to Sterling, he would go on to contest the World title, culminating in a clash with Wilfred Benitez in Las Vegas in 1981.

Hope first came to prominence in November 1974 when he defeated Larry Paul at the Civic Hall, Wolverhampton for the light middleweight title. Paul, managed by promoter Alex Griffiths, though born in Liverpool of West Indian parents, had settled in Wolverhampton where he took the inaugural light middleweight title in 1973, defeating former welterweight champion Bobby Arthur.

Paul certainly could not complain of having been held back by his colour. A firm favourite at Wolverhampton, where promoter Griffiths exploited his tremendous drawing power, his rise to fame had been meteoric – just eight pro fights before donning a

Andy Till. (*Action Images*)

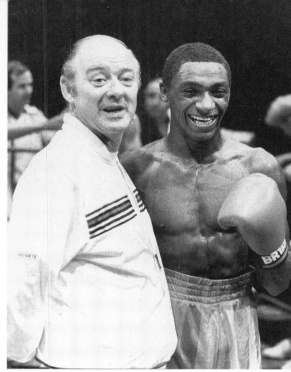

Herol Graham.

## '90s *Champions*

Sean Murphy. (*Professional Sport*)

Pat Clinton (*right*)

Ray Clarke OBE, General Secretary
BBBC 1946–86.

John Morris, General Secretary
BBBC 1986–    . (*Derek Rowe*)

Tommy Bloggs, master belt craftsman *c* 1960.

Lonsdale Belt. With a bouncy style, clever defence and powerful left hook, he looked all set to make the belt his own and, following a second win over rugged Kevin White, he confidently took on Hope. But Hope, a clever counter-puncher with a solid jab, proved far too powerful and KO'd Paul in eight rounds. Paul never did earn the belt, two subsequent attempts – against Hope and then against Jimmy Batten – ending in four-round KOs.

Maurice Hope went on to take the belt by defeating Southern Area champion Tony Poole at the Empire Pool, Wembley in September 1975. He then relinquished the title and, guided by Terry Lawless, concentrated on European and World titles, becoming World champion in 1979 by defeating Rocky Mattioli in San Remo.

Hope's background had been more humble than Sterling's. His father had been a railway porter while Hope himself worked for a time as a leather tanner. Coming to England when aged just nine, he, like Sterling, found coming to terms with racism something of a challenge. Boxing with the Repton Club in the East End, according to *Black Sportsmen*:

I had to mix and tolerate. There were a few of them who put it straight at me and I was forced into getting into rows. I remember one fellow spat in my face. I'd be in the shower and they'd push me out, actually push me out saying, 'You black so-and-so'. This shocked me because I'd left Antigua with no idea what colour prejudice was, no idea.

His response was to use the pent-up aggression inside the ring:

You'd hear someone outside the ring make comments about your colour and you raise your enthusiasm as if to say, 'I've got something to prove', and this comes as a blessing in disguise sometimes, 'cause I needed that sort of boost, like a kick in the arse.

However, if verbal abuse could serve as an incentive, the deep-seated attitudes that were the cause of that abuse were still able to thwart and undermine a black boxer's career, and Hope, while conscious one could become paranoic about such matters, felt an abiding sense of injustice:

> Where publicity is concerned I've had a raw deal. Naturally I put it down to colour. I've looked at it on both sides from different angles and colour is something to do with it.

In 1980, just prior to a big fight, Hope was quoted as saying, 'This is a white man's country and the black man is being held back', words echoed, no doubt, by John Conteh whose independent stance during the late Seventies provided one of boxing's more tragic stories. His legal and contractual wrangles with Levene, Duff, George Francis and the BBBC were presented at the time primarily as the struggle of a spirited individual against the might of the all-powerful 'establishment'.

Yet Conteh's brief involvement with Don King and his later attempts to set up a World title bout in Idi Amin's Uganda, though with the benefit of hindsight disastrous and even farcical, still indicate a desire to establish a credible black alternative to the white status quo governing the sport. Similarly, Bunny Sterling's hopes of fighting for a World title in his native Jamaica revealed a longing to receive the sort of acclaim and esteem denied him by white audiences reluctant to acknowledge his achievements and status – not to mention the purses routinely awarded to fighters with not half his ability.

For most black boxers, however, opportunities were there to be seized and exploited. Optimism was the key, and for Des Morrison, first holder of the new light-welterweight title, prejudice in boxing was no barrier: 'If you're good enough and you've got a great manager like Andy Smith, you'll make it in the end, whatever your colour.'

Morrison, a Jamaican, helped make boxing history in 1973 when he met Joe Tetteh, a Ghanaian, at Shoreditch Town Hall. It was the first time two immigrant boxers had contested a British title.

It was a rousing, exciting contest between the veteran Tetteh (thirty-two years old and seventy-four contests) and the lanky twenty-three-year-old Morrison. Morrison jabbed and moved often under pressure – indeed, he was put down for a count of eight in the eleventh – yet he gamely kept on plugging away until Tetteh's ageing legs could not keep up a sustained pursuit.

A close points decision for Morrison was not popular, but the winner preferred to dwell on the positive aspects:

> The fact that Tetteh and I put on such a good show will help a lot. You had two black men fighting in Shoreditch Town Hall – real Alf Garnett country – and the crowd were just as excited and as partisan as they would have been if Stracey were boxing another Londoner. . . .

Morrison, who had been introduced to the sport and encouraged to turn pro by another celebrated immigrant, schoolfriend Joe Bugner, would lose the title the following year at the Albert Hall to Irishman Pat McCormack – himself a long-serving battler who had waited years for a title shot.

Being an Irish citizen, McCormack had not had to 'qualify' for British citizenship in the same way as the majority of black fighters then making their mark on the British scene. He had simply taken out naturalization papers – something another prominent British champion in the Eighties, Barry McGuigan, was to do with the minimum of fuss if not with an entirely easy conscience.

McCormack would lose his title in late 1974. He stepped up a division and in December 1975 earned a shot at the welterweight crown, his opponent being another talented immigrant fighter, St Kitts-born Pat Thomas, aged twenty-five.

Thomas was an accomplished stylist who often seemed content to win on points when a KO was well within his capacity. Possessor of a cool boxing brain, he proved much too good for McCormack, opening five separate cuts on the vulnerable but courageous Irishman's face, tying him up whenever he attempted to come inside, punishing him with body shots and finally KO'ing him in the thirteenth round. It would be McCormack's last fight, but the beginning of a remarkably successful career for Thomas who, along with fellow Jamaicans Trevor Francis, Henry Rhiney and Kirkland Laing, would effectively tie up the division until Welshman Colin Jones entered the fray in 1980.

After his victory over McCormack, the city rewarded Thomas with a reception, mayor and all. Taking his Lonsdale Belt from a paper-bag, he commented: 'Everyone hopes they'll be a champion. But I never thought I'd get to feel one of these. Look, maybe, but not touch.'

In fact, both Thomas and Laing would take Lonsdale Belts outright, although Thomas would have to step up to light-middleweight to do so. Laing would need a full decade before clinching his welterweight trophy while Henry Rhiney – a tall rangy boxer whose lack of a decisive KO punch probably stood between him and a World title chance – would just miss out making a belt his own, going down to Laing in April 1979 in his third defence of his welterweight title.

In fact, that defeat completed a dramatic eclipse in Rhiney's fortunes. A gifted, smooth, underrated fighter with an extensive repertoire of punches, his well-developed frame disguised a tendency to crumble under intense pressure. Having taken the title from Pat Thomas (who then moved up a division), Rhiney proceeded to lose three bouts in succession, sending his 'marketability' plummeting.

Yet another boxer who had spent the majority of his pro-career appearing on dinner-shows or abroad, Rhiney's appearance at the Albert Hall in June 1977 (in a non-title fight with Thomas) was his first appearance in a London ring in four years as a professional. His second defence, against Billy Waith, took place at Barnsley Town Hall before 600 diners, but he must have felt the tide of his career was turning when, following a European title triumph in Germany, he was, as we have seen, lured into the ring to meet Dave Boy Green, the latter in need of a title to enhance his World title ambitions. Green duly destroyed Rhiney in just five rounds, while the British title went three months later to Kirkland Laing. By the end of the year, Rhiney had quit.

These and other fine Seventies fighters such as heavyweights Tony Moore (Jamaica) and Rocky Campbell (Antigua), light-heavy Victor Attivor (Ghana), middleweights Billy Knight and Carl Speare, and welterweights Kenny Webber and Bingo Crookes (both from Jamaica) were solid evidence of the remarkable transformation black boxers had wrought on British boxing which would continue on into the Eighties. But the most important psychological boost for black fighters at all levels came midway through the decade when that most symbolic of all divisions – the heavyweight – was stormed by a quiet, cool stylist from Jamaica, Bunny Johnson.

Johnson arrived in Great Britain in 1963 aged sixteen and was expected by his parents to take up a profession. But, as quoted in *Black Sportsmen*, the night studies soon faded: 'Quite early I made up my mind that all I wanted to be was a top flight boxer, to follow Jack Johnson in my own way and become the first black British heavyweight champion.'

Following a respectable amateur career, he turned professional in 1968 and made good progress, winning thirty-two of thirty-eight contests. Throughout 1971–2 he was among the top three heavyweights but overlooked by the BBBC when a series of eliminators was held to decide on challengers for the title then held by Danny McAlinden:

The nationality rule was a beautiful get-out for them but I had only a few months to go before I was here for ten years and would have been entitled to fight for the title. For nationality you can read racism. I couldn't interpret it as anything but racialism.

Fortunately John Conteh dropped out of the eliminating tourney and Johnson was the only credible replacement. Thus he met Richard Dunn in October 1973 in an exciting battle that saw both fighters on the canvas at various times but with Johnson, despite giving away some 23 lb, triumphing in the tenth round with a KO. Yet it would be another fifteen months before he entered the ring to meet McAlinden.

Johnson had arrived on the heavyweight scene when boxing politics appeared to have taken over completely from the real thing. The tortuous sequence of events had begun back in March 1971 with Joe Bugner's sensational and controversial defeat of Henry Cooper. Six months after the Cooper fight, unglamorous, unfancied Jack Bodell took Bugner's title after fifteen gruelling rounds; and almost a year later, Irishman Danny McAlinden completed the bizarre sequence of events by clubbing Bodell senseless in two rounds of a fight that many described as resembling a bar-room brawl.

British heavyweight boxing thus presented a split personality: Bugner had regained the European crown a few months after McAlinden's triumph and in 1973 would successfully pursue 'glamour' fights with Ali and Frazier, and defend his European title twice. McAlinden, meanwhile, being less fashionable but nevertheless the British champion, waited desperately to defend against Bugner in order to gain some credibility as well as make some much-desired cash.

In early 1973 a Bugner-McAlinden fight looked on the cards. Jack Solomons, then riding high with exclusive close-circuit rights to the World title clash between Frazier and Foreman, took control of McAlinden from ageing manager George Middleton and negotiated a lucrative £100,000 title fight with Bugner for Earls Court in July.

Unfortunately McAlinden suffered an embarrassing defeat in a warm-up contest at Solomons's World Sporting Club, injuring his arm in the process. Harry Levene – being the other major promoter involved due to his interests in Bugner – promptly cancelled the big fight, much to Solomons's anger. Bugner then moved on to fight both Ali and Frazier and a bitter argument ensued.

McAlinden, clearly anxious to rid himself of Solomons and move across to the Levene camp, refused to fight for Solomons on a non-title show, insisting he be paid £10,000 a bout as champion. The Board backed Solomons and McAlinden had to buy out his contract for £10,000, transferring to Sam Burns at the same time.

Meanwhile the Board was insisting upon a McAlinden v Bunny Johnson title fight; but it would be a long time before the fighters actually entered the ring. A title bout was arranged for March 1974 but McAlinden broke a thumb. In October 1974 Solomons succeeded in obtaining rights to stage the fight (although no one else appeared to want it) and along with Alex Griffiths he set up a promotion at the Civic Hall Wolverhampton – the first time a heavyweight championship fight would have taken place before a restricted 'club' audience of under 2,000. But McAlinden fell ill. The rearranged fight, this time for the World Sporting Club in London, also failed to happen – this time it was Johnson's turn to fall ill!

Finally, in January 1975, at the World Sporting Club, for the relatively paltry purse of £8,650 and before an audience of under 1,000, the two men met. Sadly, after so much procrastination and with so much at stake, it turned out to be a poor fight. Johnson's best boxing was done in the first three rounds when his jabs reddened McAlinden's face and a right to the heart had him staggering ominously.

McAlinden was consistently falling short with his punches and Johnson's left jab repeatedly had him wobbling. In the fourth McAlinden rallied and a left hook at the end of the round put Johnson down briefly. By the sixth, however, McAlinden's efforts had petered out. Cut under the right eye, he appeared to lose enthusiasm, while Johnson was landing with almost every punch he threw. In the ninth Johnson really opened up: a right followed by a left hook sent Danny to the floor, legs waving in the air. He looked shaky when he got up and Johnson lost little time in setting him up for the combination left hook, right uppercut which put McAlinden down again.

Danny sat on the canvas looking more crestfallen than concussed as referee Roland Dakin counted him out. He spread his arms as if to signify defeat and slowly raised himself upright as the count was completed.

Bunny himself then fell to the canvas in excitement and later climbed onto the shoulders of George Francis to have photos taken. In the dressing-room afterwards, the talk was of Bugner and even Muhammad Ali – the holy grail of every heavyweight.

There would be no bonanza, however, with either Bugner or Ali. Instead, the following September at Wembley, Johnson was first prodded and then pounded to defeat by the heavier (by 20 lb) and stronger Richard Dunn. What followed must have finally convinced him that there was little justice in the world. Not only did Joe Bugner – who had not held the title since 1971 – get a title shot at Ali, but the following May Richard Dunn did as well. . . . The two 'Great White Hopes' then met in October 1976 to share a purse of some £75,000.

There were, nevertheless, some compensations for Bunny. He stepped down a division in 1977 and over the course of the next three years won the light-heavyweight belt outright with wins over Tim Wood, Rab Affleck and Dennis Andries.

His boxing epitaph must remain the words he uttered when questioned by a reporter in the dressing-room after winning the British heavyweight championship: 'I'm sure Lord Lonsdale would have been proud of the way I boxed. . . .'

# 20

# Heavyweight Odyssey

It seems almost a boxing law of nature that British fighters above 13 stone or so rarely impress either at home or abroad. The genial but hapless shade of Bombardier Billy Wells continues to haunt the British heavyweight scene decade after decade, while any small success as has been achieved on the World heavyweight stage has usually been by men who were, strictly speaking, light-heavies – cruisers at most: Len Harvey, Tommy Farr, Don Cockell – even Henry Cooper.

On occasions a British light-heavy operating as such has proved to be a world-beater – Randolph Turpin being the supreme example. Thus it can be no surprise that during the Seventies and Eighties, with the creation of the cruiserweight division at 13 st 8 lb, along with a fractured World title scene, Britons fighting just below the heavyweight limit have provided more excitement and certainly brought home more titles.

They also provided more compelling domestic action. Conteh and Finnegan, who dominated the division between 1970 and 1975, were followed by Bunny Johnson, whose three title wins between 1977 and 1980 brought the popular and skilful Jamaican his very own belt, while the Eighties would see the light-heavyweight title shared by three men, each of whom would take a belt outright.

Tony Wilson from Wolverhampton won his in a three-fight sequence between December 1987 and January 1989, but it would be Dennis Andries and Tom Collins – hailing from faraway Guyana and Curaçao respectively – who would truly rule the light-heavyweight roost, Collins winning his belt as early as 1983,

Andries in a nine-month burst (including two wins over Collins) in 1984.

Andries would go on to contest a variety of World titles at light-heavy: an ungainly, durable, even powerful character, though never exactly a joy to behold in the ring, he would step up to cruiserweight as the Nineties began, to continue a seemingly endless career. In this he was matched only by his fellow light-heavy Collins, who would win the title for the fifth time in May 1989 and still be battling away for a WBO World title in 1991, aged thirty-six and in his fourteenth year as a pro.

The cruiserweight division, introduced in 1985, also produced a number of internationally successful British champions: Glenn McCrory, Johnny Nelson and Sammy Reeson all tilting at IBF or WBC World titles – in fact, between May 1989 and March 1990 the three men would be involved in five of the six World titles contested at the weight.

The top British cruisers, however, tended to use the British title as a passport to more lucrative action: thus, although the 'big three' of McCrory, Nelson and Angol fought twenty-two times between May 1989 and March 1991, thirteen times for various titles, including seven of eight British titles, they never managed to fight one another! The British public were hence deprived of quality domestic clashes on a par with Finnegan-Conteh, Collins-Andries or Andries-Sibson at light-heavy. Instead, they had to be content with watching the 'first' division cruiserweights regularly knocking over a 'second-string' group, namely Tee Jay (who had four unsuccessful title shots), Andy Straughn (two unsuccessful attempts) and Lou Gent (also two unsuccessful tilts, being KO'd first by McCrory and then by Johnny Nelson).

The irony is, of course, that whether successful or not, whether deserving or not, heavyweights still manage to command centre-stage, despite regularly plumbing new depths in terms of quality and performance – a depressingly predictable downward process that began its 'modern' phase more than twenty years ago.

On 16 March 1971, at the conclusion of the British heavyweight title fight between Henry Cooper and Joe Bugner, Cooper – convinced he had won – moved towards referee Harry Gibbs for his hand to be raised in victory: '. . . but he ignored my hand and turned his back on me. I thought, "Cor, stone me!" '

Bugner had taken Cooper's British, Commonwealth and European titles by the narrowest of margins, and according to Peter Wilson: 'The crowd booed and snarled like an angry animal with 10,000 heads.'

It had been a close, dour battle with neither man ever really dominating, although most experts felt that Cooper had allowed Bugner too much leeway in the first ten rounds. Thus, when he picked up the pace in the latter stages, winning two, three rounds on the trot, he was still some way behind going into the last round – and no one, not even Cooper, disputed the fact that Bugner won that round.

Unfortunately, Cooper and company felt that he had established a sufficiently large lead to have 'nicked' it, last round or not. Harry Gibbs thought otherwise, and Cooper's bitterness towards Gibbs would continue for decades afterwards. It also took the boxing public a long time to recover from the shock.

Within six months of the Cooper fight, Bugner's rawness and inexperience were revealed for all to see when he was beaten comprehensively by sturdy, unfancied Jack Bodell. It was the start of a long frustrating, exasperating relationship between Bugner and British fight fans.

In his prime, during the mid-Seventies, Bugner was undoubtedly the best heavyweight in Europe and arguably one of the best in the world. In his contests with Ali and Frazier he fought intelligent, defensive battles that had him leaving the ring to cheers. However, the apparent indifference that he (or perhaps his connections) showed for the feelings of British fight fans – as demonstrated by his blatantly cynical 'returns' and equally calculated 'relinquishments' of the title – lost him popular sympathy.

Bodell's surprise accession thus completed a threefold cycle of woe: after Cooper's and the public's, it was now the turn of the promoters' hearts to be broken as this potential goldmine of a division – in British terms at least – would continue to be sidetracked down a commercial back-alley.

The late Sixties and early Seventies had already seen somewhat desperate attempts to install a commercially 'fashionable' successor to Cooper: Billy Walker, Johnny Prescott, Joe Bugner being the principal 'Golden Boys'. But one man – George Biddles – would see many of those ambitious plans rendered unto dust.

Biddles, a licence-holder since 1926, had already handled champions such as Pat Butler, Wally Swift and Hogan Kid Bassey but in the years 1969–75, being manager/trainer of both Bodell and Richard Dunn as well as having handled both Prescott and Bunny Johnson earlier in their careers, he would have more influence than almost anyone else on the heavyweight title scene.

Bodell, from Swadlincote, was an easy-going, likeable fighter possessed of guts and determination but cursed with an awkward, unattractive southpaw style. He approached Biddles when the latter was close to retirement, asking for help with his faltering career. Biddles 'leaned' on Mickey Duff, calling in one or two favours in order to get Bodell an attractive profile-raising fight. Duff, although remarking that he needed Bodell 'like a hole in the head', obliged, and Bodell was back in business. Always a busy, eager fighter, by June 1967 he had battled his way into number one contender spot and a date with Henry Cooper.

Cooper outclassed him, ending matters in round two with a classic left hook; but Bodell and Biddles persevered, and following worthy victories over Brian London, Johnny Prescott and Carl Gizzi, Bodell found himself once again top contender.

Prior to Bodell's second title fight, however, Biddles was offered a 'final' eliminator with Billy Walker, the latter then attempting to rebuild title aspirations following resounding defeats by Cooper and Karl Mildenburger. Hard negotiations resulted in Walker taking, as ever, the lion's share of the purse (£15,000 to £8,000) but the fight proved a turning-point for Bodell.

A sell-out encounter at Wembley, it was one of the fiercest, most savage contests between two British heavyweights since Gardner and Williams met. Walker – down and almost out in the first round – battled back in the sixth to drop Bodell before more or less collapsing in the eighth under the weight of Bodell's relentless, superior attacks.

Fortune now favoured Bodell. Cooper – in dispute with the BBBC – relinquished his title and Bodell was matched with Carl Gizzi for the vacant crown which he captured over fifteen hard, unremarkable rounds. Thus, a sell-out return with Cooper saw

Bodell once again defeated but this time in a much more competitive fight, Cooper prevailing on points.

Joe Bugner now entered the fray. Bodell – guaranteed another return with Cooper – was persuaded to stand aside while the more glamorous challenger had a go. Bugner, as we have seen, pulled off the remarkable if controversial defeat of Cooper. Bodell, by a quirk of fate, now became the crowd's favourite and was cheered into the ring when matched with the new champion on 27 September 1971.

Once again, Biddles's know-how proved decisive. Bugner had been employed as a sparring partner for Bodell some years earlier and, drawing on recollections of his performance, Biddles devised a game plan for Bodell that saw him hustle and 'bull' the young champion, never allowing him to operate as he liked to off the front foot, and a bewildered Bugner was thrashed, hardly winning a round.

The problem for British boxing now was that, in world terms, Bodell had nowhere to go. KO'd by Jerry Quarry in sixty-four seconds, losing his European crown in just two rounds, he was finally crushed by Danny McAlinden's round arm swings in July 1972 after which Bodell retired. Biddles was frank: 'Bodell was by then no longer a hungry fighter. It's only human ... and I was spreading his titles out for him to make as much money as he could.'

McAlinden, by contrast, was not the busy fighter Bodell had been. Indeed, he hung on to his title for almost three years without defending, playing ducks and drakes with Solomons and Levene before Bunny Johnson mercifully (for almost everyone concerned) KO'd him in nine rounds. Sadly for Johnson, however, the heavyweight title was now a commercial nightmare.

However, enter Biddles again and with yet another 'retread' in the shape of Bradford's Richard Dunn. Dunn, like Bodell before him, had approached Biddles for help in giving his career a lift and Biddles had been able to oblige. It was by no means a simple task.

The ungainly Dunn was another awkwardly effective fighter who, when he let the punches go, could look exciting: he would probe and prod with heavy right hands before throwing over left hand smashes. Unlike Bodell, however, Dunn had a tendency to unravel in comical fashion when caught square on the jaw. Thus he was relentlessly unfashionable in a heavyweight world ruled by the peerless, matchlessly smooth and elegant Ali.

Nevertheless, by dint of shrewd coaching and clever match-making, Biddles guided the former paratrooper (who once commented when asked why he continued fighting: 'There's nowt else to do') to unimagined heights.

First Bunny Johnson – a natural light-heavyweight – was prodded and jabbed to defeat in fifteen painful rounds. Thirty-five days later Dunn crushed Danny McAlinden in a title defence and, finally, stopped Bernd August to capture the European title. Biddles now produced the coup of coups – pulling various international 'strings', he secured for Dunn a World title fight with Ali in Germany, a contest in which Dunn put up a reasonable show, earned himself many friends and, more importantly, a sizeable purse. He then earned a second bumper purse when he defended his title for the second time in October 1976 against Joe Bugner (on one of his many 'comebacks') at the Empire Pool, Wembley.

In fact, it was something of an outrageous decision by the BBBC to allow Bugner to get a shot over the heads of various legitimate contenders, their excuse being that Bugner had 'promised' to defend the title if he won it. The reality, predictably, was that, after KO'ing Dunn in one round (at two minutes fourteen seconds, a record fastest finish for a heavyweight championship), he merely used the title to eke out a little more cash on the international scene before 'relinquishing'. By the time the tedious and demeaning prevarications had ended, and John L. Gardner had squared up to Billy Aird to contest the vacant title, two more years had passed.

The division now entered the period of its lowest esteem since the Second World War. Gardner, a Lawless boxer and guided promotionally by Mickey Duff, was an aggressive two-fisted fighter, lacking a clean KO punch but able to stop the majority of his opponents by dint of relentless pressure. With a weak defence but a capacity to return punishment in equal measure, he was, in world terms, an able, game fighter but would never feature in the top ten.

His match with Aird proved little. Aird hurt him in the first round but Gardner retaliated in kind, going on to administer a four-round battering that culminated in the fifth with Aird simply retiring to the accompaniment of boos and catcalls. His tactics – which seemed to consist of imitating Ali's 'rope-a-dope' style in an attempt to absorb everything Gardner threw in the hope the latter would run out of steam – proved foolish if not quite suicidal. Following the defeat, Aird 'retired'.

Gardner then made a swift defence against Paul Sykes, Central Area champion, but a fighter of little pedigree who provided scant opposition. Gardner's progress then came to an abrupt halt. He could have gone on and defended the title for a second time, thus earning himself a belt outright, but on the advice of Duff, he relinquished the title in order to concentrate on more lucrative European and, hopefully, World title challenges. However, defeat in the USA at the hands of contender Mike Dokes was swiftly followed by retirement on medical grounds. His removal from the scene had finally laid bare the dearth of talent then on offer in Britain at this supposedly supreme weight.

In 1981 Gordon Ferris, a Northern Ireland boxer from Eniskillen – tall, rangy but apparently with no burning ambition – fought a dull fifteen rounds against thirty-five-year-old Billy Aird (temporarily out of retirement) to become champion.

Ferris's 'china-jaw' was then demonstrated when another veteran battler – Welsh/Jamaican Neville Meade – took less than a round (two minutes forty-five seconds, to be precise) to take his title.

Meade himself had few illustrious scalps to his belt. He tended to lose to men of quality and his last-ditch leap for international fame and riches ended at the hands of mediocre US fighter Leroy Boone. Though scornful of his many critics and rightfully proud that he had crowned an up-and-down journeyman's career by holding – albeit briefly – the premier prize in British boxing, Meade's only real claim to fame would be the fact that he was, at thirty-seven years of age, the oldest man to hold the title.

Two years after his single triumph, however, Welshman David Pearce stopped him in nine rounds.

Newport-born Pearce, a steelworker, was a tough, gutsy fighter with minimal skills from a genuine boxing background: all his seven brothers boxed and his father Wally had once been a booth fighter. At 6 foot and weighing around 14 stone, however, he was on the light side in the prevailing 'super'-heavyweight climate. His career would be a sad one.

Whether he won or lost, Pearce tended to ship a great deal of punishment and two years before taking the title he had failed a brain scan. He needed a second opinion before the BBBC allowed him to continue. Unfortunately, following a European championship bout in 1984, he failed for a second time and his career was over.

Pearce waged a long, bitter rearguard action, obtaining further medical opinion, travelling to Canada in an attempt to set up a return to the ring – all to no avail. In 1985 the Board formally asked him to return the belt but Pearce, convinced that he was the victim of some kind of conspiracy, steadfastly ignored the request. Thus when Hughroy Currie became champion in October 1985, there was no belt for him to wear.

At least the prominence of Frank Bruno during these troubled years (he captured the European title in 1985 and was clearly heading for a World title challenge of some kind) helped divert attention from the less attractive aspects of the heavyweight division. The British heavyweight title now appeared little more than a sideshow as Hughroy Currie and Funso Banjo's contest in October 1985 demonstrated, buried as it was beneath the gathering Bruno 'hype'.

Neither Banjo nor Currie could be accused of possessing much by way of 'charisma'. Banjo was a curious fighter with an almost impregnable defence and a hurtful punch but little obvious boxing technique or creativity. Currie, meanwhile, was not a man to impose himself on Banjo: a competent tactician with reasonable mobility, courageous and an all-round boxer, he lacked a KO punch and his performances could, on occasions, descend into untidy brawls, as on this occasion when he ground out a featureless points win over Banjo.

Currie's first defence, a KO defeat by Horace Notice, would see the heavyweight title once more firmly in the grip of the Lawless/Duff camp where it would remain for the next five years, the possession of Bruno stablemates – first Notice and then Gary Mason.

Notice was already twenty-six before he left the amateur ranks;

thus he was considered too old to develop as a world contender. He had a useful right hand and was able to take a punch, could stand and trade, and was dogged, but, like Pearce, he lacked bulk and, inevitably, class experience and his KO defeat of Currie was the result of clubbing punches rather than clean-cut explosive shots of quality.

For a time it seemed like Notice versus Tyneside and the North-East – a reflection of the resurgence of boxing in that area. Dave Garside, a mobile fighter with a good left jab, orthodox and sturdy but lacking power, was first in line. The title fight was a thriller while it lasted, with Garside down in the first round but battling back after a torrid second, only to be caught and stopped in the fifth.

Notice then took his title to Sunderland, a permanent belt at stake, and met Paul Lister at the Crowtree Leisure Centre, the latter's home territory. However, the occasion was too much for Lister who was reduced in the third to covering up on the ropes before being floored three times in succession, the final blow to the top of his head putting him down for the full count.

Notice now had a belt all his own, an achievement that must have assuaged in part some of the frustrations at remaining more or less unknown to the public at large as Frank Bruno ascended the throne once occupied by Henry Cooper as Britain's favourite boxer. But a third title defence against Hughroy Currie at the York Hall, Bethnal Green was followed by the discovery that he had suffered a detached retina and he reluctantly retired, the third heavyweight champion – and not the last – during the Eighties to suffer such a fate.

The Lawless camp swiftly provided a replacement in Gary Mason who duly took the title in January 1989, KO'ing Currie in four rounds, a feat he repeated in June that year when he stopped Jess Harding in just two rounds.

Mason would also find himself overshadowed by Bruno – the Bruno v Tyson title fight came a month after Mason's initial title win – but Mason at least believed that his chance would come. Although he had been groomed so carefully that his true ability at the highest level remained something of a mystery, he did possess an explosive right-hand punch and he could certainly take a punch far better than either Bruno or even Notice. He was limited, however, in terms of ring movement and craft; he was also prone to alarming energy losses when he would appear almost totally punched out after three or four rounds.

After his second title win, however, these questions became academic: eye-trouble threatened his career and, following surgery, he and his connections took the ambitious, perhaps foolhardy, step of accepting a challenge from the up-and-coming Lennox Lewis. A painful seventh-round stoppage finished Mason's career. His defeat also marked the end of the Duff/Lawless 'monopoly' of the British heavyweight title and heralded a new and, it has to be said, more realistic era.

Lewis's assumption of the heavyweight title came exactly twenty years almost to the day after Joe Bugner's controversial victory over Henry Cooper. And, strangely, Lewis faces the problem that many felt Bugner had failed to overcome – the true nature of his national allegiance.

Bugner, of Hungarian origin, had always remained something of an 'outsider'. Lewis, though born in Britain (in London's Forest Gate), had grown up in Canada and retains strong Caribbean links, courtesy of his parents. No amount of 'hype' concerning his love for West Ham United can conceal his Transatlantic accent, the smooth style honed on the basketball courts of Toronto, the easy grace of a natural US football quarterback.

Lewis's decision to return to Great Britain and to fight for the British title as a prelude to greater things was clearly a business decision: he needed a clearly defined constituency and a distinct mission to set him apart from the other American contenders and to present American matchmakers and promoters with a marketable product.

Yet in an odd way, Lewis's 'British' persona probably sits as comfortably on him as would a Canadian or even a Jamaican one. James Lawson has written: 'He is like a chameleon in his ability to wear any suit life requires – and a merciless ring demands.'

He at least sustained his interest in the British title long enough to win a Lonsdale Belt outright; not that his three victories would have added a great deal to his boxing education.

The Mason stoppage was probably his hardest British fight, his speed, mobility and accurate left jab proving far too much for the static British champion (whose manager, Mickey Duff, had paid £276,000 for the privilege of promoting what many regard as one of his least astute pieces of matchmaking).

In October 1991 Lewis added a second notch to the belt by overpowering and outsmarting blown-up cruiserweight Glenn McCrory in just two rounds, and in May 1992 he stopped Derek 'Sweet D' Williams in three – a right uppercut followed by a left/right combination putting Williams down and ending his interest in continuing. In winning the belt Lewis had failed to impress the cognoscenti, however, hardly surprising given his relative inexperience: little more than twenty pro contests.

However, his devastating win over contender Razor Ruddock in a World title eliminator propelled the cool, calculated, somewhat distant Lewis into the World heavyweight stratosphere ('Lewis is British and he's baaaaad!' growled his American trainer). And without doubt, Lewis has become, to quote *Boxing Illustrated*, 'the hottest thing to come out of Britain since the Beatles. . . .', although his true ability remains something of a mystery.

Sadly for British fight fans, with Lewis's relinquishment of the title, the Lonsdale Belt contest returned to earth with a bump. In a shabby, undignified contest, Norwich's Herbie Hide succeeded in thumping an unmotivated challenger, Michael Murray, to defeat. Hide then proceeded (Lonsdale Belt slung carelessly over his shoulder) to trade embarrassing insults with World heavyweight champion Riddick Bowe, who was suitably unimpressed. The depressing cycle of promise to disappointment so characteristic of the British heavyweight title had turned once again. . . .

# 21

## Grass Roots Revival

In July 1979 *Boxing News* ran a two-page spread beneath the headline: 'Style! That's the Key for Barrett and Duff', celebrating the 100th promotion at the Albert Hall by the dynamic duo.

Barrett and Duff were, on the face of it, unlikely bedfellows. Duff – son of a polish ex-rabbi who had come to the UK in 1936 to avoid the impending Nazi disaster – had himself arrived two years later. He had first taken up boxing when evacuated to a Jewish hostel in Gateshead during the war, was a successful junior amateur, reaching the London Schoolboy Championships finals and turning professional at fifteen (illegally – the age limit was sixteen), he had a sixty-nine fight pro career at light and welterweight.

He was no more than useful although British lightweight champion Dave Crowley is said to have commented of him: 'That kid knows more tricks than a monkey!' Fighting at such 'atmospheric' venues as Mile End Arena (where he was once stoned by the crowd following an unpopular verdict) he made little impact and retired aged nineteen to become a sewing-machine salesman. Within a year, however, he had become a matchmaker, first at Leyton Baths and later at that same Mile End Arena, then Shoreditch Town Hall, the Lyceum, and countless other arenas up and down the country.

His management of boxers only began in the late 1960s with Billy Knight, but his earlier involvement with the operations of Jarvis Astaire and Harry Levene had propelled him into national prominence – his raw energy, ubiquitousness and street-savvy complementing Levene's sharp instinct for business and signing deals and Astaire's astute financial knowledge and resources. By

1979 he was at the peak of his powers and with the increasing withdrawal of Levene from public appearances and involvement, Duff could almost be said to have donned the mantle 'Mr Boxing'.

Mike Barrett, on the other hand, had arrived on the boxing scene in the early 1960s with nothing like Duff's pedigree. Also an amateur fighter – briefly with Earlsfield BC – he had joined the merchant navy when sixteen, returning when twenty-two to set up a dockland business that resulted in him owning property in Woolwich, Limehouse and Bermondsey.

The son of an immigration officer (somewhat ironic when one considers the backgrounds of Levene and Duff), born in relatively genteel Whitehaven, Sussex, he came into boxing promotion on a whim, taking on matchmaking responsibilities at Epsom Baths, and later at Manor Place Baths and Bermondsey Baths. He broke into the big-time in 1962 when he became, first, matchmaker and then sole promoter at the Albert Hall. Well-spoken, immaculately dressed, he was subsequently described by *Boxing News* as 'the Beau Brummell of boxing'.

At the Albert Hall he needed top boxers and access to the international scene and so it was then he turned to Duff for help. A partnership was born which resulted in the quiet, somewhat idealistic Barrett becoming a key player in controlling the capital's top boxing programmes.

Just as with the BBBC Jubilee celebrations later that year, the 100th Anniversary stunt, complete with cake, underlined the confidence and apparent invincibility of the ruling 'elite'. But as history demonstrates, it is when empires start indulging in orgies of self-congratulation and celebration that they are at their most vulnerable. For as Marxists might say, it can be no coincidence that at almost exactly the same time Duff and Barrett were raising the champagne glasses (and maybe even pondering on where to stick the cake-knife) Frank Warren and associates were forming the National Boxing Council – an unofficial 'governing body' created to represent those presently excluded from the charmed circle of promoters, managers and fighters.

Warren, the 'enfant terrible' of the boxing world, who had risen to metropolitan fame via involvement in 'unlicensed' shows, was poised in 1979 to break into the big-time thanks to a series of audacious confrontations and bluffs. A great deal has been made of Warren's individual style and initiative; much credit for 'breaking the cartel' has accrued to him. And yet he was as much a product of the times as he was an instigator of startling changes.

The boxing world – in promotional terms – has always reflected broad economic and social shifts. Thus Solomons ruled the roost in a smaller, less diversified, almost static world of the Forties and Fifties. When the communications and entertainments industries expanded in the Sixties (with a parallel contraction of the boxing business) he lost his grip and was gradually replaced by a group of men more in tune with the tastes and technology of the time. As the Seventies drew to a close, however, fresh innovations – legal, social and technical – combined with a grass-roots revival that brought more and more boxers onto the scene to fight for more and more titles, unsettled the 'establishment'.

It has been claimed on Warren's behalf that he was able to tap a growing discontent with the stale 'glitz 'n glamour' of the promotions at the Albert Hall and Wembley, that he provided the ordinary man and woman in the street with real blood and guts contests that were once such a distinctive feature of the British fight scene.

Yet the grass-roots promotional scene in London and elsewhere had already been showing signs of a definite revival in the mid-Seventies: small-hall shows that relied on customers who paid at the door rather than dinner-jacketed 'club' members were once again thriving thanks to the persistence of smaller promoters whose pecuniary rewards were minimal.

In 1974, for instance, Paddy Byrne brought pro-boxing back to the Manor Place Baths in South London. Earlier attempts to do this had failed miserably but Byrne, with energy and determination, was making a go of it:

> I've always said that there's nothing wrong with small-hall boxing that a few good shows wouldn't cure. Just give the people the fights they want to see and they'll pay to watch them.

Byrne tackled the promotional business in direct fashion:

> A week before the show we went out and stuck 400 posters on

walls and hoardings all over London. . . . That's the side of promoting the public don't see. They think it's all big cigars and dinner suits but they don't know the half of it.

Byrne also happened to have a couple of value-for-money fighters in Pat McCormack and Paddy McGuire, men he was proud to say were not tied to either of the main promotional 'camps':

I value my independence. I like to think I'm in sole control of my fighters. If somebody offers me a fight, I can accept it or turn it down without having to refer to anybody and that's the way I want to keep it.

The culmination of his efforts would be the staging of the British welterweight title fight between Pat Thomas and Pat McCormack in 1975 at the Manor Place Baths – the first title fight south of the river since the days of the Ring.

In the Midlands, Byrne's efforts were to be matched by ex-heavyweight Ron Gray who had stepped into the shoes, as it were, of Alex Griffiths who had died in 1975. Gray operated from the Wolverhampton Civic Hall, his motives the timeless ones of promoters down the century: 'There's no feeling like walking around a ringside on fight night and seeing all the smiling faces. You know you've entertained people. . . .'

Like Byrne, Gray did his own matchmaking, wrote his own ads and designed his own posters; and his first title fight would come in 1977 when he staged the Bunny Johnson v Tim Wood light-heavyweight title clash, needless to say, before a packed house.

Gray, Byrne, Ernie Fossey at Hornsey Town Hall, Eddie Thomas in Wales, the Atkinsons at Liverpool Stadium – these and others were helping provide the fight game with the stimulus that would see it 'take off' dramatically in the Eighties. Indeed, for those anxiously seeking green shoots, by the late Seventies there were promising signs. In 1977, for instance, boxing promotions were on the increase and, although 'dinner-club' shows were still in the majority, public tournaments were multiplying. Also in 1977, it was revealed that the number of active fighters in Great Britain had topped the 400 mark for the first time since the 1960s, the number having actually dipped below 300 at one point.

The BBBC had played its part in helping to galvanize the sport at the provincial level, in particular by introducing two new weights. In fact, the decision was a rethink on the Board's part. In 1967 it had offered belts at junior lightweight (8 st 4 lb) and junior welterweight (10 st). The latter had international credibility; indeed, Britain possessed an ex-World champion at the weight in Jack Kid Berg who (though not recognized in this country at the time) had lifted the title in 1930.

Fittingly, the first-ever British title fight at the 'new' weight was held in Berg's beloved East End at the York Hall, Bethnal Green, Mickey Duff (whose own role as a small-hall promoter cannot be overlooked) promoting the contest.

The first outright winner of a belt offered at one of the new classes was Jimmy Anderson, who dominated the junior-lightweight division (later to be renamed super-feather) winning his belt via three consecutive victories in just over a year in 1968–9.

Anderson thrilled many a packed Albert Hall with his exciting blend of hard-hitting and courage and his three wins in a row remain unmatched by subsequent 'super-featherweights'. He also notched up another notable first in being Terry Lawless's debut British title holder. Anderson's pro debut came in 1964 and in a seven-year, thirty-seven-bout career he would lose just nine times, four of those on disqualifications. That did not, according to Lawless, make Jimmy a dirty fighter: 'But he was a wild puncher! He'd throw punches from wherever his arms were and they'd arc towards the body. There was nothing deliberate in it. My word, he could punch though!'

In fact, twenty-four of his twenty-seven wins would come inside the distance and it was a tremendous 'blood and thunder' affair at the Manor Place Baths on a 'live' TV broadcast that brought him to Mike Barrett's attention. Anderson swiftly became an Albert Hall regular, gaining a controversial title shot against Jimmy Revie despite having been defeated in an 'eliminator'.

He put up a brilliant performance, however, crushing the previously unbeaten Revie in nine rounds of a cracking London 'derby' at the Albert Hall in February 1968. He then had an intriguing clash with Howard Winstone whom he floored in the first round, but who climbed off the canvas to defeat him comfortably on points. In a non-title fight with World featherweight champion Johnny Famechon, he succeeded in breaking the latter's jaw though losing on points. At this stage Anderson was rated number six in the world but, incredible as it may seem today with so many 'World' titles up for grabs, Anderson never fought for any title other than the British one.

In 1970 the junior-lightweight division was abolished in the UK and, following a defeat at lightweight by Brian Hudson when Anderson was badly cut, he retired.

The Board had cited 'lack of interest' when taking its decision to discontinue the two extra weight divisions. However, with boxing activity increasing in the early Seventies, the junior-welterweight division was reinstated in 1973, only this time, following concerns that the 'junior' tag had failed to excite customers, the name was changed to light-welter.

Junior lightweight (or super-feather) would have to wait until 1986. In the meantime, the Board decided to introduce the new (to Great Britain) light-middleweight division (11 st 6 lb). With an estimated fifty middleweights and some seventy welterweights fighting in Britain at the time it was thought there would be more title opportunities and more attractive promotions for 'live' and television shows with the extra division.

In fact, the new weights almost immediately created interest at smaller venues: Wolverhampton Civic Hall, York Hall, Shoreditch Town Hall, as well as two old favourites: Liverpool Stadium and Belle Vue, Manchester, both of which were to see title action for the first time in many years.

The light-middleweight title also saw a renewal of the traditional East versus South London rivalry when, in 1977, Jimmy Batten of Millwall and Albert Hillman of Farnborough were matched at the Albert Hall, Batten having built up a strong following at Bethnal Green's York Hall while Hillman's 'home' base was Walworth's Manor Place Baths. Had they been fighting in the 1920s it would have been a Premierland versus Ring battle. Batten won an exciting contest and went on to secure a belt outright (the second light-middleweight belt won outright by the Lawless 'stable', the first having gone to Maurice Hope).

Another 'light' divisional champion, Joey Singleton, took the light-welterweight title in rapid time – under a year and just eleven pro fights – his career noteworthy for the fact that it involved the revival, albeit temporary, of the 'Graveyard of Champions', Liverpool Stadium, as a championship venue.

After an interlude during which Dave Boy Green was champion, the light-welterweight belt came back south when Colin Power, a Harrow Road boy who had come to prominence via Ernie Fossey's fight bills at the Hornsey Town Hall, took the title in October 1977 and the belt outright in February 1979.

Fossey, of course, would become Frank Warren's right-hand man as his head trainer in the 1980s, and it is significant that Warren achieved considerable success in the new divisions as the battle developed between himself and the 'old guard' of Duff and Barrett.

Where the light-middles were concerned, it was Warren's boxer Prince Rodney who took a belt outright in the early Eighties with wins over Londoners Batten and Cable. Rodney's was an erratic career, spoiled by injury, his smooth 'show-off' style bringing accusations (always denied) of arrogance.

Warren also promoted and managed the division's other 'glamour-boy', part-time male model Gary Stretch, who could have taken a belt outright had he not become disillusioned with the game (not to say Warren, too), eventually heading for the USA and a career in films.

Stretch was a flashy, flamboyant boxer who fought at speed and whose smash-bang tactics were somehow characteristic of Warren's men in general. Stretch was adept at slipping punches, however, and would swing hooks in from all angles; but he had to struggle hard to wrest the belt from a more traditional pro-fighter, Gary Cooper. Cooper, aged thirty when the two met, had provided veteran trainer/manager Jack Bishop with his first-ever Lonsdale Belt champion, and though Stretch floored Cooper twice early in their title clash, Cooper refused to 'lie down'. Instead, he proceeded to give the younger challenger an exciting, tough fight – so tough that Stretch's nose was broken and his hand damaged before he finally prevailed on points.

However, it would be at light-welter that Warren would, as manager and promoter, achieve his greatest coup – guiding Essex fireman Terry Marsh first to British, then European and finally World titles.

The division's domestic 'king' throughout the Eighties, however, was Clinton McKenzie, for most of his career a Duff man but, at the end, fighting for Warren. In all, he would take part in eleven title bouts – ten of them consecutive, a record for Belt contests – at the weight, winning seven of them. He would also win two Lonsdale Belts outright (the last man to do so and thus joining a select band of only eight men this century). Yet when he stepped up to international level, he invariably lost. Despite his great determination and sound defence, he lacked a KO punch: thus, his fights were usually wars of attrition as he gradually overcame the opposition with gnawing jabs and precision combinations.

Terry Marsh also lacked a KO punch but he developed a strategy based on tremendous will-power and psychological strength that, as he put it, 'broke fighters' hearts. Lots of fighters go for the throat. I go for the heart. Go for the heart and you crack the mind. Then you finish the body.'

Marsh was no overnight sensation. He was born in February 1958 just off Cable Street – classic boxing territory. In fact, fifty years earlier, another great little fighter, also a junior-welterweight and a World title winner, Jack Kid Berg, was born not a short walk away on the same street. The parallels do not end there. Berg's title win in early 1930 clinched 'renegade' Jeff Dickson's arrival in British boxing's big-time. Marsh's victory would prove as important for Frank Warren.

Ironically, Clinton McKenzie's manager Mickey Duff had advised his man against fighting Marsh for the British title, pointing out the latter's awkwardness. Experts felt, however, that although Marsh's flashing left hand might cause problems, Clinton would have too much expertise and class to allow Marsh much of a chance. As McKenzie admitted:

I'd underestimated him. I had no respect for his punching power and he looked so skinny that at first I thought I'd blow him away. But he kept catching me off-balance. I remember pinning him against the ropes in round seven or eight and I let everything go at him. He was the hardest bloke I ever hit in the stomach. I could feel my punches sinking in. I could hear him groaning. How the hell he got through that, I'll never know. He was a very tough guy. . . .

Although Marsh was almost out on his feet during the last tumultuous round, he received a unanimous points decision, having given a perfect exhibition of boxing on the retreat, proving that guts and determination plus sound technique can still prevail over hard professionalism.

There was a great deal of sympathy for McKenzie, however. As he put it later: 'Marsh came from nowhere. He had a couple of fights and all of a sudden he was the man. When I fought him I'd been going ten years and never really got recognized.'

Having taken McKenzie's title, Marsh moved on to take the European title in October 1985, defending twice before forfeiting. In March, 1987, in a circus tent in Basildon, Essex, he defeated Joe Louis Manley to become IBF light-welterweight king.

For Warren, it came at the perfect moment. Barry McGuigan had been defeated a year earlier and Marsh seemed set to fill the gap he had left in a way that Lloyd Honeyghan – Britain's other World title holder – could not. The triumph was short-lived, however: one defence followed, before Marsh embroiled Warren in squabbles and controversy concerning his health and finally gave up the game.

Clinton's career, meanwhile, continued at domestic level. Defeated by Tony Laing (Kirkland's brother) and then by Tony McKenzie (no relation), he would wait until the title had passed to Lloyd Christie (brother of Errol), who won a Lonsdale Belt in under ten months in 1987 before facing Clinton in January 1989 at Cocks Moor Wood Leisure Centre, Kings Heath.

Financial reasons had forced McKenzie out of retirement though, sadly, he would receive less than £5,000 for his pains. It was, however, not a matter of money – it was the title he coveted most of all:

It was just like the movies. My last chance, everything on the line. My little boy Leon was there shouting for me. It went the distance. It was close. I was so tense waiting for the decision. I wanted it so bad. I was there in the ring thinking,

'Have I done enough, have I done enough?' The referee put my hand up. . . .

# 22

# Warren Butts In

On 22 January 1988 Harry Levene died in his luxurious West End flat just off Marble Arch. Levene had been cloistered away for some years before his death, rarely venturing out although keeping in touch with events. Only the continual appearance of his name on various Duff/Barrett promotional banners kept his public memory alive.

The son of an immigrant cabinet-maker, Levene had been eleven years old when the first Lonsdale Belt had been contested and sixteen when he had managed his first boxer – a role he had concentrated on for most of the inter-war years and into the 1950s.

Significantly, given his 'maverick' personality, Levene's boxers had been an odd, if classy, assortment, few of them Lonsdale Belt winners while under his management. This was because they were either ineligible to fight for a British title, being Australian (George Cook) or Canadian (Charlie Berlanger and Larry Gains) or American (Augie Ratner and Gene Tunney); or they were itinerant tradesmen travelling the world in search of cash (Danny Frush, Ernie Jarvis, Fred Archer); or they were past their prime by the time Levene picked up their contracts in order to help them squeeze a few more hefty pay packets out of the game before retirement (Jock McAvoy, Jackie Brown, Jack Kid Berg, etc.).

This vast and colourful experience at the sharp end of the game would be put to good use when Levene finally emerged in the 1970s as the principal boxing impresario in the country – a role he played ruthlessly but with great style and panache. Always something of a 'loner' in purely social terms, he was usually at the heart of whatever storm was breaking in the boxing world and no doubt would have given Frank Warren – just then, in 1988, approaching the peak of his entrepreneurial career – more than a run for his money.

Warren's rise during the 1980s had been swift: by early 1980 he had forsaken the 'outlaw' NBC and had accepted an invitation from the BBBC to take out an official promoter's licence – a mistake, according to Jarvis Astaire, who thought the Board should have refused Warren such a privilege.

Soon he was nose-to-nose with Mickey Duff concerning the implementation of the 'fourteen-day rule', one of a number of unofficial conventions that had effectively sewn up big-time shows for decades. Warren lost the first battle but would ultimately win the war.

Almost simultaneously he had managed to gain a foothold in TV by utilizing a Joe Bugner 'comeback', a foothold he transformed in 1982 into a full-scale contract with ITV that would soon breach yet more 'conventions', in particular those governing the transmitting of 'live' shows. Programmes such as 'Fight Night', 'Seconds Out', not to mention regular 'Mid-Week Sports Special' slots followed; and there was little the old 'cartel', let alone the BBBC, could do to prevent his progress.

For too many years the Board had been content (or had had no option, according to one's point of view) to oversee or 'police' the quasi-official promotional arrangements that so suited those who had drawn them up. Just as the Board had considered itself unable to resort to courts of law where the so-called 'cartel' was concerned (Duff, Levene, Barrett and Solomons had done nothing illegal, after all), so the Board was now uncertain where it stood regarding Warren and his various activities.

In the 'free-market Eighties', any attempt to place restrictions on his freedom to carry out his business in the manner he so chose would almost certainly have come to grief. As Ray Clarke, Board secretary between 1972 and 1986, commented:

> In the Sixties and Seventies the Board had more powers than they do today. There was no Restrictive Practices Act, no Office of Fair Trading. We could allocate tournament dates which specifically affected major promoters which included Jack Solomons and Harry Levene. There were differences of course but,

by and large, they accepted our decisions. Nowadays, it's a different ball-game. Now the lawyers have come in on the act and it's a shame.

Which is why the old cliché that the Board, by offering Warren a licence, hoped to 'control' him, misses the point of Warren's progress. The Board could not 'take him on' (despite all the scurrilous accusations/allegations of past misdemeanours, most if not all fiction, anyway) without exposing not only its own many inadequacies but also its own ambiguous legal standing. Warren's alternative 'governing body' might have been considered by some as a joke but its very existence demonstrated that official sporting governing bodies, being self-appointed, are always at the mercy of the 'Emperor's New Clothes' syndrome: all it takes is for one among the crowd to blurt out the obvious and the illusion of power is shattered.

Thus it is no exaggeration to say that the Board needed Warren almost as much as he needed the Board. However, like Harry Levene in the late Twenties, being a member of the club does not mean one has to obey all the club rules. And whether Warren did what he did out of a sense of altruism or sheer self-interest, within a couple of hectic years he almost singlehandedly carried out a thorough deregulation of professional boxing.

If we compare the season 1974–5 with that of 1984–5, a measure of some of the changes wrought can be ascertained. Championship boxing in the former season was dominated by two men handled by Duff and Lawless: John Conteh, whose World title bouts at Wembley straddled Christmas, and John H. Stracey, whose successful European title challenge at the Albert Hall heralded a World title bid at the end of 1975.

On the British title front, belts were contested at all weights bar welter at a variety of venues but principally of the dinner-club kind. In London the only public title fights were two staged at Barrett's Albert Hall, while two more took place in dinner clubs: one at Solomons's World Sporting Club at Grosvenor House, another at the NSC's Café Royal.

Outside London, Solomons was involved in a title promotion at the Nottingham Ice Rink, while other title fights were held in Glasgow and Wolverhampton (both dinner-club shows) and one

'Champs Camp', Phil Martin's four Lonsdale champions: Paul Burke, Maurice Core, Frank Grant and Karl Thompson. (*Harry Goodwin*)

Randolph Turpin's belt at auction, 1974. (*Press Association*)

at the Liverpool Stadium. Overall, it was a scene dominated by Lawless, Duff and Barrett, with Solomons and one or two others pitching in where they could.

Ten years on and things had been radically transformed: of thirteen British title fights in that 1984–5 season, Frank Warren was involved – either as manager or promoter – in at least six. In London, his *public* venues staged four title fights: three at the Britannia Leisure Centre, one at the Alexandra Pavilion. And while he controlled only one British champion (Terry Marsh, who would go on to take a World title in 1987), already that season he had promoted two of the three World title fights held in the UK: Colin Jones v Don Curry in Birmingham and Charlie Magri v Sot Chitalada at the Alexandra Pavilion. He had also made a large but unsuccessful bid to stage Britain's top fight that year – Barry McGuigan v Eusebio Pedrosa, a Duff promotion but an Eastwood boxer.

The old guard were still prominent, of course, Duff being manager of Duke McKenzie, who took his first flyweight Lonsdale Belt at the Albert Hall in June, Sibson and Mark Kaylor selling out Wembley the previous November, but it was clearly a more open, more fluid scene than a decade earlier.

That Warren's arrival resulted in a rerun of the 1960s, with boxing's promotional establishment once again divided into antagonistic camps hardly able to speak to one another, let alone co-operate in business terms, must not be seen as an inevitable consequence. With the sport expanding, with more boxers, more promotions, more titles on offer and with TV (or rather ITV) taking a constructive and financially beneficial interest for the first time in decades, there was more than enough to go round.

Sweet reasonableness, however, has never been considered a quality worth encouraging in the area of professional boxing, whereas jealousy, overweening pride and sheer greed have traditionally been the dominant character traits of those who have risen to the top in pro-boxing's promotional hierarchy (traits conspicuously absent, it must be said, among boxers themselves).

Thus Warren's progress was bitterly contested every foot of the way, each victory he achieved acting as a stab in the heart of those on the retreat. Warren's 'scorched earth' policy did not help matters, of course. For instance, his success in removing entirely the policy whereby a reasonable interval between major tournaments was maintained (thus avoiding splitting potential audiences to nobody's advantage) created a situation where virtual anarchy could and sometimes did break out.

Of course, had the old guard not insisted on using the fourteen-day rule to try to exclude him (and others in the past) entirely, then such tactics might not have seemed necessary. In the event, it became an all-or-nothing struggle that did little for the image of the pro-fight game.

Thus the boxing scene to which Harry Levene bade farewell after ninety long years would not have been unfamiliar to him: headlines proclaiming 'Promoters At War!' as major London shows clashed, the BBBC wrestling with an up-and-coming promoter over rules and regulations, and controversy over the poor quality of imported boxers.

One major difference, however, between Levene's heyday and the promotional scene of the 1980s was that the new promotional wizards – Warren and later Barry Hearn – were men possessing considerably less knowledge and certainly less experience of the actual trade of boxing than their rivals and predecessors.

Jack Solomons had been a boxing manager and small-hall promoter and matchmaker for some twenty-five years before assuming the mantle of big-time promoter; Harry Levene, too, had been around the fight game at a much higher level for even longer, while Mickey Duff had actually been a pro-fighter for a number of years and had made matches and managed for a decade or so before reaching the top. Warren, by contrast, had come into the game after a few years promoting what were, by anyone's standards, some rather scruffy, unlicensed shows.

Thus it would be some time before Warren could match his considerable skill and success outside the ring with comparable expertise and triumphs inside it. In the crucial money-spinning divisions, Duff and company usually held most of the aces.

During the Eighties, for instance, the welterweight division was dominated by Colin Jones, Kirkland Laing and Lloyd Honeyghan – all of whom won Lonsdale Belts outright. Jones, managed by Eddie Thomas but promoted by Warren, failed, albeit courageously, in three World title attempts, the last when stopped by

Don Curry at the NBC in Birmingham in 1985, Warren's biggest promotion to date.

However, Kirkland Laing and Honeyghan – both in the Duff camp – captured the public's imagination, Laing because of his puzzling inability to fulfil brilliant potential, Honeyghan because of his priceless ability to rise to the occasion. Laing would win five British title fights and lose three; Honeyghan, marshalling his fluent skills, pace, variety of punch and overall ringmanship to marvellous effect, demolished the same Don Curry who had defeated Colin Jones – this triumph probably the greatest achievement by a British boxer since the days of Ted Kid Lewis.

In the middleweight division, a similar situation prevailed: despite another Warren man – Roy Gumbs – taking a belt outright early on, the Eighties were dominated by Tony Sibson, initially a Burns/Duff man, and Herol Graham, managed and trained by Brendan Ingle.

Gumbs was deprived of his title by Duff/Lawless fighter Mark Kaylor, a West Ham 'bomber' who also put paid to the considerable ambitions of yet another Warren hopeful, Errol Christie. Graham, meanwhile, took the title in April 1984, KO'ing in one round Warren-hopeful Jimmy Price.

Graham was a quality middleweight who should have achieved more at world level than he did. His no-risk style may have been something of an acquired taste and very much in contrast to the rest of the division, but his defensive reflexes, his tendency to appear to take crazy chances by sticking his chin out and swaying in and out of range, in defiance of all traditional boxing manuals, made him a connoisseur's delight.

He looked so awkward when throwing punches, lunging at long range, hooking from strange angles, and yet his punches – his southpaw right in particular – hurt (his respectable KO ratio is testament to that) and he could also, for much of his career, take a good punch. Ironically, it was a single right hander from Julian Jackson when the two met in November 1990 for the vacant WBC World title that probably put paid to his world ambitions. Graham had been close to victory, well ahead on points when KO'd.

A second European title defeat against Sumbu Kalambay was followed not long afterwards by the loss of his British title to

Frank Grant in October 1992, the only time in his forty-nine-
fight career that he had lost to a British fighter.

Harry Warren wrote in a tribute to Graham:

> Maybe, in the final analysis, he was simply too nice for the
> harsh business he was in; had he possessed a bit of spite and
> venom and been hard enough to stop the emotional side of his
> nature getting in the way of the biggest fights of his career he
> may have been the kind of champion his talent merited.

Sadly, Graham never met a quality British contender in a British title fight. Sibson, Watson, Benn and Eubank either avoided
him or had alternative, more lucrative prizes to pursue. The issue
came to a head in early 1988 following Tony Sibson's retirement.
An attractive couple of eliminators had been mooted including
Nigel Benn, Michael Watson, Johnny Melfah and James Cook.
Before the action could begin, Mickey Duff withdrew Watson,
saying he 'didn't believe in eliminators'. Subsequently, Benn met
Watson for the Commonwealth title a year later, while Cook and
Melfah went in with Graham in 1988, Graham dispensing of
each man in five rounds.

This tendency of top men to avoid one another, thus depriving
British fight fans of some potentially great Belt fights, would place
a question-mark over the role of the Lonsdale Belts in general
during the Eighties and Nineties, as TV, allied with a variety of
'governing bodies', came to play an even greater role in boxing
politics.

The problem would not be so acute in the lighter weight divisions – lightweight, bantamweight, super-feather – where the class
of British fighters during the Eighties appeared significantly lower
than in earlier decades.

At lightweight, after Charlie Nash had retired, the title was
scrapped over by some good domestic class men, Scots such as
Alex Dickson from Bellshill and Steve Boyle from Glasgow and
Londoner Ray Cattouse; George Feeney won a belt outright as
did Tony Willis from Liverpool, while Carl Crook from Bolton
won a belt in record time – 161 days.

A tall, upright stylist, an accurate counter-puncher, durable,
cool and adept at 'tying up' an opponent when matters became

rough, Crook would lose only a couple of fights in a career of over thirty contests, although his international horizons were limited. Following a third successful Belt defence against Brian Roche in June 1991, Crook failed to overcome European champion Antonio Renzo and thus was unable to move forward to a World title shot.

A fourth successful defence against Steve Boyle was followed in 1992 by a resounding defeat at the hands of busy, muscular Billy Schwer – younger by six years, a hard hitter and able to 'bull' his way past Crook's spoiling tactics. In an enthralling contest, Crook was put down three times in round nine and, dazed and bewildered, was unable to come out for the tenth.

It was a similar tale at bantamweight, where no one appeared to match the qualities of Alan Rudkin and Johnny Owen, stars of the Seventies. Owen's four wins in a row between November 1977 and June 1980, as well as Commonwealth and European triumphs, had seemed the prelude to world success. Beaten only once – and that decision highly controversial – in twenty-seven contests before his fatal clash with World champion Lupe Pintor in September 1980, Owen – a Welshman managed by Dai Gardner – was an awkward pressure fighter who could use both long and short punches to good effect, his right-hand shots being particularly hurtful.

Unusually for a long-limbed fighter, he was adept at mixing at close quarters where he pumped away furiously firing both arms from waist level to ribs or straight into the chest and solar plexus. He professed a penchant for fighters who brought the action to him:

> I like my opponent to attack me so that I can use my long reach to push him back as he comes forward. I've got longer arms than most bantams so I can straighten them up before they get within punching distance of me.

He took his belt outright in June 1979. By then the BBBC had decided that a fighter could only win one Lonsdale Belt outright. Owen commented: 'I can't win another one nowadays so I'll have to hang onto this. The British title means everything to me.'

Fifteen months later he was battered into a coma in a World

title challenge against Lupe Pintor in Los Angeles – the only British belt holder to die from injuries sustained inside the ring.

Hugh McIlvanney wrote, while Owen lay in a coma in hospital:

It can be no compensation to those in South Wales and in Los Angeles who are red-eyed with anxiety about Johnny Owen to know that the extreme depth of his own courage did as much as anything else to take him to the edge of death.

He remained in a coma for almost two months before dying in early November 1980. None of his successors would promise – or deliver – as much as Owen. John Feeney, for instance, who took the vacant title in 1981, would have some twelve title fights at British, European and Commonwealth level but would win just two – his Lonsdale Belt victories. His successor, Hugh Russell, held the title for just two months before losing it and dropping to flyweight (where he won a belt outright). Feeney then returned, defeated champion Davy Larmour and then lost to Ray Gilbody who in turn managed one successful defence and had two unsuccessful tilts at the European title before losing the Lonsdale Belt to Billy Hardy. Hardy would then dominate the division in similar style to Crook at lightweight, although Hardy at least managed to challenge for a World title.

Hardy's record series of successful title defences took place at the Crowtree Leisure Centre, Sunderland, promoted by the local Deans brothers who had tasted earlier success in a rejuvenated North-East boxing scene with heavyweights John Westgarth and Paul Lister.

Hardy certainly packed them in: an all-action fighter who rarely failed to put on a show, he stopped Ray Gilbody in three, John Hyland in two and outpointed Ronnie Carroll to take the belt in a two-year campaign that included a European title defeat in Italy. Despite dominating the British scene, Hardy made no headway abroad at bantamweight, retiring, still undefeated at home in mid-1991.

Bantamweights certainly broke some records, however: the Feeney v Russell bout was the last fifteen-round title fight in Britain; Larmour, at thirty-one, was the oldest man to hold a bantamweight title; while Russell's brief tenure as champion (thirty-six days) was only matched by Frank Goddard's twenty-three days in 1919.

For unenviable records, however, the inability of super-featherweight champions to defend their titles successfully must take some beating. From January 1986 right through to early 1993, thirteen men tried and failed to hold on to the crown – all the more remarkable when placed alongside Jimmy Anderson's record in the late Sixties.

The first title fight at the newly revived weight took place in January 1986. Promoted by Frank Warren at the Guildhall, Preston, the new title got off to a typically jinxed start with scheduled contender Najib Daho having to pull out and his replacement, John Doherty, taking the title.

Doherty (no relation to his first title victim Pat Doherty) was the first man to take a belt outright after Anderson, though it took him the best part of six years to do it. His first reign was brief. The Bradford man was matched with Pat Cowdell at St George's Hall, Bradford in April 1986 and was stopped in six rounds.

It was the last phase of a tremendous fifteen-year boxing career for Cowdell, who already possessed a featherweight belt, won in 1980. He had retired in 1982, claiming he had lost enthusiasm for the game, but within a year was persuaded by the Lynch brothers to resume his career. In July 1984 he won the European super-featherweight title (thus far, the only international success achieved by a British fighter at the weight).

Cowdell was the classic British fighter, doing all his work off the jab, who rarely threw a punch other than a left for the opening round or two of a fight, during which time – especially as he entered the veteran stage – he could be vulnerable. Once into the fight, however, left-hooks, right uppercuts and crosses, combinations all flowed, and with his long arms and superb sense of distance he could drive opponents back, picking them to pieces with stinging, accurate blows that would gradually render them defenceless.

Having nipped in ahead of Daho, however, Cowdell felt obliged to make a quick defence – too quick, as it turned out. Five weeks after stopping John Doherty, Cowdell squared up to Daho on an ITV 'Fight Night' show. It was a chaotic, bizarre affair with

Cowdell being floored in the first twenty seconds, caught cold by a fast-starting, hard-hitting challenger.

Cowdell later claimed that Daho had pushed him down a second time before KO'ing him with a big left hook; also that Daho's vociferous supporters had swarmed onto the ring apron (the seating being on a level with the ring itself) and getting too close to the action.

It was, nevertheless, a reward for the long-serving Moroccan-born Daho who had been a professional since 1977 – a nine-year, forty-six-bout fight odyssey through the small halls and clubs of Britain that had resulted in this unfancied, unheralded journeyman being catapulted briefly into the big-time.

Manchester-based Daho, managed by Jack Trickett, was the first Moroccan to challenge for a British title: a Berber from the mountain regions, he fought as a boy in various village markets between the ages of nine and fifteen and, by the time he met Cowdell, was a battle-hardened veteran, estimated to be about twenty-five years old.

As would be the case with all super-feathers, though, Daho's reign would be brief. In October 1987 at the Aston Villa Leisure Centre, Cowdell, though wobbling in the early rounds, outboxed and eventually KO'd Daho in the ninth round. For Cowdell, the end was almost in sight. Now thirty-four, he made a strong bid to become the first man to win a Lonsdale Belt outright at two separate weights, taking on Frank Warren's boxer Floyd Havard on a Warren bill at Aberavon, South Wales.

Havard was a smart-boxing southpaw with fast hands and typical Welsh grit. He had been carefully brought along by Warren and there were uncertainties about his real punching power and ability. Upright in style (he was an ex-ABA champion), feet close together, he tended to skip about a great deal and was considered unlikely to take Cowdell's title.

But Cowdell could not overcome the age factor. For the first six rounds he was in control, amassing points steadily as the younger man searched for a way to cope with his vastly more experienced opponent. But in the seventh, weariness was forcing Cowdell to hold and press down on the younger man's neck. In round eight, Havard strode in, placing his punches with power and precision. Cowdell had nothing more to offer: he took some sixteen blows without replying before falling to the canvas, and when he rose referee Larry O'Connell decided there was little point in his continuing.

Cowdell announced his retirement from the ring following the ceremony to place the belt around Havard's waist.

# 23

## Titles Galore

Barry Hearn once outlined his boxing ambitions in the following terms:

> Ten world champions in ten years, then that will be enough. I will monopolize boxing. That's not an ambition: that's automatic.

Born in Dagenham in 1948, son of a bus-driver, he became an accountant, then a financial adviser before moving into snooker in the 1970s. With his Matchroom 'stable' of players, and with Steve Davis the standard-bearer, Hearn more or less created the modern TV snooker phenomenon that was such a feature of the 1980s.

His involvement in boxing began in 1987 with a co-promotion with Duff and Barrett of the Bugner-Bruno fight:

> That fight made a million quid ... I mean, that's a lot of money ... At the time I thought all big shows were like that and I wondered why more people weren't in the game.

A couple of years and the loss of a million or so pounds later, he understood, but by then he was hooked: with a 'stable' of over thirty boxers and responsible for more than seventy promotions a year, he was a significant force in the fight game.

A principal plus for him and the key to his continued survival was his close involvement with Screensport, the satellite station that stood on a par with Sky and Eurosport (with which it merged in 1993) where boxing was concerned. Satellite transmission would be a crucial new factor in the late Eighties and early Nineties.

But Hearn represented something more than new technology. He was a major promoter without an axe to grind. Having come through the hole blasted by Warren, he would carry none of the latter's scars and none of the old guard's resentments:

> My fighters work for anyone. If Duff wants one of mine, it's only a phonecall away. I'll ring him and say, 'There's a great fight on, that's what people want to see.' But he comes back – 'We want this, we want that'. Jesus, he's got a bad attitude.

What's more, Hearn's 'unusual' business approach of what he himself termed 'total up-front honesty', was startling to some in the fight game accustomed to skulduggery and double-dealing as par for the course:

> When I negotiated Bugner-Bruno I gave Joe's manager Bill Mordy the 12.5 per cent we'd agreed. I couldn't understand his amazement. I didn't realize a lot of others stitched up everyone else.
>
> The secret is to negotiate until a common ground is found. And I obey Rockefeller's rule: always leave a dollar behind for someone else. If you are good to people, pay them what you said, on time, they'll come back for more. People don't understand that I deal straight, that I stick to what I say. For them it's like a game of poker with a new player and they don't know his game.

For Hearn, fighting is a business pure and simple. The word crops up regularly whenever he talks of his promotional activities, but its true significance lies in the fact that he is unburdened by boxing's long traditions. He is completely at ease in the new 'pick 'n mix' title world where half a dozen 'world' governing bodies offer a plethora of titles at a bewildering number of weights – not to mention 'continental' titles, 'international' titles, on into infinity.

For Hearn this is logical and good for business, a situation he considers 'the greatest thing that has ever happened to boxing'.

When there was one champion reigning over a traditional weight division he felt it led to monopoly and restriction: 'One or two people could control a championship and keep others out of the frame.' Now, he insists, boxers have a choice of titles to go for and a choice of weights: 'You don't have to kill yourself for half a stone . . . and no one is held to ransom. If someone won't fight, then you choose another title. . . .'

Hearns's philosophy is perfectly illustrated when one looks at two busy weight divisions, the middle and featherweight. With the addition of super-middle, boxers between 11 and 12 stone have the choice of a wide variety of titles to aim for and Britain – in April 1993 – could boast nine champions: two Lonsdale Belt holders, one Commonwealth, one European, two WBC 'International', one WBA 'Penta-Continental' and two World champions.

As for the featherweights, if we include men fighting as 'super-bantams' (a division only recognized in the UK in mid-1993) there are six title-holders between 8 and 9 stone, including a Commonwealth, a Penta-Continental, a WBC 'International' as well as one 'World' title-holder – Paul Hodgkinson at WBC.

In all, there were, in April 1993, thirty-five title holders spread across thirteen weight divisions, not to mention another thirty-eight Scottish, Welsh, Irish and Area title holders. Thus, one in ten British professional boxers can boast a title of some kind – a much higher percentage if one were to count only regularly active professionals.

In sheer business terms, this proliferation of silverware provides promoters and TV companies with more attractive contests to sell – although rarely do the public actually see the fights they *want* to see, i.e. those *between* various title claimants rather than a series of ultra-safe 'defences' that are often an insult to the paying customers.

What is more, the proliferation of titles and the variety of alternative routes to sizeable purses cannot be said to have improved quality at the top. In certain divisions – in particular, the super-featherweights, where only one champion was able to defend his title successfully in over six years – there is a strong argument to suggest that the restless movement of men up and down divisions has broken rhythms, interrupted steady preparation and sacrificed necessary continuity of experience in the quick dash for cash and spurious glory. It might also be the case that, with weight divisions so close together, the existing pool of class contenders becomes diluted, thus making titles easier to come by.

With the introduction of super-middleweight in 1989 and super-bantam in 1993, the number of weight divisions in Great Britain increased to fourteen and, at every level, Lonsdale Belt activity has never been busier. In fact, even the flyweight division – not so long ago declared 'moribund' – has been producing regular champions, in sharp contrast to the Sixties and Seventies when Walter McGowan was awarded a belt after just one victory and when it took John McClusky seven years to earn his belt outright.

In fact, when Charlie Magri was awarded his flyweight belt in 1987 it was a gesture by the BBBC for his outstanding contributions to British boxing in general – his single win in December 1977 (in only his third fight as a professional) being his only British title contest before his defeat by Duke McKenzie almost ten years later.

During his reign as champion, Magri had found nobody of sufficient calibre to challenge him. But as the Eighties began, the flyweight title scene rapidly altered. Although five years were to pass before the title Magri had vacated was next fought for, there would be no fewer than six flyweight title fights and for the first time in eleven years a belt would be won outright inside the ring.

In January 1984 champion Kelvin Smart was challenged by Hugh Russell who, having caused a surprise by dropping down from bantamweight, caused another by forcing the favourite Smart to retire after seven rounds. Within a year, Russell had stopped both Danny Flynn and Charlie Brown to earn the fastest flyweight belt since Jimmy Wilde.

Following Russell's retirement, Duke McKenzie beat Danny Flynn to assume the crown, then met and defeated Magri in 1986 in a fight that confirmed McKenzie as a world-class contender. He then relinquished the title, as did his successor, Dave Boy McAuley. The two would eventually meet, but for a *World* title, while McAuley's successors – Pat Clinton and Robbie Regan – would both take belts outright in swift succession. Thus the flyweights would produce as many outright winners between 1979 and 1992 as in the previous forty years.

The featherweight division, though much healthier in terms of quality contenders, also saw a rapid turnover in belts during the Seventies and Eighties, though it was some time before a British featherweight came near the class of Howard Winstone. Jimmy Revie did tremendously well to subdue Alan Rudkin twice but fell to veteran Welshman Evan Armstrong with the belt within his grasp.

Armstrong, a good, tough pro, battled his way to win a belt outright, then Alan Richardson and Dave Needham scored two victories apiece. The title now became rather like a revolving door with men moving in and out at high speed – so rapidly, in fact, that featherweights broke the existing record for the fastest outright win no less than three times between 1979 and 1991.

Pat Cowdell's three wins between November 1979 and May 1980 established 204 days as the new target; Robert Dickie reduced that by a day during 1986 before Colin McMillan smashed it in 1991. Paul Hodgkinson made more leisurely progress towards his outright belt, while Barry McGuigan could probably have won a belt for himself with his eyes closed had he or his handlers been so inclined.

McGuigan's retrospective views on the Lonsdale Belt are interesting. Like a number of Irishmen before him, he made a calculated decision to become 'British'. He was blunt enough about it:

> I didn't see anything complicated about taking out (British) citizenship. It was just a quick way to get through the red tape and get to the top: win a British title, then a European and then the World.

Experts were divided, however, feeling that McGuigan could have gone straight to a European shot without taking the risk of upsetting his more Republican-minded supporters, but McGuigan asserts that it was Eastwood who pressed on with the idea: 'Sure, it's only a piece of paper anyway', Eastwood is supposed to have said.

The existing British competition at featherweight was fairly weak; indeed, McGuigan's first title fight, against Vernon Penprase, was very much a mismatch, Penprase being floored and cut before being stopped in round two.

With the title won, McGuigan turned to bigger things, winning the European championship and, by late 1984, was in line for a World title shot. He was then, inconveniently he thought, asked to defend his British title against Clyde Ruan, the British number two, a fine boxer but, like Penprase, not in McGuigan's class.

It was, to use McGuigan's phrase, 'a time-wasting exercise', a fight in which he had all to lose and nothing to gain – except, perhaps, another notch on the Lonsdale Belt. Ruan lasted four uncomfortable rounds before being KO'd by a left hook that 'sent him clean off his feet'. McGuigan then went on to his World championship, relinquishing the British title in the process. His subsequent comments are revealing:

> Looking back, it wasn't worth the trouble. I didn't even get a Lonsdale Belt. Ray Clarke, who was Board of Control secretary at the time, promised me one but I never heard any more about it.

Citing the Magri case, McGuigan felt that he deserved a belt, despite the fact that his British nationality meant nothing to him:

> Any rational person could see that it was a career move, nothing more. The fact is, I'm Irish and everybody knows that and nothing changes that. . . .

This conveniently overlooks the commercial nature of the decision. In the eyes of the world McGuigan was British, a more compelling label – whatever one's political point of view – than being simply Irish.

What is more, McGuigan held the British title for only two years, Magri for five, and though perhaps not in McGuigan's class there *were* men active at featherweight during his reign who could have given him a worthwhile contest: Pat Cowdell, who took on (and was comprehensively demolished by) Azumah Nelson – a fighter conspicuously 'missed' by McGuigan during his tenure as World champion; and the young Jim McDonnell who became European champion in succession to McGuigan in November 1985 and who ultimately ended McGuigan's professional career in May 1989, stopping him in the fourth round of a super-featherweight World eliminator.

Perhaps Cowdell, McDonnell – even Robert Dickie – were no more available for a British title fight than McGuigan during these years: all making 'career moves' of their own in order to maximize their earning potential. The fact remains, however, that a belt and a title ought to be won in the ring, not in the mind. Lennox Lewis has demonstrated the sense of combining action in the ring with hard-nosed commercial calculation and appears to have handled the complicated national identity issue with slightly more tact than McGuigan.

If McGuigan had really craved a Lonsdale Belt, then he should have taken a leaf from his successor, Robert Dickie's, book. Dickie beat John Feeney in a close, bitterly fought title contest in April 1986. Three months later, former champion Steve Sammy Simms was KO'd in five, and three months after that, in October 1986, it was John Feeney again when another hard-fought points win established a new Belt 'record' of 203 days.

Dickie's career then hit a couple of unfortunate snags: injuries, first in a road crash then in the gymnasium, led to the BBBC stripping him of his title, after which he moved up to super-featherweight and enjoyed a brief tenure of the title in March 1991.

Meanwhile, after Peter Harris and Kevin Taylor had battled to decide who should take the vacant title, Harris triumphing on a tumultuous night at Afan Lido, Liverpool's Paul Hodgkinson stepped up to assume the mantle McGuigan had let fall.

A talented, non-stop puncher out of the McGuigan 'stable' (he was once known as the 'clone from Clones'), 'Hoko' took just twelve pro-fights to take the title and some sixteen months to secure his own belt before moving on to World title challenges. His successor, the brilliant, flashy Colin McMillan, with wins over Gary de Roux, Kevin Pritchard and Sean Murphy, would take just 161 days, a new record.

The speed with which such talented men take their belts and then move beyond the domestic scene is clearly necessary from a financial point of view. Television, in particular, renders irrelevant the regular 'learning' fights that champions and potential champions once undertook.

Nevertheless, the dash for glory and the careful, cynical matchmaking now made more viable by the proliferation of international titles means more and more meaningless contests – leading to uncertainties as to the true quality of many contemporary 'champions'.

The sight of Crawford Ashley being comprehensively thrashed by Michael Nunn (albeit at a weight far too low for the Yorkshireman); of Paul Hodgkinson being dismantled by Mexican Gregorio Vargas; of shock international defeats for such apparently brilliant prospects as Pat 'The Flash' Barrett, Colin McMillan and Derek Angol: all suggest that there is no substitute for sustained top-quality opposition if a boxer is to succeed at the very highest level.

However, if international pro-boxing presented a perplexing, sometimes bewildering spectacle, the domestic boxing scene in 1993 was both healthy and strangely familiar – traditions of all kinds being revived or renewed. In 1993 Manchester boasted more Lonsdale Belt-holders in one gym than in the great days of Harry Fleming and his Collyhurst 'stable' – Phil Martin's Champ's Gym in Moss-Side accommodated four belt-holders. Sadly, another tradition lives on – that of media bias against 'provincial' success – TV companies turning their backs on Martin's promotions, preferring instead the 'metropolitan' glamour of Warren, Hearn and Duff.

The eternal accusations of syndicates and monopolies were reheated and served up again in 1993 to the accompaniment of writs and weary denials; a British heavyweight champion made a doleful defence of his title and then challenged the world; and small hall-shows continued to thrive but made their promoters no money.

A Boxer's Union – the fourth this century – was formed with great determination, and to complete the litany of familiar sights and sounds, the British Medical Association launched yet another attack on the sport.

Ex-champs continued to do what ex-champs have always done: take on that one fight too many. Lloyd Honeyghan, Dennis Andries, Carl Crook, Glenn McCrory, Duke McKenzie – all lost fights the fans wished they had never embarked on in the first place.

And, all the while, rugged domestic battles for British titles continued apace: Wally Swift Jnr and Andy Till providing a second absorbing encounter at light-middleweight, Francis Ampofo and James Drummond at flyweight, Drew Docherty and Donnie Hood at bantamweight also serving up gutsy, exciting contests – while twenty-eight-year-old Sean Murphy, whose fights are never less than rousing affairs of the heart if not the head, took a featherweight belt outright with a memorable victory over Alan McKay, grinding the latter down in a head-to-head war of attrition.

In the light of such struggles, suggestions that the Lonsdale Belts now come too easily, that in the general race for assorted silverware they have become devalued as symbols of excellence, only insult the present holders, and misunderstand the true significance and importance of the belts today.

Whether won at lightning speed, held but briefly, or secured after years of relentless toil, the belts remain a symbol of straightforward sporting aspiration and – more important from a spectator's point of view – of pleasing continuity. For there is something deeply, psychologically satisfying in being able to behold the 'undisputed' British champion – a need so perfectly understood by the NSC at the turn of the century.

For how much longer the British Boxing Board of Control can protect its precious symbol from the forces of commercial greed and anarchy is unclear. What *is* certain is that if the Lonsdale Belts are ever consigned to the dustbin – as certain 'World' belts have recently been – then the sport of pro-boxing will follow fairly swiftly afterwards.

# 24

## The Glittering Prize

In a time of declining values and standards in pro-boxing, the Lonsdale Belt continues to fascinate fans and fighters alike, not least because, in aesthetic terms, it can justly be considered a cut above those ridiculous, saddle-like monstrosities, the inflated dimensions of which perfectly mirror the overblown pretensions of the various 'world' governing bodies responsible for awarding them.

Thanks to John Morris, secretary of the BBBC, the famous old trophy has, in recent years, been restored physically to something like its pre-war glory.

Morris, who took over from Ray Clarke in 1986, has been described by Julian Critchley as modern boxing's 'stout defender'. An ex-schoolboy boxer, a publican for ten years, he also ran a freelance sports agency in Northampton and was boxing correspondent for United Newspapers.

As a journalist, he possesses an instinctive feel for the way things ought to look and be presented and, as a keen student of sporting history, he understands the importance of tradition. Thus, one of his first moves on becoming secretary was to 'resurrect', in physical terms, the Lonsdale Belt itself.

It had, he felt, gradually deteriorated as a tangible object of desire. It no longer looked or felt as 'special' as it once had. The enamel portrait of Lord Lonsdale, for instance, had become little more than a caricature, while the actual construction of the belts had suffered due to 'modern', streamlined production methods.

Morris approached Fattorini's, the jewellers, to take responsibility for producing the belts, returning where possible to the original designs, and a new, refurbished belt emerged.

The original belts had been made by Mappin and Webb, London jewellers, at their Birmingham workshops – a contract begun by the National Sporting Club in 1909 and continued by the BBBC when they took responsibility in 1936–7.

The NSC belts were made of 9 carat gold with an enamel centre-panel showing two boxers in fighting stance surrounded by a chased oak-leaf border. The institution of the BBBC belts saw changes in the design, the principal one concerning the main centre-panel or badge which now contained an enamel portrait of Lord Lonsdale, surmounted by a lion (Lonsdale having consented to allow his name and image to be used in perpetuity).

Although also of 9 carat gold, the last of these to be launched by the Board was the lightweight belt won by Eric Boon in 1939 – and the last to be won outright was the heavyweight belt secured by Henry Cooper in 1961, first won by Tommy Farr in 1937.

After the Second World War, the gold was replaced by hall-marked standard silver gold-plate but the belts were still being made by hand, the laurel-leaf border, the engraved inscriptions, the four national emblems of shamrock, thistle, rose and daffodil (where once there had only been rose) all chased from sheet silver and fixed onto sheet metal back-plates, each panel and emblem fixed inside wire-frames and castings. Small enamels showing scenes in the boxing ring were incorporated (similar to those on the NSC belts, though smaller) on either side of the centre-panel while the main links (hinge-knuckle joints, mitred joints and oval wires) were separate items requiring diligent hand-soldering. In fact, the whole thing amounted to some 393 hand-made parts involving 387 separate soldering operations.

The enamels themselves were a separate operation entirely, the image of Lord Lonsdale being hand-painted onto a surface of glass coated on metal, the enamel paint (of metal oxide powder mixed with oil) being coated with clear enamel, this then being fired in a kiln.

Hand-burnished to a bright finish, backed the full length with a specially produced red, white and blue banded ribbon, it was, and remains, a triumph of old-fashioned craftsmanship and traditional design.

Sadly, little is known of the men who originally designed and made the belts except that for fifty years or more one man –

George Norton – was the principal belt maker. He was the son of a master craftsman from Doncaster who had a workshop in Meadow Street, Birmingham and whose own work had been bought by the Victoria and Albert Museum in the 1880s. Norton Senior died in 1914 and George Junior continued the tradition and was still at work on the Lonsdale Belts as late as 1958, when Jack Solomons invited him to London to see his first championship fight.

After the war a skilled silversmith and instrument-maker called Tommy Bloggs became closely involved in producing the belts and he would continue working on them until Mappin and Webb ceased production in the early 1970s. A prize-winning exhibitor of, among other things, filigree palm-trees and silver candelabra, Bloggs was a meticulous, dedicated craftsman who – unusually – kept all the drawings and sketches concerning the making of the belts, a unique record now held in Sheffield Library.

In the 1970s, however, when Mappin and Webb closed their workshops in the Midlands, the belts were put out on a 'factoring' system, individual craftsmen such as Bloggs and Norton now being considered too expensive and 'old-fashioned'. Inevitably, of course, the quality of the belts declined – at which point enter John Morris with his insistence on a return to original specifications.

Costing some £4,000 each, with half a dozen on order at any one time, it can be seen just how expensive 'tradition' is. The Board now charges all promoters of larger shows a £400 belt 'levy' to help cover this substantial and ever-increasing financial burden, all the greater because of the increasing number of belts won outright and thus having to be replaced.

With the proliferation of 'modern' belts, however, there is rarity value in those originally issued by the NSC before its demise in the mid-Thirties, their whereabouts the subject of rumour and legend.

As artefacts they are unique, irreplaceable; not, however, priceless, their worth in monetary terms very much dictated by fashion and the economic climate. Nevertheless, surprisingly few of the twenty-two original belts have actually been sold in the open market; happily, the majority remain within or close to family circles, and only a handful have completely disappeared from view. Thus the old idea that most were melted down for their gold by desperate, destitute ex-champs can be completely discounted.

Twenty-one men won a National Sporting Club belt outright; one belt, however (that of Digger Stanley) was bought back by the Club and reissued to Johnny Brown, while two belts remained unclaimed – Al Foreman's lightweight belt and the light-heavy-weight belt first fought for in 1919.

Foreman's belt, as we have seen, was pawned and then retrieved by promoter Jeff Dickson who offered it to the winner of the Jack Berg v Harry Mizler lightweight title fight in 1934. Neither fighter recalled seeing the belt and champion Berg was certainly not presented with it. In fact, it surfaced again in possession of Ted Broadribb and is thought to have been passed on to Jack Solomons. Solomons offered the young Brian Curvis a Lonsdale Belt in the 1950s if he won a crucial bout but whether this was Foreman's belt is unclear.

The light-heavyweight belt had an interesting history. John Harding, manager of the revived NSC in the late Thirties, found the belt in the Club safe and in 1937 offered it as a prize to the winner of a *Daily Mail* sponsored 'open' heavyweight competition. Jack Smith from Worcester, a novice at the time, won it and, according to Gilbert Odd, as the belt was being presented Len Harvey – whose name was the last to be inscribed on it yet who had never been formally presented with it – stood up and protested: 'That's my bloody belt you're giving away!'

Smith nevertheless kept the belt and had a useful professional career at heavyweight just before and after the Second World War before emigrating to New Zealand – taking the belt with him. When the Queen visited the country in the 1970s, Smith presented her with it; the Palace later decided that the BBBC was the best place for it – and today it hangs on the Board's committee room wall.

Another 'Lonsdale' Belt – in fact, one issued for an Empire title and won by Johnny King – was also appropriated by the resourceful John Harding and, despite protests from the BBBC, was eventually presented to Joe Louis following his defeat of Tommy Farr in 1937. The idea was to launch a 'world' series of Lonsdale Belts but, like the NSC itself, the idea soon sank without trace.

The rest of the original belts have led relatively quiet lives. The Mighty Atom Jimmy Wilde's belt has for many years now been in the possession of Midlands scrap-metal merchant Sam Bowater who bought the belt along with that once belonging to bantamweight champion Dick Corbett.

Strangely, apart from bantamweight Johnny Brown's belt – still in proud possession of his son, Ed Brown – these three are the only belts of the eight won outright at fly and bantam that are traceable: those of Joe Fox, Jim Higgins, Johnny King and Jackie Brown have not been sighted for some years. There are those still alive, however, who can recall seeing Fox's belt adorning the window of his tobacconist shop near Birmingham in the 1930s, and some can still recall seeing Jackie Brown carrying his belt about in a paper bag, happy to show it to any interested person he met.

Of the thirteen remaining belts, from featherweight up to heavyweight, only Freddie Welsh's lightweight trophy (last seen being handed over to Tony Canzoneri in New York in 1931 by Welsh's widow) and Johnny Basham's (also sold to an unknown American in the 1950s) remain untraced.

The four featherweight trophies are in the hands of families and friends of the boxers concerned. The Peerless Jim Driscoll's is with his niece, Kitty Flynn, having been lovingly handed down through three generations of her family; while Tancy Lee's is in the possession of his daughter, Maria Traynor.

Both the above belts have been extensively used to raise money for charity – indeed Tancy Lee would carry it all over Scotland during his lifetime, wrapped in a towel and placed in a bag. His daughter recalls: 'Time without number he came back without it plus the towel but it always got brought back.'

Nel Tarleton's NSC belt is with his son on Merseyside while Johnny Cuthbert's is with the wife of an old family friend in Sheffield, the late William H. Shepherd, who bought the belt in the Seventies when Johnny needed some cash and who made a point of letting that great little competitor have access to it whenever he wished.

Jack Hood's welterweight belt remains with his widow, while of the middleweight belts, Pat O'Keefe's is with his great nephew, Alan Stratton (who has lovingly preserved Pat's memory in a privately produced booklet); Len Harvey's is owned by promoter Mickey Duff's son; while Jock McAvoy's is with northern promoter/manager Jack Trickett – another case of a friend taking a belt and helping out the boxer financially.

Dick Smith's light-heavyweight belt is with boxing collector Charles Taylor, purchased from dealer Maurice Baldwin, while the two heavyweight belts – those of Jack Peterson and Bombardier Billy Wells – are also in good hands. Peterson's remains with his family, while Wells's belt was purchased from the family in the early Seventies and presented to the King's Artillery Regiment. It now takes pride of place amongst the latter's silver collection at Woolwich Barracks, probably as perfect a place as any for a trophy whose owner and provider were so closely involved with the armed services.

From time to time either an NSC or a BBBC belt will appear at auction and cause a stir in boxing circles. 1993 saw a remarkable six belts put up for auction. Those of Jimmy Wilde and Dick Corbett from NSC days were ultimately withdrawn, not having reached their reserve price, while Henry Cooper's famous trio of heavyweight belts and Randolph Turpin's light-heavyweight trophy were knocked down at Sotheby's for remarkably modest sums.

Turpin's had been auctioned back in 1974 and raised some £10,000. In 1993 the same belt – the first to be won outright by a coloured boxer in this country – went for a mere £8,000.

Cooper's belts raised well below £50,000 in a sale that occasioned a great deal of sympathy for 'our 'Enry'. With considerable press and TV coverage of the event, it was like watching a part of the nation's heritage being pawned, although the collective sense of loss was not shared – on the surface at least – by Cooper himself.

Practical and down-to-earth to the last, he insisted that he was simply trying to secure a pension and a peaceful retirement for himself and his wife – ironically one of the reasons why the belt system had been introduced in the first place.

For Henry Cooper at least, the belts finally proved to be of practical as well as of symbolic value.

# Appendices
## First NSC and BBBC Belts

*First NSC Lonsdale Belts*

| | | |
|---|---|---|
| 8.11.09 | Freddie Welsh w.pts.20 Johnny Summers | Light |
| 20.12.09 | Tom Thomas w.ko.2 Charlie Wilson | Middle |
| 14.2.10 | Jim Driscoll w.rsf.6 Seaman Arthur Hayes | Feather |
| 21.3.10 | Young Joseph w.dis.11 Jack Goldswain | Welter |
| 17.10.10 | Digger Stanley w.ko.8 Joe Bowker | Bantam |
| 24.4.11 | Billy Wells w.ko.6 William (Iron) Hague | Heavy |
| 4.12.11 | Sid Smith w.pts.20 Joe Wilson | Fly |
| 9.3.14 | Dick Smith w.pts.20 Dennis Haugh | Light-heavy |

*First BBBC Lonsdale Belts*

| | | |
|---|---|---|
| 16.9.36 | Benny Lynch w.ko.8 Pat Palmer | Fly |
| 24.9.36 | Johnny McCrory w.pts.15 Nel Tarleton | Feather |
| 19.10.36 | Jimmy Walsh w.pts.15 Harry Mizler | Light |
| 15.3.37 | Tommy Farr w.pts.15 Ben Foord | Heavy |
| 27.4.37 | Jack McAvoy w.ko.14 Eddie Phillips | Light-heavy |
| 31.5.37 | Johnny King w.ko.13 Jackie Brown | Bantam |
| 25.10.37 | Jock McAvoy w.ret.11 Jack Hyams | Middle |
| 21.2.38 | Jake Kilrain w.ko.8 Dave McCleave | Welter |

# Outright Winners

| | |
|---|---|
| FEATHERWEIGHT | Nel Tarleton, Ronnie Clayton (2), Charlie Hill, Howard Winstone (2), Evan Armstrong, Pat Cowdell, Robert Dickie, Paul Hodkinson, Colin McMillan |
| S. FEATHERWEIGHT | Jimmy Anderson, John Doherty |
| LIGHTWEIGHT | Eric Boon, Billy Thompson, Joe Lucy, Dave Charnley, Maurice Cullen, Ken Buchanan, Jim Watt, George Feeney, Tony Willis, Carl Crook |
| L. WELTERWEIGHT | Joey Singleton, Colin Power, Clinton McKenzie (2), Lloyd Christie |
| WELTERWEIGHT | Ernie Roderick, Wally Thom, Brian Curvis (2), Ralph Charles, Colin Jones, Lloyd Honeyghan, Kirkland Laing, Del Bryan |
| L. MIDDLEWEIGHT | Maurice Hope, Jimmy Batten, Pat Thomas, Prince Rodney |
| MIDDLEWEIGHT | Pat McAteer, Terry Downes, Johnny Pritchett, Bunny Sterling, Alan Minter, Kevin Finnegan, Roy Gumbs, Tony Sibson, Herol Graham |
| L. HEAVYWEIGHT | Randy Turpin, Chic Calderwood, Chris Finnegan, Bunny Johnson, Tom Collins, Dennis Andries, Tony Wilson, Crawford Ashley |
| CRUISERWEIGHT | Johnny Nelson |
| HEAVYWEIGHT | Henry Cooper (3), Horace Notice, Lennox Lewis |

# Bibliography

*The Home of Boxing*, Bettinson and Bennison (Odhams Press, 1922)

*Seconds Out!*, Fred Dartnell (T. Werner Laurie, 1924)

*Gloves and the Man*, Eugene Corri (Hutchinson, 1927)

*Recollections of a Boxing Referee*, Joe Palmer (1927)

*Fighting Is My Life*, Ted Broadribb (Frederick Muller, 1951)

*Jack Solomons Tells All*, Jack Solomons (Rich and Cowan, 1951)

*White Ties and Fisticuffs*, Gerard Waller (Hutchinson, 1951)

*Noble and Manly*, Guy Deghy (Hutchinson, 1956)

*Bella of Blackfriars*, Leslie Ball (Odhams Press, 1961)

*The Noble Art*, ed. T. B. Shepherd (Hollis and Carter, 1962)

*Old Holborn Book of Boxing* (Gallaher Ltd., 1969)

*Henry Cooper: An Autobiography*, Henry Cooper (Cassell, 1972)

*Finnegan – Self Portrait of a Fighting Man*, Chris Finnegan (Macdonald and Jane's, 1976)

*Freddie Mills*, Jack Birtley (New English Library, 1977)

*McIlvanney on Boxing*, Hugh McIlvanney (Stanley Paul, 1982)

*Black Sportsmen*, E. Cashmore (RKP, 1982)

*The Hamlyn Encyclopedia of Boxing*, Gilbert Odd (Hamlyn, 1983)

*British Boxing Yearbook*, ed. Barry Hugman (Newnes, 1986/92)

*Buchanan: High Life and Hard Times*, Ken Buchanan (Mainstream, 1986)

*The Manchester Boxers*, Denis Fleming (Neil Richardson, 1986)

*Jack Kid Berg*, John Harding (Robson Books, 1987)

*The Fighting Irish*, Patrick Myler (Brandon, 1987)

*The Fight Game In Scotland*, Brian Donald (Mainstream, 1988)

*A Victorian Earl in the Arctic*, Shepard Krech III (British Museum Publications, 1989)

*My Bleeding Business*, Terry Downes (Robson Books, 1989)

*A London Life*, Peter Jones (1990)

*Fighting Was My Business*, Jimmy Wilde (Robson Books, 1990)

*Johnny! The Story of the Happy Warrior*, Alan Roderick (Heron Press, 1990)

*Ted Kid Lewis*, Morton Lewis (Robson Books, 1990)

*Ten and Out*, Peter McInnes (Robson Books, 1990)

*The English Boxing Champions*, Bill Matthews (Arthur H. Stockwell, 1990)

*Lords of the Ring*, Harry Lansdown and Alex Spillius (Heinemann, 1991)

*Pat O'Keefe*, Alan Stratton (1992)

Newspapers:

*Boxing News*
*All Sports Weekly*
*Topical Times*
*Sporting Life*

Minutes of the British Boxing Board of Control

# Index